Tips for Time Manage

1. Hold meetings standing up—no one will stay very long.

2. Fine everyone a dollar per minute for being late to meetings. Put the money into a pot for a party at the end of the year.

3. Use different-colored paper for various reports to improve recognition (try blue for final budgets, yellow for blueprints, green for memos, etc.).

4. Use symbolism to communicate your ideas.

5. Develop strategic alliances to hand off some of the work that is not your core.

Words of Wisdom

1. It always takes two times as long and costs three times as much as you anticipate.

2. It takes five calls to close an average cold call for a sale.

3. Eighty percent of your business will come from 20 percent of your customers.

4. Eighty percent of your business will come from 20 percent of your products.

5. A happy customer will tell five people about you. An unhappy customer will tell 25 people.

6. Every company can cut another 5 percent.

7. Not making a decision is still a decision—a *bad* decision.

8. If you do nothing, that's what will happen.

alpha books

Use Common Sense

1. Get a number *and* a date, or you don't have a commitment.

2. Develop two budgets—one for internal purposes and one for outsiders.

3. Work hard to keep your current customers—they are your best customers.

4. Put a sunset provision in every plan so that things automatically die unless there is a compelling reason to continue.

5. Focus.

6. Plan on the 11th-hour crisis.

Lower Costs

1. Set up your own advertising agency—you will get the 15 percent discount normally given to agencies.

2. Barter—trade your excesses and unsold merchandise or services to other companies. Match up excess with needs. This is often cheaper than dumping merchandise.

3. Use technology—get more information, do less travel, and have less need for secretaries and administrative help.

4. Reduce the number of employees, because you can reduce more than salary. Reductions save fringe-benefit costs, telephone costs, supplies costs, space costs, and fixed-asset investments.

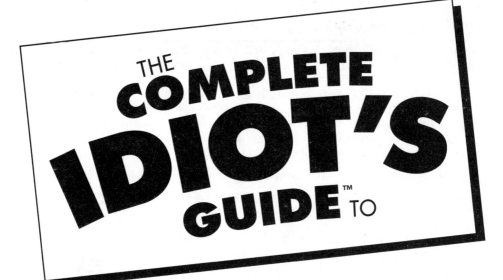

THE COMPLETE IDIOT'S GUIDE™ TO

Business Management

by Hap Klopp

alpha books

A Division of Macmillan General Reference
A Simon & Schuster Macmillan Company
1633 Broadway, New York, NY 10019

Copyright©1998 Hap Klopp

International Standard Book Number: 0-02-861744-4
Library of Congress Catalog Card Number: 97-071176

00 99 98   8 7 6 5 4 3 2 1

Interpretation of the printing code: the rightmost number of the first series of numbers is the year of the book's printing; the rightmost number of the second series of numbers is the number of the book's printing. For example, a printing code of 98-1 shows that the first printing occurred in 1998.

Printed in the United States of America

Alpha Development Team

Brand Manager
Kathy Nebenhaus

Executive Editor
Gary M. Krebs

Managing Editor
Bob Shuman

Senior Editor
Nancy Mikhail

Editorial Assistant
Maureen Horn

Development Editors
Kate Layzer
Lynn Northrup

Production Team

Production Editor
Robyn Burnett

Copy Editor
Lynn Northrup

Cover Designer
Michael Freeland

Cartoonist
Judd Winick

Designer
Glenn Larsen

Indexer
Chris Barrick

Layout/Proofreading
Tricia Flodder, Aleata Howard, Lisa Stumpf

Contents at a Glance

Contents

10 Goal Setting—Setting the Bar and Raising It a Notch or Two   87

Part 3: Organizing Your Team   99

11 Aligning Your Team and Minimizing Friction (So You Can Sleep at Night)   101

Foreword

The Foreword is supposed to whet your appetite for reading the book you've just picked up, so you must already be interested in the subject—business, and how to get along with it. *The Complete Idiot's Guide to Business Management* will give you a mixture of basics and fun, which is a good way to find out what is really important about work while you're investing your life and your time and your soul in the practice of business.

The humor part is not incidental. I think it's good armor and keeps reality from getting to be overwhelming. Good humor is the right frame of mind in which to enter this activity; otherwise, although it's basically serious, and you run the awful risk of taking it—and even yourself—too seriously. The road to seriousness is paved with dull days, and Hap Klopp is good at adding touches of magic and sustenance to ordinary Tuesday-after-Tuesday, for instance, and the inevitable Wednesday-after-Wednesday following that.

Hap has been destroying routine since the very beginning—and so have I, so I recommend it. Routine is the enemy, and it comes equipped with repetition, rustiness, disrepair, deflation, no fun at all, and (eventually) no results. That road is a business road and it's a dangerous and familiar one.

Here are some recipes for the variation of daily life, for the preservation of self, for the understanding that customers are the real inspiration of every successful business, and a host of other business lessons shared by a man who cares and cares, and moves and dares—and that's worth reading about.

Why shouldn't reading about business be a pleasure? Why shouldn't work itself bring pleasure? There is no evidence to compare with the excitement of people working with synchronized enthusiasm. This book helps balance the technical, economic, "business" learning through which business readers plod. A little breath of fresh air sustains us all, and this book has it.

Peter Glen

Peter Glen is the author of the best-selling *It's Not My Department*, (Morrow and Co.) and *10 Years Of Peter Glen*, (ST Publications), as well as a contributing editor to *VM & SD* magazine. Peter, considered America's First Customer Critic, is the star of a video entitled *Customer Service: Or Else!* (Enterprise Media). He is a renowned lecturer and consultant to some of America's largest and best companies including Nike, Benetton, Squibb, Transamerica, Esprit, and Charles Schwab.

Introduction

The first thing to do is to look in the mirror. Say hello to the new boss…not the same as the old boss. Oh no. Definitely not the same. After all, you always said that if you were in charge, you would change things. Make 'em better. Right? So, here you are. That's right, take a good long look in the mirror. There is the new manager, smiling at the challenge. Here you are. Meet the new boss.

Management is about action. This book is about action, and action plans that get results. We're not idiots. We know that our charge as a manager is to get results—better results. We all understand that management is a quest for better results. I wrote this book to share my experiences and to help.

The world is ready to be conquered. If you are disciplined and driven, if you are honest and compassionate, if you are passionate with a plan, you can accomplish anything. This is a book about dreams. This is a book about conquests—and I give you the methods.

In *The Complete Idiot's Guide to Business Management*, I will teach you to do more with less and to do it quicker than the competition. This book is a foundation of managing, covering all aspects, and it includes easy-to-use charts and graphs. This book ties all of these tools together, while at the same time providing an overall logical approach to the chase for success. This is a book about winners.

I love winners. Sports, life, business. There is something, *something,* about those stories. An ebb and flow and then an electricity. I love winners, and I love their stories.

Business stories, in reality, are merely a series of linked recoveries that have been elegantly defined in hindsight. This thing called time doesn't stop, not ever. Things go good. Things go bad. Things go good again. And the stories bring us forward. We plan, and act, and react, and then learn. We always learn. I certainly do, and I want to share what I've learned.

I've learned how to avoid some pitfalls, and how to deal with others you will encounter. More importantly, I've learned to recognize opportunity and I know how to make the most of it. I know that managing is hard work, and that it can also be fun. In this book, I offer my tools and methods and a philosophy. In this book, I offer victory.

How to Use This Book

The Complete Idiot's Guide to Business Management helps you develop a feel for business and shows you how to apply your unique attributes to the day-to-day role of management. I will help you control the job, rather than have it control you. I have divided the book into six parts:

Part 1, "Preparing Yourself to Be a Manager," covers the basics of management as a concept and as a career. I cover how to learn to feel comfortable in your new role and what it takes to get your ideas accepted.

Part 2, "Instilling a Sense of Purpose," deals with the passionate side of managing—how to get the most out of your people. It explains the difference between leading and managing and shows you how to combine the two to guarantee your success.

Part 3, "Organizing Your Team," addresses how to get a group of humans to work toward a common goal. I show you how to get your team clicking and how to improve the performance of individuals on the team.

Part 4, "Dealing with Finances," is a clear explanation of the value of keeping score in business. In simple language, I describe the methods used to keep track of results and ways to help make your operations more efficient and more profitable. I give you tools, shortcuts, and methodologies to reach goals. I explain in common sense terms the reports that you need and how to use them.

Part 5, "Managing Sales and Marketing," explains the difference between the two terms and how to use each effectively. These chapters help you discard the theory that sales and marketing are expenses, and instead show you how and why to treat them as investments.

Part 6, "What to Do When Problems Arise," talks about what to do when your hopes and dreams clash with reality. In these chapters, you learn what to do when you attain success, and how to handle the problems that will inevitably crop up.

Extras

In addition to the detailed explanations you will receive in each chapter, I offer four little extras to brighten your reading and give you gems of wisdom. These boxes give you extra information:

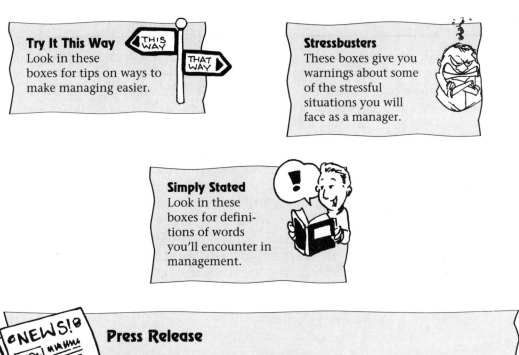

Try It This Way
Look in these boxes for tips on ways to make managing easier.

Stressbusters
These boxes give you warnings about some of the stressful situations you will face as a manager.

Simply Stated
Look in these boxes for definitions of words you'll encounter in management.

Press Release
The information in these boxes includes interesting tidbits from the real world that will help you understand your world of management.

Acknowledgments

To those who accept only the best and damn all the rest

Special kudos to Margot, Matt, Kelly, and now Dave who ride along with me on my quixotic roller coaster of exploration for perfection in business and in life.

Plus my heartfelt appreciation to Brian Tarcy, Dick Staron, Kathy Nebenhaus, and all the people at Alpha Books for giving me the opportunity to articulate my view that management can be simple, elegant, and best of all, a lot of fun.

Thanks also to Paul Sigler (aka Wally), David Tarcy, Paul and Heidi Perekrests, Dan Ring, Vaughn Sterling, Gregg Alexander, Maureen Anders, and Seneca and Martha Anderson. And, of course, Denim, Derek, Kayli, and Marissa.

And I wish to thank all those people with whom I've worked—for good or ill, you've all taught me what I share here.

Trademarks

All terms mentioned in this book that are known to be or are suspected of being trademarks or service marks have been appropriately capitalized. Alpha Books and Macmillan General Reference cannot attest to the accuracy of this information. Use of a term in this book should not be regarded as affecting the validity of any trademark or service mark. The following trademarks and service marks have been mentioned in this book:

Absolut, Air Jordan, Beefeater Boeing, Budweiser, Burlington, Chevrolet, Coke, Columbia, Cornell University, Dayton Hudson, Dilbert, Dun & Bradstreet, Energizer, Ensure, Ernst & Young, Giro, Gore & Associates, Gore Tex, Harvard University, Head Skis, Holly Hansen, IBM, International Designer Accessories, J.C. Penney, Jaguar, Jan Sport, Kresge, L'Eggs, L.L. Bean, Lanier, Levi's, *Life*, Look, *MAD* magazine, Marmot, McDonalds, Mickey Mouse, Microsoft, Milliken, Moonstone, Muzak, National Speakers Bureau, Netscape, *New York Times,* Nordstrom, The North Face, Opti-Con, Oracle, Patagonia, Powerbar, Reebok, Regis McKenna, Royal Robbins, Scott, Semco, Seminole, Stanford University, Sun Micro Systems, Sunglass Hut, Toastmasters, Tour de France, University of Pittsburgh, Wal-Mart, the *Wall Street Journal,* Wild Roses, W. L. Post, Woolrich, Yahoo!, and YKK.

Part 1
Preparing Yourself to Be a Manager

The difference between genius and mediocrity is that genius anticipates, and mediocrity just reacts. That's all.

Everyone has seen managers who work 18 hours a day but are still always behind. These so-called managers, these professional victims, are always "almost there." Or so they say.

On the other hand, we have also all witnessed the success stories of managers who take everything in stride and live wonderful, successful lives. They are always ahead of the power curve and have all the necessary numbers at their fingertips, even if it's just on an envelope. They have vision. They are organized. They "get it."

This first part of the book will give you your foundation as a manager. You will learn the two types of management, how to analyze your business, and how your business fits into the world at large. I'll also talk about how to start to get control of your job, and how to organize your day.

Dive on in. Success awaits you!

Chapter 1

So, You're Going to Manage a Business

> **In This Chapter**
>
> ➤ What is management?
>
> ➤ Goals, strategies, and policies
>
> ➤ The two styles of management
>
> ➤ Why your people skills are the key

One day, someone from Human Resources comes up to you. Or maybe you get a call. "They've made a decision. They want to see you." The HR person is smiling. The next thing you know, you have a different kind of life: the life of a manager.

Alternatively, you may have awakened one morning and realized you are tired of working for others. It's time for you to control your own destiny by running your own business. It could be starting up a franchise. It could be a one-person operation. Or it could be a many-person operation. Whatever. You've just promoted yourself to a manager.

It can be pretty exciting to know that you are going to manage a business, or a large division of a business. It can also be a bit scary. But, as Mark Twain once said of Wagner's music, "It's not as bad as it sounds."

Hey, you'll probably even get a raise. How bad can that be?

Management is about responsibility. If responsibility doesn't scare you off—if, in fact, it invigorates you—then you're ready to start thinking about management—what it means and how it's done. In this chapter, I'll describe the two types of management styles and a few basic approaches. Polish your people skills! You're going to need them.

Everything Changes

Being a manager is just different. Different from being an employee. A lot different, in fact. When you are a manager, your success depends on how others perform. You are the boss, and when you are the boss, the buck stops with you. No passing! If you want to manage a business, you can't be afraid, and you can't be a fool. At least, not if you want to *keep* managing a business.

If you manage a business or division, or if you aspire to be a manager, you probably have a manager's temperament. What does that mean? It could mean any number of things, but at its core it means you want to make decisions.

So here's what you do next. Put on your best power outfit—even if it's jeans and a sweatshirt, though I doubt it—and keep reading. It's time to put those clothes to use.

You thought you were working hard before. Back then there was quitting time. If not, there was overtime. Now, there is *not enough* time. And that's just the first change. Next comes relationships. You're a boss now; your friendships will be tested by jealousy and second-guessing. You will probably lose some friends, gain others, and learn a lot about a lot of people. You'll learn even more about yourself.

That's a perk, not a pitfall. From responsibility follows growth. And you better believe in yourself, because many people are counting on you. Good management depends on confidence as much as ability. A manager must be confident in his or her ability to handle people and money.

What Is Management?

As a concept, "management" is simple, really. If other people do good work, you've done a good job. *C'mon,* you think. *You're kidding me.* It's not a joke. All you have to do is get others to do good work. Piece of cake, right?

Sure. Just wait. Management is hard work.

There is one other component to management—it's this green stuff called *money*. Heard of it? In business there's rarely enough of it. It will be up to you to make choices about allocating money to the proper channels. Welcome to the antacid culture.

So, do you really want to do this? Do you have any idea what you are getting into? Are you ready to be a manager? To find out, take a look at the check list on the following page.

Are You Ready to Be a Manager?

❏ Do you like people?

❏ Are you willing to work 100 hours a week?

❏ Are you dissatisfied with the way things are?

❏ Do you think you can change things?

❏ Do you feel like crying about sales your company missed?

❏ Can you put up with people second-guessing your decisions?

❏ Do you thrive on pressure?

❏ Would you take the job even if there were no more power?

❏ Would you take the job even if there were no more money?

If you checked 7 or more, you are probably ready to be a manager. If not, take the day off and think again. If you think you're ready, or if you think you aren't, there's a good chance you're right. Another way to assess your managerial desires is to examine your traits against the common traits of a good manager. The nine traits of a good manager are:

1. Demonstrates leadership

2. Is resilient

3. Thrives on pressure

4. Is organized

5. Is thick-skinned

6. Believes in himself

7. Knows herself and her business

8. Respects others

9. Displays patience with a sense of urgency

Management is pressure-packed and adrenaline-filled. It's more than the hard work of the employee. Those were just hours; now there's pressure, too. When things go wrong, even when others make mistakes, the job of the manager is to take responsibility.

Decisions, Decisions

So, management is about people and money. You've got to handle both.

But what is a manager? What do managers *do*?

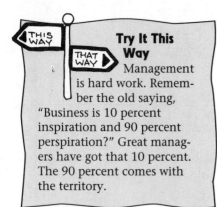

Try It This Way
Management is hard work. Remember the old saying, "Business is 10 percent inspiration and 90 percent perspiration?" Great managers have got that 10 percent. The 90 percent comes with the territory.

They make decisions.

Management is a never-ending process of getting things done. It's a vocation. When you are good, you are dedicated, and when you are dedicated, you eat it, sleep it, breath it, and dream it. You take your decisions seriously. Management is a lifestyle, where the next crisis is always just around the corner and your mind better be sharp enough to beat it.

Most of the issues you will be dealing with will be financial and human. Ultimately, though, management is about *getting things done.* That means your first task is to decide *what* you want to get done.

Reach for the Reachable

What is your goal? What do you want to accomplish? That's a management decision.

There are two kinds of goals: *quantitative* and *qualitative*. Quantitative goals are about numbers. Many managers focus on quantitative goals to the exclusion of qualitative goals. Qualitative goals, while more difficult to measure, define the company and differentiate it from its competition. Both sets of goals are of equal importance and are complementary to the overall success of the company.

Simply Stated
Quantitative goals are about numbers and measurable results. *Qualitative goals* are about a more intangible kind of success—what's special or different about your company. You need to think about both types of goals.

Managers set goals and then work to make sure that the company, department, or division they manage reaches those goals. It's like when you were in school and you needed to get your homework done: Set a goal, reach the goal. Think of it as advanced math and advanced social studies—except that now you're in the school of life, the big leagues. There are real consequences. You could lose your job, your friends. Scary, but real.

The rewards, though, are equally real. Satisfaction, a feeling of accomplishment, increased opportunities, a larger paycheck. Set a goal, reach the goal, reap the benefits. That's management. We'll be talking more about setting goals in Chapter 10.

Strategies to Reach Goals

Once you've defined your goal, the next step is to develop a strategy for how to get there. A strategy is a big-picture look at how you will approach your task. The best strategies are adaptable to change. Business is based on people, social systems, and technology; that means it can't stay static, and neither can your business strategy. Chapter 10 will take an in-depth look at developing sound and flexible strategies.

Policies to Support Strategies and Goals

Finally, you need policies in order to implement your strategies. Policies create the environment that allows you to succeed.

When you have goals, a strategy, and policies (pursue them in that sequence) you are ready for action, which means allocating resources. Resources in business are money and people. Only when you've followed these four steps can you begin to do the work of business: to produce.

Press Release

Change is more present in our lives now than ever before. For example, did you know that 99 percent of all technology ever invented was invented in the last 20 years? Or that more technology will be invented in the next five years than was invented in the last 20? The advances in technology are exponential changes and will continue to be so. Better be prepared to roll with the punches!

As you go along, you are constantly measuring your actual performance against your planned performance—your goal, or part of it. If there is a significant deviation, you take corrective action.

The Role of Common Sense

Learn and study as much as you can, but don't forget your greatest strength: your common sense, also known as your instincts. After all, business is mostly about people. It doesn't require years of experience as a manager to understand people. It requires common sense. Common sense takes account of other people's gifts, needs, and motivations in planning for business. You want to build a team, right? Good. Use your common sense.

Here's an example. I've found that the best way to manage people is to treat them the way you wish you had been treated when you were an employee. What would have made you work harder? Care more? There you go. Those are your policies.

When I talk about common sense, as I will throughout this book, that's what I mean. Of course, judging from all the screwed-up businesses out there, common sense may not be as common as it used to be.

Try It This Way
Develop a feel for your business through personal involvement. Be there, do some of it, experience it; don't leave it to someone else.

It's easier to avoid the pitfalls if you know what they are. Here are some common pitfalls that can undermine your reliance on common sense:

➤ *Arrogance.* The title of manager is not a license to be condescending to others. You could see the same people on the way down that you saw on the way up.

➤ *Fear.* Don't be afraid that people will find out you are not perfect. You're not, and they already know it, so relax. And don't use the "when in doubt, shout," approach. *Instilling* fear doesn't work, either.

➤ *Hunger for power.* A quest for power is not common sense, and most people will recognize this. As Lord Acton said, "Power corrupts; absolute power corrupts absolutely."

➤ *Misconstruing the role of manager.* If you don't understand your job, you won't understand a common-sense approach. You are not a dictator, and no one will let you be. That's just—well—common sense.

Dealing with Priorities

To succeed, you have to be ready to make decisions. Lee Iacocca said, "If I had to sum up in one word what makes a good manager, that word would be "decisiveness." Managers decide what is to be done. They decide when it will be done, and by whom. Managers set priorities.

Managers need to be organized and they need to be energized. It is not a job for the lazy or disoriented. So before you even begin to figure how to handle your new position, you need to understand that a promotion to manager is not a jackpot that lands you on Easy Street. It is, however, a jackpot of opportunity. What you do with your opportunities is up to you.

Management is:

➤ Clarifying goals

➤ Organizing people and resources

➤ Setting the environment for success

➤ Regularly measuring performance

➤ Taking necessary corrective actions

➤ Celebrating successes

The Two Types Of Management

There are two basic, proven types of management that apply whether you have one employee or thousands. If you're stepping into an established corporate culture, as you probably are, you may not have much choice about which style you'll adopt, but we'll discuss them in the next sections anyway.

If you are lucky enough to be starting your own business and have a tabula rasa (blank slate), you can choose your style. My simple advice is to choose the one that is consistent with your personality. It will be the most honest and easiest for you and will therefore get you better results.

Stressbusters

If you are taking over the management of an established firm, division, or department, steer clear of sweeping changes, which can cause short-term chaos. Start off working with the existing style of management. Once you've gained people's confidence and gotten some results, you can begin to introduce changes.

Big Culture Management: The American Way

The first type is *Big Culture* management. Big Culture's hallmarks are an orderly style of execution and a predictable goal. A system of checks and balances ensures that very few mistakes are made.

Big Culture management doesn't take risks; it makes calculated decisions. It has precise ways of operating, and you must fit the mold for it to work. You can't be a maverick in a Big Culture, but if you can figure out how to fit in, you can do great things.

A Big Culture management system is usually, but not always, found in a big company. This kind of management is characterized by lots of meetings, lots of teams, and shared responsibility. Power is clearly delineated, there are many layers of management, formal decisions are made with approvals from superiors, the span of authority is clearly defined, and even product introductions are done in an orderly way and approved by many people.

A Big Culture is a lot like the military, where position equals authority. The assumption is that if someone has a position, she must also have talent. Big Culture management believes in process first. If everything is done right, the results will inevitably follow.

Of course, dinosaurs are proof that big isn't always better.

Press Release

The U.S. military claims that a manager's maximum effective span of control—the maximum number of people he or she can directly control—is six people. This is because of the time limits of a manager as much as anything else. The best way to prove them right is by trying to manage too many people.

If you know how to tap into it and you are good at making it run, the sheer size of a large corporation can add power to your ideas. Yes, it is formal. Yes, *do it by the book* will be your mantra. But doing it by the book is just a way of making sure the gears mesh. When they do, and when you can harness that power, you have great opportunity.

Entrepreneurial Management: A Style, Not a Stage

Stressbusters

Think twice before trying to be an entrepreneurial manager in a large firm. Entrepreneurial management works most easily in smaller organizations, where coordination is not so key and where employees are younger, more flexible, and not so troubled by chaos and change.

The second kind of management is the so-called *entrepreneurial style*. Entrepreneurial management believes in maximizing opportunity. Entrepreneurism is about making fast decisions with limited information. It has a high tolerance for risk and a strong capacity to deal with ambiguity. Entrepreneurism is opportunistic. The mantra of an entrepreneurial manager is *Go for it!*

This style believes that chaos is good if it results from the pursuit of excellence. It is set up for speed and flexibility to ensure that opportunities are not missed.

Entrepreneurial management is so willing to be a leader that it will put up with restarts and changes of direction if it will maximize opportunity. It is not a stage of management, it is a style—targeted at the quicker world of the 1990s. Entrepreneurial management does not shrink from risk. According to this approach, the greatest failures are mediocrity and missed opportunities.

At its extreme, entrepreneurial management can seem like total chaos: every office running things its own way. Microsoft is a good example of that. Entrepreneurial management believes in results first.

IBM and Microsoft—Two Big Companies, Two Styles

Two giants of the high-tech field have shown that both styles of management work.

IBM, also known as *Big Blue,* is the classic Big Culture company, with layers and lines of authority and lots of rules. IBM insists on an orderly introduction of products, clear titles, dress codes (it used to be white shirts and suits, but they're beginning to loosen up some), and very thorough research before trying new products in the market. The focus here is on certainty: IBM relies on its large resources rather than speed or risk to gain dominance. And it has worked. In 80 years of business, the company followed a smooth line from its beginnings (cash registers) to the high-tech world of computers. A logical and orderly introduction of products ensures that no one product could threaten the entire product line if it failed, and that there will be minimum cannibalization of existing products.

Microsoft, on the other hand, has grown to have an even greater market value than IBM using an entrepreneurial approach with an informal infrastructure. Some people don't have a desk in their office, they have drums, yes, like a drum set. Others have a desk and can often be found sitting cross-legged on top of it. It's not unusual to see an employee in a backwards baseball hat working directly next to another employee in a three-piece suit. The style and informality of the company allows it to change directions quickly and to stay vibrant.

In a weekend retreat, for instance, the top management of Microsoft decided that the company was mistakenly ignoring the Internet. That weekend, the biggest computer software company in the world changed direction. Their new focus was Windows 95, with a direct interface with the Internet. The company committed itself to becoming a leading Internet content provider, spending $1 million every few weeks to achieve their goal. And it worked.

There are two ways to look at this story. One way says that IBM has never been capable of making such changes so quickly: That's one reason it's no longer the top high-tech company. On the other hand, as many companies have flopped after changing directions at a weekend retreat as have succeeded.

It Still Comes Down to People

Since management is mostly about people, it's essential that a manager be a good motivator—someone who can inspire, encourage, and lead. There aren't very many easy days once you become a manager, but then, there aren't very many boring days, either.

People are unpredictable. Their outside lives affect them—so do their attitudes and goals. You cannot take one view of someone and assume that forever and ever that person is going to play the same role. Whatever the structure of your organization, you still have to deal with people all the time: motivate them, guide them, and point them toward the goal. You have to be a cheerleader, encourager, and visionary. You have to *get things done*.

Stressbusters
A sure way to fail is to try to please everyone. You can't, so don't try.

The Least You Need to Know

➤ Managers get things done by making decisions about how to allocate people and money and by inspiring employees to be as productive as they can.

➤ Common sense will take you a long way as a manager. Analysis is good, but in the end you have to trust your gut.

➤ Big Culture management relies on checks and balances and is designed to avoid mistakes.

➤ Entrepreneurial management is a fast-acting style with a high tolerance for risk and a great appetite for opportunity.

Where Do You Start? At the Beginning

So. You're a manager. Where are you going to start? For that matter, *how* are you going to start? Slow down, that's my advice. No ball player expects to get into the Hall Of Fame in his first game. Don't try to take on too much on the first day on the job, and don't expect to be perfect. You don't need to be *good,* just good enough. Good enough to survive, and good enough to beat the competition.

To use another analogy from sports (can you tell I'm a sports fan, or am I being too subtle?): In basketball, great rebounders are not always the tallest players, nor are they necessarily those who can jump the highest. Great rebounders are the players who know where the ball is going and who get there before anyone else. Anticipation. Knowledge. Instincts. Great basketball players have all three, and so do great managers.

Lace up your wing-tipped sneakers! This chapter is going to clue you in on why you need to analyze your organization, and how, and why frame of reference is crucial. This chapter is about The Basics.

Begin at the Beginning

You want to get a handle on managing your firm or department, but you aren't sure where to start. That's normal. It's also (fortunately) temporary, especially if you read this book and take my advice seriously. For now, remember to breathe, and get to work finding your frame of reference.

Simply Stated
A *frame of reference* is a context within which facts and ideas can be correctly interpreted.

Frame of reference? What the heck is that? Simple. It's your context. What's going on in your business, and why, and where you fit in. To have a frame of reference, you need knowledge. Now's the time to find out everything you can about what your company (division, department…) makes or produces, what service it provides, or whatever function it is that you are going to manage. The more you learn, the more confident you'll feel.

Know Your Product or Service

Use the products. Use your competitor's product. Read critiques and product reviews. Make your business your business.

Perhaps your business is to make, sell, or service widgets. But do you really know widgets? A great widget manager really knows widgets, especially *her* widgets. That manager understands the widget business, studies the widget market, and spends half the day dreaming of ways to make a better widget. I'm generalizing, but you get the idea. When I say "know your product," I mean become consumed by what you do and become the most knowledgeable person in the world on the subject. If widgets are your business, know everything you can about widgets.

Whatever your product or service, ask yourself this:

➤ *What is unique about my offering?* If there is nothing different, price is probably going to be the tool to knock everyone else out of the market.

➤ *What feature of my product or service will sustain it in the future?* If it has no such feature, and you aren't prepared to wrap up your operation, you'll need to invest in R&D (Research & Development) to come up with something new, or figure out a marketing plan that will make people believe that what you have is needed.

➤ *What is the cost of my service/product relative to my competition's?* Cost is crucial.

Know Your Employees and Believe in Them

Meet with your employees regularly, both formally and informally. Give them a chance to speak up. Learn their capabilities, their limits, and what drives them. Know them as people, too. They have to believe in you, and they have to know that you believe in them. All of that starts with a personal, human connection. At the same time, you're quietly taking people's measure. Is she the one you can count on to meet deadlines? Is he less than committed to the company? Can she handle change? These are the kinds of understandings you will be cultivating in your life as a manager.

Ask yourself these questions about your employees:

> ➤ Are they currently reaching their potential?

> ➤ What are their aspirations?

> ➤ Do they have growth potential?

> ➤ Do they have energy?

> ➤ Do they have enthusiasm?

> ➤ Are they looking to disturb order?

> ➤ Do they relate to my goals?

Stressbusters
Don't use ESP management. You want to know what's going on: Ask! You want people to know what you are thinking: Tell them! Research your organization thoroughly and then clearly state what you expect.

Know Your Customers and Offer Them Satisfaction

You're working for your company, but you do that by getting to know your customers and what they need. Meet them, visit their facilities, and invite them to visit yours. Ask them questions. By presenting yourself as open to suggestions and criticisms about the company's products, you'll build strong relationships and gain important knowledge of the market.

Getting to know your customers and taking their needs seriously is simple business sense. It's also the key to growth. Attracting new customers is essential, of course; but to gain ground the company also has to build customer loyalty by offering superior products and services. In most companies, the *Pareto Principle,* which states that 80 percent of business comes from 20 percent of the customers, applies.

As you examine your customer base, ask yourself:

> ➤ Does the Pareto Principle apply? If so, how can I use it to target my energies and my expenses?

Simply Stated
The *Pareto Principle,* which projects that 80 percent of business comes from 20 percent of the customers and 80 percent of your business comes from 20 percent of your products, gives you a tool to prioritize your actions, and is a guide of where to focus your resources.

➤ How large is my share of the market? Who am I reaching, or not reaching? Who is using my product—and who in the pipeline am I actually selling to?

➤ How financially healthy are my customers? Can I improve the economic health of the relationship with my customers and create a win-win relationship?

Know Yourself

Evaluate your own performance with a performance review. Ask your employees and trusted friends what they consider your strong and weak traits. Measure yourself against your written objectives.

As you learn more about yourself, you can start to figure out how you plan to get things done as a manager.

Try It This Way
To be comfortable in a management role takes some soul-searching. Make a list of traits you want to build in yourself and those you'd sooner avoid. Meditate, go for long walks, talk to someone whose opinion you respect. Make this a time of personal growth.

Ask yourself:

➤ Am I motivated by the job?

➤ Am I tough enough to make the right decisions?

➤ Are my management skills organizational or charismatic? (Don't panic if you can't do both. If your strength is "reading" people and motivating them, you can always hire someone to organize.)

➤ What is my plan for this job? Is this the pinnacle or just a stepping stone?

Keep your sense of humor. You have to be able to laugh. If you don't, all the tools and techniques in the world probably won't help you. Business is often a theater of the absurd: You may as well enjoy it!

Analyzing Your Business

What do you manage? Yes, you manage a business or a division called *whatever,* but what do you really manage? Now's the time to get that straight, because you'll need to understand exactly what you have in order to present it in the best possible light. *Get the facts straight first. You can put your own spin on them later.*

Is Your Company Union or Non-Union?

If there is a union in your company, you'll want to know a lot about it. *Read the union contract.* Unionized companies usually have more formalized rules for hiring, firing, layoffs, and compensation than non-union companies. These issues, along with tenure, formal reviews, and formal acceleration within the company, will all be covered in the union contract. So will the pay structure. There's less scope for abuse at a union company, but also less flexibility for management.

Unions add a third party to any employee communication, one with its own agenda. Sometimes this third-party contribution is beneficial, sometimes not. It does tend to slow down communication. If you have a union, I suggest you:

➤ Meet with your labor lawyer and review past problems and differences of opinion.

➤ Meet with the union representative in your area for an open discussion of each other's needs.

➤ Listen to all sides of the issues—everyone (employees, lawyers, Union officials, your boss or board, and so on).

➤ Don't assume anything not based on fact.

Are You Considered a Boss or a Peer?

Perception is reality. How you present yourself to your employees makes a huge difference in how you manage. If you are perceived as a peer, you will inevitably be tested by your employees to find out where your limits are. Promotion from peer to manager changes relationships, and you'll probably go through a period of adjustment as new boundaries are established.

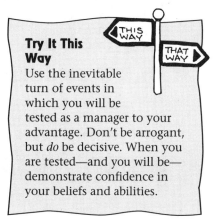

Try It This Way
Use the inevitable turn of events in which you will be tested as a manager to your advantage. Don't be arrogant, but *do* be decisive. When you are tested—and you will be—demonstrate confidence in your beliefs and abilities.

Even if you are new to the company or department, it's important to establish yourself from the outset as a boss and a leader. To manage effectively, you need to command respect. This depends on the two fundamental traits of honesty and decisiveness. You not only have the right but the responsibility to make decisions, and you have to let people know you intend to do exactly that.

Does Your Company Have Strong or Weak Financial Resources?

Business requires resources—especially money. The more you have, the easier it is to make changes. Money allows you more opportunity to implement your ideas and programs; it also provides a cushion when the wrong decisions are made. With a large budget, you may be able to implement a grand strategy—a major advertising campaign, for example.

If your resources are weak, you'll just have to compensate with creativity and quick action. You'll have to become an urban guerrilla. The point is to understand the financial

17

situation of your company or division so you can plan your strategy. Case in point: A small hair-care products company hired a sales manager from Proctor & Gamble. The manager was gifted, but he was used to large corporate budgets, and he just couldn't adjust his approach to the realities of a small company. Start with reality and take it from there.

Does Your Company Have Strong or Weak Human Resources?

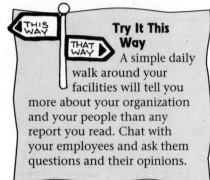

Try It This Way
A simple daily walk around your facilities will tell you more about your organization and your people than any report you read. Chat with your employees and ask them questions and their opinions.

"I've got the best employees in the business." Everybody says that. Don't worry about who's right. Ask yourself, what do our competitors have that we don't?

A few tangible things can make a difference when it comes to your employees—education and specialized technical skills, for example. Those who are respected in the industry—who have been elected to committees, or who have published in technical journals—undoubtedly deserve special consideration. In the end, though, the thing that really counts is performance. Trust your gut.

If Your Organization Is Shrinking...

Is your company growing? Shrinking? Staying about even? If your organization is shrinking, your responsibilities and concerns are likely to be dramatically different from what they would be if it were growing.

For a manager, shrinking presents particular dangers, especially in the area of employee morale. I'll discuss morale in more detail in Chapter 9, but for now, just remember that one of the tasks of a manager is to offer encouragement and foster the feeling among the employees that they're working for a winning company.

Here, in brief, are some other potential problems for a shrinking company:

Simply Stated
Overhead is any cost of goods or services that is not directly related to its production. Utility bills, salaries, and mortgages are all examples of overhead.

➤ *Overhead that is too high for sales levels.* You'll need to slash expenses to be in line with the most pessimistic forecast.

➤ A *loss of key employees.* Consider starting an employee retention program. Meet with key employees, find out their main needs and concerns, and address any and all that you can.

➤ *Diminishing motivation.* Don't argue about it—that only ratifies the feelings. Find something new to motivate your employees. Give them something they can control: Offer evaluations and bonuses based on performance.

➤ *Underutilized assets.* Use them or sell them.

If Your Organization Is Growing...

Growing organizations have a very different set of problems. They have great morale, but they're usually very chaotic. Despite the confidence, the odds of success are not wonderful. Spending tends to be poorly controlled, power grabbing wreaks havoc, and too many people are focused on tomorrow instead of today.

The policies you set regarding pricing, advertising, staffing, and so on, must reflect the company's situation. Here are some of the common challenges a growing company faces:

➤ *Expenses are growing faster than sales.* Draw up budgets and hold people to them. Set targets below expectations (last year's numbers, or 80 percent of projected growth). Hold some money in reserve and agree to spend it after you get results, not before.

➤ *Poor communication.* Make sure the lines of authority are clear. Put together cross-functional work teams, set up a suggestion box, and institute an organizational newsletter.

➤ *The group is going in too many directions.* Prioritize; then eliminate the lowest priority. Require a written analysis of any new directions before launching.

➤ *Customers are being undervalued.* Send teams of employees out to meet with customers; invite customers to come and tour your facility. Measure customer service functions regularly.

➤ *Employees are engaged in power grabbing.* Redo your organizational chart and announce that everyone will be held accountable for the duties assigned to them and for making the company successful by working amicably with their business associates. If someone violates the standard, fire him or her. This sends a powerful and effective message.

➤ *Cash needs are growing faster than the organization can generate cash.* Consider raising prices to slow growth and increase profits.

Your approach to managing will have many things to take into account, but your company's stage of growth (or non-growth) is one of the most essential considerations.

The Best Type of Management: Simple Management

The more complex the organization, the easier it is to mess up. Set up an intricate and complex strategy, and there's a good chance something will go wrong. There are too many moving parts. It doesn't matter whether your style is Entrepreneurial or Big Culture: If you make it complex, you increase your chances of failure.

Good management is simple. If you have a good philosophy, you should be able to explain it to your employees over a cup of coffee. A good philosophy is something that will work when things go wrong, because face it (I hope you are ready for reality here): Things will go wrong.

It's been said that "A" students make the best professors, "B" students make the best accountants, and "C" students make the best managers. That may or may not be true, but I do think that "C" students know better than to try and deal with everything. It frees them to focus on the important stuff. Those who know and have experienced their limitations realize the need to do what they do well and not try to overreach. They often feel more comfortable delegating and realize that they can't do everything themselves. They trust their employees' abilities and assign projects and tasks to them. You don't have to be a genius to be a manager. You just have to be bright enough to know your limitations.

Try It This Way
Don't waste your time trying to make everything 1 percent better. Focus on making the important stuff significantly better. It will make a bigger difference in your company—and in your performance as a manager.

Focus. There's no better word to describe management. Some things, *some things,* make a difference. Smart, in business, is sometimes dumb, and dumb is sometimes smart. Managers know the difference. Good managers know that smart is usually simple.

The Least You Need to Know

➤ To succeed, you must know your product/service, your employees, your customers, and yourself. This is fundamental.

➤ Some aspects of your organization (financial resources, personnel resources, union or non-union, industry cycles) are determined before you take over. Understand them and manage accordingly.

➤ Your group's stage of growth will have a major impact on how you manage. Shrinking organizations offer different challenges and opportunities than growing ones.

➤ Simple, straightforward management gets the fastest and best results.

Seeing the Whole Picture

In the midst of the complexities of managing a business, it's easy to forget that the big, wide world is still going about *its* business, too. And yet what happens outside the office doors has a direct and shaping effect on what goes on inside. You need to know about the forces and events that affect your organization, and be ready to respond accordingly.

In the right market it's easy to be a genius. Most organizations rise in a rising market. The manager in charge will come out looking great. Unfortunately for him (or her), when the market shifts, perspective does too. That same manager may look a little less like a genius and a little more like a regular person.

This chapter will help you understand and anticipate some of the forces out there that can make a difference to your organization.

The Big Picture

No organization is an island—more like a boat on the tide. The tide of what? Social, political, and economic forces, to give some trivial examples. Interest rates. The world economy. Recession. Growth. Public policy. Get my drift? No matter how seaworthy you are, you can't wave away the big picture.

Your internal plan is important, but make sure you factor in what is happening globally, economically, and in your particular industry. The world has a bigger effect on you than you will ever have on the world. Read. Study. Analyze. Educate yourself.

Most trends are driven by sociological events and demographic shifts. That's why it's sometimes better to be lucky than to be clever—provided you're prepared when luck comes your way.

Press Release

The Baby Boom generation, consisting of those born from 1945–1960, is the largest demographic group around. As this group ages, opportunities are following them. Hair coloring, hearing aids, health products, and retirement communities will boom. The second largest group to follow is the children of the Baby Boomers known as the Echo Boomers.

A Story of Success

Here's a story about a company that followed a larger trend to great wealth.

Stressbusters

Early in this century, the buggy-whip business began to decline. The problem wasn't design flaws, pricing mistakes, or bad management; society just happened to be turning from horses to cars. Companies that got caught by surprise didn't survive. Keep an eye out: Technology creates new buggy whips every year.

RGI, a Norwegian company, was in the fishing industry, an industry fraught with problems. When the fishing was good, everyone was catching fish. The market was flooded and prices were depressed. When the catch was low, prices went up, but there weren't enough fish to sell. On top of all that, some prime fishing areas had become so overfished that the areas were no longer prime.

Many fishermen were going bankrupt and selling their boats.

So RGI began buying up boats at depressed prices and upgrading them, turning them into some of the best fishing boats in the world. Sounds crazy, right? Why make great boats in a depressed market? Keep reading.

RGI's upgraded boats could travel to wherever the fishing was good. They were equipped with the latest in flash-freezing equipment so that the catch would never spoil. That meant the fishermen could travel farther, and even more importantly, they could ship the fish to markets around the world—wherever the prices were best.

RGI didn't have to be able to control a trend to profit from it. The owners of the company now travel the world in Gulf Stream jets.

Many Trends Are Intuitively Obvious

Sometimes you stumble upon information. That's why it helps to keep your eyes open. Let me give a personal example.

I work in the adventure travel industry. In fact, I'm the founder of The North Face Company. A few years ago I was out hiking and noticed for the first time that about half my fellow hikers were women.

This started me thinking. Something was definitely wrong. Not only my own business, but the whole outdoor industry, both manufacturing and retail, were selling at most about 33 percent of our goods to women. We were obviously missing the market.

Why? I started asking the women I met on my adventure-type excursions. The answers I received were intriguing and a bit embarrassing.

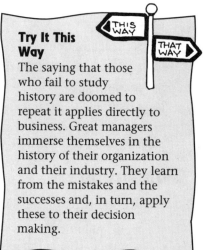

Try It This Way

The saying that those who fail to study history are doomed to repeat it applies directly to business. Great managers immerse themselves in the history of their organization and their industry. They learn from the mistakes and the successes and, in turn, apply these to their decision making.

I was told that the clothing that was made and sold in my industry didn't fit women very well and didn't look good either. We were offering a unisex look, and not every woman wanted that look. Besides that, our stores were macho, testosterone-oriented places staffed by male salespeople. We had created a sort of elitist atmosphere where women were treated with condescension. Ouch.

In the midst of my embarrassment, I spotted an opportunity in my oversight. I went to a small company called Wild Roses, which was designing outdoor clothing specifically for women. I asked if they would like an investor. They were thrilled.

I was thrilled too. I invested and helped them promote their product. The company was run by women, had women designers and salespeople, and made its clothing specifically for women. This company found a niche that no company, including my own, was going after.

Try It This Way

Take advantage of sociological shifts. More and more families have two wage earners these days—by necessity. Time has become a precious commodity. Shopping services, take-out foods, and other conveniences are among today's hot opportunities.

The success of Wild Roses has been phenomenal.

I could have concentrated on my numbers, cutting expenses and increasing sales margins. But I'm sure glad I didn't.

When you look, the big picture is usually pretty clear. Use it to your advantage. Economic trends, unemployment trends, regional trends—watch and dream. Be creative.

The Four Trends

Four trends are currently shaping the way of the world. Well, okay, there are more than four, but these are biggies:

➤ Globalization

➤ Technological growth

➤ Downsizing

➤ The high-speed society

Let's look at each of these trends in more detail.

Globalization

The world is getting smaller. Consider the following:

➤ Communications systems have become remarkably efficient. Travel, too, is getting faster—and cheaper. American popular culture is more and more the popular culture of the world.

➤ Improvements in communication and travel mean that companies can shift labor and production anywhere on the globe—wherever the most efficient markets are to be found. This means that even the smallest companies now face global competition.

➤ Products and services can be moved efficiently to virtually every market. Tastes are becoming less regionalized. Just look at the proliferation of ethnic foods in restaurants and grocery stores.

➤ Brand names like Levi and Nike are as prevalent outside the USA as inside.

Don't panic. Look at globalization as an opportunity. The key is to read and stay in touch with the global market. You don't have to be good enough to beat everyone—only your competition. If you understand the global aspect of your industry, you will have a better-than-fair chance for success.

An old story illustrates this well. Two guys are camping in a meadow when a big grizzly suddenly appears. One man jumps up and runs; the other puts on his running shoes.

"Why are you doing that?" yells the first guy. "You won't outrun the bear at that rate."

"I don't have to outrun the bear," his companion replies. "I only have to outrun you."

A final word about globalization. The world is breaking up into three distinct trade groups: the European Union, the North American Free Trade Agreement (NAFTA), and the Far East (principally Japan).

Agreements, like NAFTA and the Common Market, stimulate trade within each region but work to exclude or discourage trade between regions. This doesn't necessarily reduce opportunities, but it does make international business extremely complicated. When in doubt, seek expert advice.

Technological Growth

Remember when no one had ever heard of the Internet?

Now people are saying it's the greatest new opportunity to come along in decades. Whether or not that turns out to be true, it's certainly a great opportunity right now. The future is anyone's guess.

The advance of technology is already changing society in profound ways. Even the rate of change is increasing—dramatically. In Chapter 1, I pointed out that more technology will be invented in the next five years than we've seen in the past 20. Stop and think about the advances of the last 20 years, and then try to imagine what the next five years will be like if these predictions come true. The opportunities for some companies will be incredible. Others will fall by the wayside.

This is no time to be timid. Learn to use the Internet to your advantage, or hire someone who can. Technology is leveling the playing field, forcing big companies to think and act like small companies in order to stay competitive.

But bigger companies do still have some advantages, not the least of which is money. Don't wait for technology to be proven. Nowadays, companies that have the resources to stay ahead of the curve are smart to make the most of them.

Let the buyer beware, however. One problem with rapid technological change is that accounting rules and tax laws haven't kept up. The way they're written, you're forced to depreciate your hardware investments over a longer period of time than the actual useful life of the products. Your only option is to take a lump-sum write-off when you dispose of old technology and move on to newer products. It's frustrating, but don't let it stop you from investing in more up-to-date products.

Stressbusters

When it comes to technology, you don't want to fall behind, but neither do you want to be a guinea pig for new products. The trailing edge of the leading edge is where I like to be.

Try doing a payback analysis on purchases. Figure out how long it will take you to recover your investment, including the extra write-off, then compare that to your existing situation. That should make the decision easier.

Finally, a word about software. Does your company need a custom-designed system? It might and it might not. Before you invest, find out what's presently available off the shelf. Much of it is more than adequate for most companies, and surprisingly adaptable to your specific needs.

Downsizing

> **Simply Stated**
> In a *strategic alliance* between two organizations, one uses the other one's services in a specific area—accounting, for example—to perform tasks that were formally done in-house.

Cut costs, raise profits. That's downsizing in a nutshell. Many organizations are reducing payroll to increase profits. Who gets to deal with the effects of these decisions? Managers, of course. You may need to make these decisions yourself.

Meanwhile, the policy of cutting employees is forcing many organizations to form *strategic alliances* to augment their internal staffs.

The response time of an organization increases from strategic alliances, but the feeling of control diminishes.

The High-Speed Society

Entire businesses have been created in the past few decades on the concept of speed. Fast food and overnight deliveries are just two examples. Even if your organization does not belong to these speed-driven sectors, you probably still need to go faster.

He who hesitates is lunch. As a manager, you have to make quick decisions with less information. This non-stop acceleration can cause a manager some apprehension. Reluctance is common, but nothing could be worse. The wolves won't even wait for dinner.

The Life Cycle

All industries follow the same basic pattern of growth and maturation. This cycle is illustrated by the curve shown in the following figure.

Industries typically start slowly with limited growth. At some point they begin to grow rapidly, until they reach maturity with a slowing of growth. Where is your business in the cycle? If you have industry figures (which most of us don't), this is easy to calculate. Otherwise, I recommend that you do some research. Industry magazines, annual reports, and libraries are all useful sources.

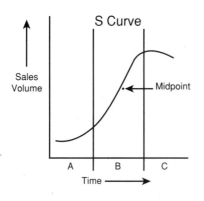

The typical product life cycle.

Where Are You in the Cycle?

Think about what stage your business is at:

➤ *Stage A: Product-driven.* Competition is not very keen; demand is likely to be greater than supply. The company's energies are directed toward increasing consumer awareness of the product or company. In Stage A, companies are typically small and simple to run.

➤ *Stage B: Growth.* Growth is usually fueled by some external event that causes sales to skyrocket. This is a tremendously exciting stage for companies. A good product is no longer the only requirement for survival; effective management and decision making become crucial as decision makers multiply and the pace of operations picks up.

➤ *Stage C: Maturity.* Sales growth slows down. Production overtakes demand, and the consumer drives the market. Because of the high level of competition, cost efficiency becomes imperative. This is the stage at which industries are consolidated. Some companies are acquired; others go out of business. It is exciting for the survivors, but traumatic for the others.

Knowing where your company is on the curve gives you several advantages. You'll know just what to focus on, you'll be able to make reasonable predictions about where your company is headed, and you'll even be able to make some sense of the conflicting information coming out of your industry.

Take another look at the curve. Do you see the spot marked "midpoint"? This is the point at which growth begins to diminish. The company (or industry) is still growing, but at a decelerating rate.

Midpoint on the S-Curve

How do you know when your business has arrived at the midpoint? Here are some of the signs:

➤ The market shifts from a product-driven to a customer-driven industry.

➤ Products are many, successful brands few.

➤ Professional managers take over from entrepreneurs.

➤ High-specialty products yield to lower-commodity products.

➤ *Sourcing* emphasizes cost-effectiveness instead of convenience.

➤ The industry press shifts from success stories to stories about acquisitions and failures. There is a subtle but noticeable shift from optimism to pessimism.

Simply Stated

Sourcing is the procurement of goods or services to facilitate the running of a business. An example is buying products, or components of products, for resale.

All businesses follow this pattern. The only variations are in sales volume and in the length of time a business takes to complete the cycle. The more technological the shift, the slower the evolution. The shift from fresh food to frozen food was slow and deliberate; the shift from wooden golf clubs to metal and then titanium was just the opposite.

Know Your Competition

What's the competition up to? For that matter, who are your competitors? Take some time to identify them and to analyze their strengths and weaknesses. You may gain some insight about opportunities you could be pursuing, or ways in which your business could be improved. You may also be able to anticipate your competitors' strategies and position your business accordingly. The more you know, the better you'll manage. Even anecdotal information helps.

Of course, there's a risk in too much competition analysis. It can lead to paralysis—or worse, mimicking a competitor's strategy. But it may help you avoid head-on, nonproductive collisions with your competition.

When I was running The North Face, my outdoor adventure company, I watched one of our competitors use competition analysis extremely effectively. Columbia wanted to expand in the industry, but the competition was pretty formidable—not only my company, but Patagonia, Helly Hansen, Moonstone, Marmot, Woolrich, and a host of others. All were focusing on one narrow niche of the market—high-priced and highly functional sports clothing.

Instead of trying to compete with all of us, Columbia took a different path. First it did a market matrix analysis. A market matrix analysis is a simple graphing technique that plots the positions of various competitors. The following figure shows the graph Columbia used to find its industry niche. Just change the identifiers on the x and y axes to suit your own needs.

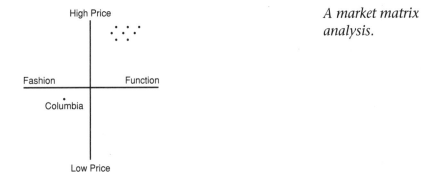

A market matrix analysis.

Columbia noticed a saturation of competition in the high-priced functional quadrant (upper right-hand corner, where the dots are concentrated).

To differentiate itself, Columbia decided to offer more fashionable garments at lower prices. Their "Bugaboo"—a jacket with zip-off sleeves—was priced under $100, for example, between 50 and 100 percent less than the competition equivalent.

Having chosen this quadrant, Columbia wisely allowed it to dictate their entire operation—from sourcing to margin to sales to financing. In 25 years, Columbia has grown from virtually no sales to over $300 million in sales. Not bad!

The Least You Need to Know

➤ No company exists in a vacuum. You can't control economic and social forces to suit your company, but you can benefit from them if you pay attention and stay flexible.

➤ Watch the four big trends: globalization, technological advances, downsizing, and the high-speed society.

➤ Organizational growth follows an S-curve of early growth, accelerated growth, and slowed growth (maturity).

➤ Studying your competition can tell you where the opportunities are.

Chapter 4

Getting Your Arms Around the Job

In This Chapter

➤ What a manager needs to survive

➤ Ways to deal with being busy

➤ Approaches to decision making

Any job is overwhelming when you first start. There's so much to learn and so little time to learn it. This is especially true for managers.

That's why one of the hardest and most important aspects of your job to learn is how to allocate your time effectively. It's your only defense against the ticking clock. Allocating means making intelligent decisions. Everything will seem urgent at times, but a good manager knows that spending all day putting out fires just guarantees more fires the next day. At the same time, you don't want to lose track of what's important while you deal with what's urgent. Remember, you are a manager because someone thinks you have vision. Prove that person right and you will succeed.

This chapter is about learning to take control of the job. It tells you what you need to survive, and how you can train yourself to make smart decisions. Sure it's overwhelming, but don't panic. Just read on.

Three Tools for Survival

When you're a manager, you face a lot of tests—some from others, some from yourself. You can wilt or you can survive—and I, for one, prefer survival. But where do you start? How do you begin to get your arms around the job of manager and to take control?

My advice is to start with an honest self-evaluation. Do you have the three essential qualities of a good manager?

➤ Vision

➤ Self-confidence

➤ Self-motivation

My view of these qualities follows. See if you agree with me.

Vision

People don't follow people, they follow visions. As a manager, you have the task of articulating your vision of the company, of your employees, and of yourself. Vision comes first from knowledge of yourself, second from knowledge of your organization and industry. I can't say this often enough: *You were hired for a reason.* Someone, somewhere believes in your ability to make decisions and to articulate a clear vision. If you don't have a vision, you will have a tough time—an impossible time—managing. Your employees expect you to have vision—Vision? Yes, an image of a better future. What would that look like?

You've probably been studying the organization and the market for some time now, and have developed a perspective based on knowledge. If you haven't, that's your top priority. First figure out what's up; then you can begin to think about where it's all going.

Try It This Way
Call a strategy meeting of your key people to talk about new directions for the organization. The people "in the trenches" almost always have great ideas about how to make the organization grow. Don't be afraid to ask questions or to listen. That's part of your job.

That's vision. Vision addresses where the organization is going and how it should be run. It's your concept of how to make the organization better, grounded in your research about where it has already been.

When I founded The North Face, it was based on the vision of a changing society. It was the Vietnam era and people were changing their lifestyles. They were moving away from the cities, traveling more, and looking for inspiration.

Establishing The North Face, which produced sleeping bags, packs, tents, and functional clothing, allowed people to comfortably commune with nature. It was the perfect response to the needs and changes we saw in society. It also formed the nucleus of our plans for the future.

Your vision of how the organization should be run will be your distinctive contribution as manager. There's no one style that guarantees success. On the contrary, I've seen many styles succeed. The only guaranteed formula is this: Follow your heart. It's the only way to succeed.

Here are three common styles of managing:

➤ *Delegate.* "We need to get things done, so I want you to do this, and you over here to do that, and you two to do this thing."

➤ *Dictate.* "Do it! Right now! Do it now or you're fired!"

➤ *Build consensus.* "So, what does everybody think? How many are in favor of this? Okay, Mark, tell me why. Jane, what do you think about that?"

What kind of manager are you? I'm a delegator. That's the style that works for me—and I mean *for me.*

You are not me. You are you. You're the person you have to trust. Don't believe me or my style. You can only trust yourself.

When you've been a manager for a while, you'll begin to notice that the people who work for you have chosen to do so. Those who don't like your style will vote with their feet. And that's good. You're building a team.

Self-Confidence

You don't have to be right all the time. Accept it and move on. Self-confidence is the ability to make wrong decisions as well as right ones and to know that's okay. Hey, everybody makes wrong decisions. Don't be afraid of it. *Often wrong, never in doubt* is one of my mottoes. It works for me. It works for every successful manager.

When you're a manager, you have to make decisions which a lot of people will then question. Good. Good for them, good for you. You're not going to get unwavering agreement very often. When it happens, buy a lottery ticket, because it's obviously your lucky day.

The point is, you're not the only person with the answers. A good manager is a good listener. Why? Because good decisions depend on input. When things don't succeed the way you hoped, deal with it and move on. Believe in yourself, and others will too.

A friend of mine had an electronics company based on some proprietary patents. When his partner left in a dispute, he was faced with the possibility of a lengthy and costly battle over these patents and potentially damaging delays.

He never missed a beat though. He hired a bulldozer, dug a huge hole in the back yard of his business and buried all the products. He had no idea what kind of product he would produce next, but he did know that he couldn't, and shouldn't, look back. He knew the same energy invested in moving forward would get infinitely better results. And it did. He is now a millionaire many times over from that business, a business based almost entirely on self-confidence.

Try It This Way You can improve your self-confidence when you start out as a manager by making small decisions first and sharing large decisions with others.

Confidence comes from information, among other things. If you know what you're talking about, you'll feel a lot stronger about making a decision. Try following these confidence-building steps:

1. Define the problem/opportunity.
2. Research causes and solutions.
3. Lay out the facts.
4. Prioritize the choices based on what is best for the company.
5. Make a decision.

Self-Motivation

Stressbusters If you don't make things happen, no one will. Do nothing and nothing will happen. Do something, and something will happen. Do it quick enough and you'll always have time to make it even better.

Inspire yourself and you'll inspire others. Count on it.

Are you motivated? Do you rush to work eager to meet the challenge of your job? If not, it could be time for some serious assessment. Maybe you really don't want the job. That feeling is going to come across to others. Could it be time to make a change? Rest assured, there are plenty of jobs out there just waiting for someone like you—someone who loves their work.

Test your self-motivation by answering these questions:

1. Do you love to go to work in the morning?
2. Do you get frustrated at inefficiencies in your organization?
3. Do you feel like screaming when you lose to another organization?
4. Do you constantly seek to change and improve things?

If you answered yes to all of these, you have proper managerial motivation. Focus on these attributes and take on the world.

If your motivational lag is short term, figure out the cause and correct it. As a manager, your job is to bring a high level of motivation to your staff, and that is only possible if you have and exude that level of motivation yourself. Once again, this is common sense.

Guess What? You're Going to Be Busy

There is never enough time. Every manager knows it. Some get up at 4:00 a.m. and still don't have enough time to get things done. No matter what they do, they feel as if they're falling further and further behind. So they stay later, try to work faster. Help! Stress!

There is a better way. It has to do with how you parcel out your time. You can't do everything—so start with the most important things, and then do the next-most important. *Prioritize.*

Simply Stated
Prioritizing is ranking your tasks from most important to least, then focusing on those at the top of the list first.

Make a list of everything you have to do and then rank the items on the list: 1, 2, 3…Focus on the most important; if you can, hand off the lower-ranked tasks to others. Some things will simply be left undone.

Simplify—Starting with Committees

Complexity is the nemesis of efficient management. Complex things take time, your most precious commodity. Two of the most common time-gobblers in business are reports and committees. Some are necessary but I have found many are not. We can all save a lot of time by eliminating those that are not necessary.

Think about committees. A group of people get together and try to make each person's input mesh with everyone else's. It's a nice idea in theory, but in practice too often leads to a mish-mash of compromise.

With committees, simplicity is harder to achieve. Not only do decisions take longer to reach, they tend to be based on irrelevant factors—personal friendships, pleasing co-workers (so they will be easier to work with) individual personalities, and so on. Decisions should be based on results.

Try It This Way
Want to make your committee meetings decision-oriented and fast? Make a no-sitting rule: Meet standing up.

Committee dynamics usually put the focus on consensus, whether or not that consensus favors the best solution. Consensus is good, but not when it's achieved *at the expense of* results.

"Search the parks in all the cities," someone once said, "and you will not find one statue of a committee." It's an interesting point. Committees are extremely helpful for the sharing of information and getting a two-way discussion going, but they don't necessarily make for strong leadership.

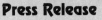

Press Release

A few years ago, the Museum of Modern Art almost launched a $100,000 study to determine which areas of the museum were most popular. The committee that decided this thought it was a good idea, but at the last minute, one member had another thought. The committee achieved its goal by asking the janitors where they did the most cleaning.

Stressbusters
The equation that works best is generally one part analysis and three parts action.

Try It This Way
Reading and analyzing reports is a time-consuming but necessary part of being a manager. You can simplify the process by requiring that every report begin with a one-page summary of its contents.

Reducing committee inefficiency is just one way to simplify. In the next chapter I'll be talking about a few other ways, including organizational charts, employee feedback systems, and financial reports. You can even simplify your phone system—but for that you'll need to talk to a phone company.

Reports can be beneficial or confusing, but too many reports are just plain overwhelming. However, analyzing why so many reports are being churned out can be very enlightening and amusing.

➤ Is it because your team fears face-to-face confrontations?

➤ Is it because people want something on paper so they can cover their backsides?

➤ Is it because your team is more academic and not so much results oriented?

➤ Is it because your people are more literal than verbal?

The causes are many, but the result of too many reports is always the same—paralysis. As a manager, you have to cut out excessive reports and the reasons for them. You need to create an environment that is "results oriented" and conducive to efficient decision making.

Delegate

Getting other people to do things is an essential role of a manager. That's what delegating is—taking work from your desk and assigning it to someone else.

Of course, it's a lot more involved than that. I break the delegation process into three steps:

1. Assign specific tasks with specific timetables.

2. If you are assigning a task to a team, assign a leader.

3. Make sure everyone understands the objective, how much work is involved, how results will be measured along the way, and what the final goal is.

Never forget that, although you are passing along responsibility, you really have full responsibility.

Manage by Exception

One way to keep tabs on your areas of responsibility is to set standards and then measure performance against those standards. If a standard is met within a range you consider reasonable, great. You can let that function alone. Significant deviation, however, either above or below the standard, deserves attention.

Management by exception means paying just as much attention to positive variances as negative ones. If sales are over budget, for example, you may soon run out of inventory. If sales are way under budget, you'll soon find your bottom line profits are also substandard.

Decide to Make a Decision

So, you're a decision maker. Do you know how to make decisions? How are you going to learn to do it effectively? Quick, decide!

What kind of team do you want? How do you plan to lead? These aren't easy questions. Sometimes you approach them with a pen and paper, sometimes via a quiet room or vigorous exercise, sometimes with a trusted confidant. In the end, the decision is yours.

To do this well, you have to know yourself well. The big stuff counts, but the small stuff will get you. You have to make decisions all day, every day, in a timely and rational style. The last thing you want is to be going back and revisiting old decisions all the time.

Nor do you want opportunity to pass you by.

> **Stressbusters**
> When it comes to making decisions, perfection = paralysis. You don't have time for exhaustive research and analysis every time you make a decision. Sometimes you just have to leap. After all, while you're analyzing, your competitors are probably *doing*. Taking a risk is preferable to doing nothing.

If you're having a tough time feeling comfortable about decision making, don't panic. Try my foolproof three-step approach:

1. *Set clear goals.* What are you trying to accomplish? Write it down as completely as you can. The more thoroughly you define your goal, the easier it will be to make decisions that support that goal.

2. *Conduct research.* Ask around, look around, read around. Gather numbers, if they are available. Go find stuff out.

3. *Lay out the facts.* That means organizing the research so that it's easier to analyze and act on.

Finally, trust your intellect—and your gut. Make choices. This is the moment where you prove your worth.

The Discipline of Decision Analysis

There's a mathematical side to some kinds of decision making. One technique I have used with great success is a widely taught discipline called Decision Analysis, which involves analyzing alternatives and assigning each one a value. Decision analysis helps you to make logical choices based on the probability of a given event.

Consider this example. Let's say a manager is trying to figure out how to allocate the time of her sales staff. There are three types of accounts: big buyers, who place few orders but generate $100,000 profit when they buy; medium buyers, who place more orders but generate an average of only $50,000; and small buyers, who place more orders still but generate only $25,000. So far, so good.

Now assume all of her competitors are pursuing big buyers. Based on past experience with this market and common sense, this gives her only about a 10 percent chance of success with that market.

Medium buyers have fewer salespeople chasing them, but they are always looking for a better deal. With this crowd she has a 25 percent chance of success.

Small buyers are not being chased. Based on her experience with small buyers, she assumes an 80 percent chance of success.

From this information you can construct the following equation:

Channel of Sales	Result	Probability	Expected Value
	(a)	(b)	(a) × (b) = (c)
Big Buyers	$100,000	10 percent	$10,000
Medium Buyers	$50,000	25 percent	$12,500
Small Buyers	$25,000	80 percent	$20,000

The solution now becomes obvious: She should focus on the small buyers.

Of course there are no guarantees. There aren't many in life, apart from death and taxes. But logic and reason are a good foundation for instinct.

The Business School at Stanford University (650-723-1670) offers a two-day course in decision analysis. You might want to check out what schools in your area are offering.

I Decide to End This Chapter

Management is making decisions. Once you get your arms around the job, you have no choice: You've got to start making the tough calls. Remember, if you make the wrong decision fast enough, you can still correct it. How's that for comfort?

Like this: I decide to end this chapter right now.

Nope, I changed my mind…Okay, NOW it's over. See? It works.

The Least You Need to Know

➤ Know and believe in yourself. Believe you have the ability to learn and adjust.

➤ To make the best use of your limited time, practice simplifying your approach and delegating your work.

➤ Techniques like management by exception and decision analysis can be extremely useful. In the end, however, it always comes back to your gut. Who are you?

Chapter 5

Organizing Your Work and Your Day

In This Chapter

➤ Two approaches to time management

➤ How and when to plan your day

➤ Three time sneaks and how to avoid them

You think your day is planned—then the phone rings. You answer it and suddenly you're trying to think your way through a crisis. At that moment the mail is dropped on your desk.

As you talk, you open the mail. Hey, something just gave you a great idea. That's an opportunity you really want to pursue. You make a note of it while you go on trying to get a handle on the crisis.

You're keeping track of the facts, factoring in the trends, managing someone's personality, and checking your e-mail all at the same time. There's a note from your lawyer about the acquisition. Everything is in place except for one tiny detail: The price has gone up.

Welcome to the world of business, where everything always goes as planned, provided you planned for chaos. This chapter is about how to take control of your time—how to organize meetings and phone calls, how to deal with competing demands, and how to get through a crisis. Learn to work with time and you can control it. Otherwise it will control you.

Making the Most of Your Time

Management is a marathon, but it's also a 100-yard dash. To deal with both you need a plan and a system of organization. There's no single right way to do this, although there are plenty of wrong ways. Basically, anything that uses up time unproductively falls in the second category.

This is one area in which you can definitely learn from others. Talk to other managers and ask them what tricks they use to maximize time. Some people like to use a day planner organizer. Some find time management classes helpful. There are lots of approaches. Time is your most precious asset, and your organization's most precious asset too. Invest it with great care.

Here are two basic approaches to time management. Which works best for you?

Start with What You Dislike

Saving the most enjoyable work for last helps some race through the drudgery quickly instead of dawdling and procrastinating over it. For members of this camp, looking forward to the fun tasks provides energy for dealing with the less-fun tasks.

Press Release

Leonardo da Vinci took a unique approach to maximizing his time. He sketched with his right hand and wrote with his left simultaneously. He didn't accept the standard ways of doing things as the only way to do things. As a result, he found time where it appeared there was none.

Start with What You Like

The other approach is to start with what you enjoy. This is the one that works for me. The enjoyable work energizes me and establishes a pattern of problem solving that carries me through the less exciting work. If the fun tasks are also the most important, even better.

This approach works especially well if you don't mind a few things always dangling and being unfinished. By the very nature of this approach, you may be so excited by what you are doing that you will never get around to dealing with all the detail.

Got the Plans?

Here's a simple strategy that you might not think to try but that really works. Make your to-do list the night before. You don't want to begin your day trying to figure out where you should start and what you should do first. You want to hit the ground running. Having the next day charted out before you leave your office means you can make the most of your time away from the job instead of worrying about work. Enjoy a ballgame or the opera or your children. (Yes, effective managers do have lives outside of work!)

The format I use to plan my next business day is simple and effective. A daily to-do list, such as the one shown below, gives me a snapshot of my workload. I then work from the top down and check things off as I complete them.

Daily to-do List

Call:

Matt Smith	(212) 555-5555
Mary Jones	(508) 555-4444
Denny White	(312) 555-3333
Jane Brown	(970) 555-2222
Kelly Green	(415) 555-1111
_____	_____
_____	_____

Meet:

10:00: Staff Meeting, Conference Room

2:00: Insurance Agent, his office

_____

_____

Do:

1. Write fax to European sales reps
2. Do research on competitors
3. Pay consultants
4. Prepare for board meeting
5. Prepare for trade show; make travel plans
6. _____
7. _____

My phone calls are "ranked" from the Eastern time zone to the West to make sure I call during business hours. This is especially important when you are doing international business. (It won't help you or your business very much to call someone in the middle of the night!) Also notice that I leave extra spaces in each section to accommodate anything that may arise during the day.

The meeting portion of my schedule is self-explanatory—I just need to know when to be where.

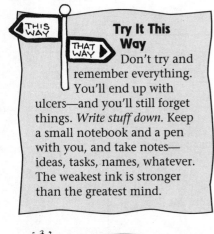

Try It This Way

Don't try and remember everything. You'll end up with ulcers—and you'll still forget things. *Write stuff down.* Keep a small notebook and a pen with you, and take notes—ideas, tasks, names, whatever. The weakest ink is stronger than the greatest mind.

Stressbusters

Too rigid a schedule can be just as bad as no schedule. Sometimes you need to take care of emergencies and urgencies as they come up, even if you had other plans for your day. Leaving some flexibility makes dealing with such eventualities significantly easier.

The "Do" portion of my schedule is organized from most important to least.

I have a rule that if anything in the "Call" or "Do" section stays more than one week without any action, I eliminate it from my worksheet. If I am ignoring it, I probably won't get around to it anyway, so there's no point keeping it on the list. If it's important, it will probably surface again.

Surviving the Squeeze

Demands on your time and presence are coming from above and from below—from the boss, board of directors, investors, and from your employees. Unless you have been cloned (still unrealistic, unless you are a sheep), you can only be in one place at a time. Yet you have to be responsive.

Here are some tips for dealing with competing claims on your attention:

1. If someone is in your office and the phone rings, answer the phone and tell the caller you're in a meeting and that you'll call him back. The person calling doesn't know you have a visitor and may be put off by your voice mail or your continuing lack of availability, while the visitor in your office will know you are receiving a call and understand.

2. Anticipate the possibility of meetings overlapping or conflicting, and block out time in your schedule for rescheduling. A delayed meeting is better than a canceled meeting. Your employees will be glad you found time to meet with them, even if they had to wait.

3. When you reach someone's voice mail, don't just ask them to call back. Tell them when you called, why you called, what you would like them to do, and when you want them to call back. Be specific.

4. Send faxes in the evening. The rates will be lower and the fax will be fresh on the recipient's desk in the morning.

5. Before you place an international call, send a fax. Tell the person when you will call and what you want to discuss.

6. If you have a cellular phone, make good use of it. It's not JUST for looking cool. It's also so you can be stuck in traffic and with the person you are calling at the same time. A phone call is not as good as a face-to-face meeting, but it will allow you to spread yourself around more.

7. Each day, make it known that you will be available at a certain time. You'll be interrupted less often, guaranteed.

Press Release

Northwestern Mutual Life, the giant insurance company, has a rule that no internal calls are made on Thursdays. This gives employees one whole day to handle other matters without being interrupted. If an urgent matter comes up, employees can send e-mail, though they are encouraged to make sure it is really urgent.

When a legitimate conflict arises, use common sense. Decide which meeting/call/contact is most urgent and explain the importance to the person you have to delay. If you're on the same team striving for a common goal, the person will understand that it's not a question of who's more important, but who can help the organization the most. Even if they don't understand, you at least know that you will be measured on results—only results.

Obstacles to an Organized Day

No matter how well organized you are, you are going to run into conflicts. Every day you'll have to find time for things you simply don't have time for. In other words, you will be expected to do the impossible and make it look routine on a daily basis.

Three huge obstacles will test your ability to get your work done. Those three things are:

➤ Meetings

➤ Information overload

➤ The appearance of crisis

Meetings—Do I HAVE To?

The best way to handle the problem of meetings is not to have them. Okay, that may not work too well. But you really do want to minimize the time you spend in meetings so you are free to spend it on more productive endeavors.

Here are some ways to accomplish this:

➤ Set a firm time limit on the length of a meeting. Most people can't concentrate for more than two hours anyway. Schedule a meeting for just before lunch and no one will feel like prolonging things.

➤ Send out a written agenda in advance.

➤ Write up the results of the meeting and distribute them to every participant with a request that they edit as necessary and get back to you.

The third step is especially important if you don't want to feel as if the time you spent in a meeting has been wasted. Something that happened to me illustrates this point especially forcefully.

Once, at a sales meeting, I made an announcement that the percentage of sales paid in commissions to our sales reps would be reduced because sales were rapidly escalating and we were beginning to incur all sorts of additional costs to support those growing sales. I went to great lengths to explain that, in real dollars, their pay would still go up if they performed well. The only thing being cut was their percentage. There was a lot of silence, which I interpreted as grudging acceptance, but a couple weeks later I received visits from two sales reps, both of whom had been at that meeting. Both asked me if the rumor was true that their percentage commission was going down. They told me they had heard the rumor from other sales reps. Apparently the two reps had heard nothing and the others who informed them had misconstrued what I said. The moral is, just because you say something doesn't mean people heard you.

Information Overload

It's not hard to find yourself buried beneath the information avalanche. The irony is that most of the information you receive is worthless—or at best overdone. Most is longer than it needs to be. Encourage brevity and clarity in office memos and reports.

Try It This Way

Put an hourglass on your desk and turn it over when you begin phone calls. Try and get to the end of your calls before the hour is up.

Routine response formats for matters that come up regularly can be great time-savers. Form letters and memo templates are two examples: No sense reinventing the wheel if you don't have to.

If you have someone to screen your phone calls or mail, give that person authority to make decisions for you. Just be sure to get copies of whatever is sent out on your behalf. Reviewing and signing letters and faxes before they are sent gives you a measure of control. But after awhile, you may not even have to review these things.

Block out a certain part of the day for NOT taking calls. Make sure everyone in the organization knows about this.

A final way to limit information overload is to respond promptly to faxes on the original fax paper. Just hand-write on the original and send it back. This spares you the trouble of constructing a formal response and spares the recipient having to refer to the original fax.

Eliminating Crisis

Everyone loves a good crisis. Well, not really, but there's certainly nothing like it for testing your managerial skills. The first thing to remember is that many crises aren't. Often they're just problems to which someone has been tempted to overreact. These sorts of situations require deft handling: The employee wants your attention, and yet you know that the more responsive you are to a crisis, the more crises you will face. This is bad for you and bad for the collective psyche of the company. It can even undermine your authority as a manager.

Make it known to your employees that anyone wishing to bring a problem to your attention must be ready with a suggested solution beforehand. This will force people to stop and think instead of flying off the handle. (Whether you adopt a particular solution is up to you.)

The important thing is not to be rushed into making a judgment because someone else perceives a crisis. When people know you will not automatically respond, they will stop using the crisis technique to get your attention.

> **Stressbusters**
> Never react to a fax or letter in an emotionally charged manner. Give yourself time to calm down and construct a reasoned, professional response. You'll have less explaining to do later.

Keep track of which people are bringing you crises. When you see a pattern of behavior that relies on crises, counsel the person on how better to deal with the situation.

When legitimate crises do occur, and this will happen, remember not to put it on the back burner but to deal with it in a professional way. Some things to keep in mind when a crisis occurs are: don't panic, ask for a written summary of the situation, ask for a prioritized list of solutions, and most important, make a decision.

The Least You Need to Know

➤ Decide what you want to do first: the tasks you like, or the tasks you don't like. Which works best for you?

➤ Coming up with your next day's schedule the night before saves a lot of time.

➤ Don't let meetings, information overload, or constant crises rob you of your valuable time.

Part 2
Instilling a Sense of Purpose

Life is short.

Management is a chance for you to do something electrifying. You must believe that, or why bother? Don't do it just for the paycheck, because no matter how much it is, if you're not into the job, the money won't be worth it. There is too much to do in management for you not to enjoy it.

In this part of the book, you'll learn how your motivation will become the motivation of your employees. It's important to find what it is that makes you burn, so you can make them burn, too. These chapters are about passion. You will learn about leading, and discover how to find your core. I'll discuss managing your manager, because for you to succeed, you will need their approval. And finally, I'll talk about setting goals. Life is short. Make it your goal to make it great.

Learning to Lead

In This Chapter

➤ The many faces of leadership

➤ Leading with vision

➤ Finding your leadership style

➤ Bringing out the hero in your employees

➤ Making it all work together

You've gotta have style—management style. This means more than just giving out assignments. You want to encourage people to do their best. Your role is not just to manage, but to inspire.

This chapter is all about leadership. It covers pragmatic things like method, communication, and timing, and some harder-to-pin-down things like style, presence, and how to bring out the heroes and heroines in your team members. Leadership involves many complex steps, but the concept behind it is a simple one: You need to get people to believe in you and your vision. Follow me, I'll show you the way.

Managers Take the Lead

Don't be shy. Shyness and leadership go together about as well as hot fudge and mayonnaise. I'm not saying you have to be some tub-thumping preacher. If that's not your style, don't even try it. But you do have to be a leader, because that's your job. Besides, life expands or shrinks in proportion to one's courage.

Leadership in management means getting everybody working together amicably for a common goal, often (but not always) defined by you. It's team building, and you're the coach. Leadership isn't synonymous with management, but it's pretty hard to manage without it.

Part Visionary, Part Administrator

You've got the people. You've got the resources. You've got the product. What more do you need? Someone to run things. That's where you come in.

Business leadership means figuring out how to use those people and those resources to realize a vision and a goal. It's not the ride-in-on-a-white-horse kind of leadership—not usually. It's an ongoing set of responsibilities that combine roles like visionary, administrator, teacher, and boss to achieve goals. What are those responsibilities? You already know, but for the record, they are:

➤ Understanding the goal

➤ Identifying tasks

➤ Breaking up tasks

➤ Linking tasks together

➤ Encouraging people

➤ Evaluating people

➤ Taking corrective action

Quite simply, leadership is seeing that things get done.

Press Release

Years ago, workers were given control of an assembly line as part of a study on productivity. The workers varied the speed depending on the time of day. The production line ran fast in the morning, slower after lunch. Workers liked it that way. So did management—once they realized that a measure of control made the work force more productive.

Set the Tone

You are the battery pack of your business unit. Your style, your moods, your techniques drive the company. This was brought home to me in a powerful way at a consulting job not long ago.

When "Joe" called me, he sounded despondent. "We've got a problem with sales and earnings," he said. "Can you help?" We made an appointment and I went out to see him. I like to interview as many people in a company as I can, but I try to see the manager first. The manager sort of sprinkles holy water on the consulting project.

When I walked into Joe's office, I felt as if I had stumbled into a funeral in progress. He had a long frown and a sad, monotonous voice. Although he wasn't past middle age yet, his eyes looked old and beaten.

"You look like you hate your job," I said.

"You got it," he growled. "I can't stand coming here in the morning."

"Why don't you quit?"

Joe's was a doomed smile. "Only 15 years until retirement," he said.

No wonder sales were in trouble. Joe couldn't even find the soapbox, let alone get on it and motivate anyone.

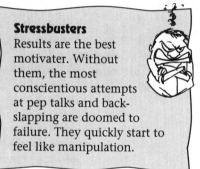

Stressbusters
Results are the best motivater. Without them, the most conscientious attempts at pep talks and back-slapping are doomed to failure. They quickly start to feel like manipulation.

If you have enthusiasm, it will show. If you don't, well, the results will show that too.

Though This Be Motivation, Yet There Is Method in It

As you know from your years as an employee, motivation is much more than empty cheers and hurrahs. Leadership needs to be intentional; it needs a method that will get people working harder and better. It's like old-fashioned dancing—the kind where one partner leads and the other follows. If you're leading, and you know where you're going, your partner will find it much easier to follow, and you'll both enjoy the dance. If the lead dancer feels unsure of himself (or herself), no one has any fun.

Here are the 10 steps I've developed for motivational leadership:

1. Define the responsibility of all subordinates.
2. Forecast the future.
3. Set specific objectives to be achieved.
4. Establish a plan of action to reach the objectives.
5. Set up timetables.

6. Establish budgets broken down by individuals who report to you.

7. Identify checkpoints along the way to the goal.

8. Measure performance against your standards.

9. Take corrective action when necessary.

10. Achieve your objectives.

The key is good communication and clear assignment of responsibility—particularly the quantifiable, financial responsibilities that are tied to the goals of the company.

Uh...What Did You Say?

What a difference good communication makes! Articulate your goals so they can be understood, and you're on the way to success.

What exactly are your expectations? Communicate them in quantitative terms. "Amanda, you are responsible for…" *what?* Well, some folks are responsible for bringing in profits, and others are expected to control costs. Of course, revenues and expenses aren't your only concerns, but they're good starting points.

Profit centers are areas of responsibility where an individual is responsible for revenues as well as costs. A division like sales and marketing is one example of a profit center; another might be is a geographic subset of a division. Whoever is in charge of a profit center is accountable when it comes to the profit or loss of that center. The following form is useful for evaluating and guiding your employees, as you need to do regularly.

Evaluating a profit center's performance.

PROFIT CENTER - DEPARTMENT						
Month						
Sales		Monthly			Year to Date	
	Actual	Budget	Difference	Actual	Budget	Difference
Cost of Goods	$ %	$ %	$	$ %	$ %	$
Gross Margin						
Expenses						
Largest Budget						
2nd Largest						
3rd Largest						
4th Largest						
etc.						
Total Expenses						
Contributions						
Accounts Receivable						

The following cost center form is similar and can be used to measure responsibility and progress for employees who only have control of expenses—departments such as finance, office management, or shipping.

COST CENTER - DEPARTMENT						
Month						
	Monthly			Year to Date		
	Actual	Budget	Difference	Actual	Budget	Difference
Expenses	$ %	$ %	$	$ %	$ %	$
Largest Budget						
2nd Largest						
3rd Largest						
4th Largest						
etc.						
Total Expenses						

Evaluating expense controls at a cost center.

Using these forms allows your people to rate their own performance regularly, long before you sit down with them to go over results. Frequent reviews are important, though. Once you get your system of measurement in place, I recommend assessing progress once a month, with a major review annually. Where are you in relation to your goals? Numbers are important, but don't forget to look at percentages, too.

Someone—that's *one*, singular—needs to be in charge and responsible at each profit and cost center. Go over things with that person once a month, offer guidance and support and develop corrective action, if necessary, but then *get out of the way*. People need to have authority equal to their responsibility. A good leader doesn't micromanage.

Be a Visionary

Vision is important for a leader. You don't need to be way ahead of everyone—a step or two will do. Your people need to know and trust your vision. They need to have confidence in you.

Important patterns in business are often repeated, but the world does change. Keep an eye on the trends (see Chapter 3). If you can figure what is repeated and what is changing, you can make predictions about the future of your organization. That's vision.

Simply Stated

A *profit center* is a grouping of revenues and expenses for which one person is held responsible.

A *cost center* is similar to a profit center except no revenues or profits are included because the person in charge of this is only responsible for cost control.

Try It This Way

When accountants lean on you to organize expenses their way, stand firm. It's important that you organize your reports, your headings, and your sub-categories to reflect how you run your company, division, or department, and in a way that *you* can understand.

Press Release

Vision is not always recognized as such. Fred Smith, founder of Federal Express, was given a "C" on his economics paper at Yale. The subject of his paper? The development of an overnight delivery service. Great ideas and great visions are often not clear to everybody. But like Fred Smith, we should not let that get in our way!

Products have a predictable life cycle or path that they follow. One way to chart the future is to become familiar with this cycle and use it to plan your organization's activities. Have a look at the following graph and see whether you can pinpoint where your product is in the cycle.

The life cycle of products.

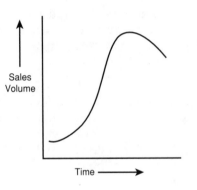

If you know where you are on this cycle, you can make a reasonable decision about how much more to invest, if anything, and what the return might be. You can also decide when to stop making a product.

The cycle doesn't vary. The only thing that distinguishes one company's product from another is volume of sales and how long it takes for the cycle to be completed.

Since all good products must come to an end someday, it stands to reason that to stay in business you're going to need new products. By studying the cycle, you can get to know when it's time to introduce new products, seek out new markets, or extend the life cycles of your existing products. Graphically, the process looks something like what's shown in the following figure.

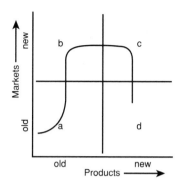

The quadrants of a product life cycle.

Quadrant a is the alpha, or startup, phase. R&D and marketing demand a lot of cash, and you may lose money for a while. Prices are not normally under pressure during this phase. Despite negative cash flow and tepid profits, companies keep plugging along, waiting for the anticipated growth phase.

Quadrant b is the break-even phase. Old products are meeting new markets. Profits are great, cash flow is good; there is little need for investment, except to fund inventory and sales. This is the growth phase.

Quadrant c is a cash cow. No further investment is needed. The product is humming. Profit margins will probably be squeezed, but there will be profits.

Quadrant d is a dog. Business is down, the product is dying, and you are at risk of getting stuck with inventory. This is a cash trap: It's time to exit the market.

Get the idea? With this information, you can confidently lead your product design and sales team toward the future.

Democratic, Autocratic, or Clueless?

There are many styles of management that work. The one that works for you is the one that allows you to be true to yourself.

A lot of people prefer a democratic approach, in which employees are encouraged to ask questions, make suggestions, and generally have some input. I like this style because it involves the team in the decision-making process and gives them a good feeling about me, themselves, and most importantly, the company. It makes them feel more invested.

The one time this does *not* work is in a crisis. That's when you need to assume an authoritative role. For this you must know and trust your own instincts.

Another popular management style is the autocratic. Take charge. Don't worry what others think. You're the boss: Act like it. Trust yourself completely. If necessary—and it probably will be necessary from time to time—show people the door. Now, I don't prefer this style myself. But if this is you, that is who you should be. It can and does work.

The worst thing is to be clueless. Many of us have worked for or with someone like this. They waver. They waffle. They're autocrats one moment, consensus builders the next. They're doomed. Employees can spot cluelessness a mile away. If you fall prey to this malady, suddenly everyone's agenda will be more important than yours. No one will believe in your instincts once they come to see that you don't believe in them yourself.

Figure out who you are and stay true to yourself. Be somebody.

Turn Your Employees into Heroes

No one is perfect. Not your employees, not yourself. You can dwell on the negatives or focus on the positives; I say it's an easy choice.

Make your employees winners. Make them feel and act like winners. Make them proud partners of the organization. Happy, motivated, self-assured employees deliver results. You don't have to have a degree in psychiatry to understand that the way people think about themselves is a prime determinant in their success. The more you can make heroes of your employees, the more heroic their actions will be.

Here are some ways to make your people feel like heroes:

➤ Simplify your message—complexity confuses and often paralyzes people.

➤ Assign responsibility equal to people's skills—don't doom your employees to failure.

➤ Give meaningful work—let people know they are valuable.

➤ Give recognition and praise to successes—appreciated employees are motivated employees.

➤ Have a larger purpose than just making money—allow employees to have an emotional as well as an economic attachment to the organization.

➤ Never reprimand in public.

➤ Always praise in public.

Managers who take all the credit for successes and blame all the failures on others don't make for very popular leaders. Those who cultivate a sense of teamwork do much better. Don't think "you" and "I"; think "us." Not only will your group will be stronger for it, you'll get better results. Hey, this job isn't about *your* ego. It's about team building.

You need your team. If you didn't, you probably wouldn't have them. But you do have them, so take advantage of the skills and drive they bring, and celebrate their successes.

One man knew this lesson well. Interestingly, he is remembered as one of the great lone adventurers of all time, although he knew better than to call himself one.

Edmund Hilary was a beekeeper in New Zealand when he decided he wanted something more. So he set out to climb Mt. Everest.

He had one companion, a Sherpa guide, Tenzing Norgay. Now, Norgay was a friend as well as a guide. When they climbed, they climbed together, and arrived at the summit at the same time.

When they returned, Hilary was proclaimed a hero and was even knighted, to be known forevermore as Sir Edmund Hilary. But Hilary refused sole credit. His equal, he declared, was Tenzing Norgay, a Sherpa guide. It was quite a statement for a time when people of European descent mostly took their superiority for granted. But Hilary didn't care what others believed. He knew what he believed. He knew about teamwork.

Hilary gave back, too. He used his new fame to raise money to help the Sherpas build schools and hospitals.

Hilary was a hero because he allowed Tenzing Norgay to be one. You can do the same with your employees.

Timelines on the Wall

But how do you lead a whole team of individuals who depend on one another for many things, but who hear, each in his or her own way, a different drummer?

Answer: You use a timeline.

The timeline is where the rubber meets the road—where the abstract is quantified according to time and results. It's a translation of the motion of business into static ink.

Timelines are great for giving you a read on your employees, following projects from week to week, and helping you integrate all the work in progress. But their real effectiveness lies in the fact that they're up on your wall for all to see. Timelines create a powerful sense of motion. They let everyone know where everyone stands on every project.

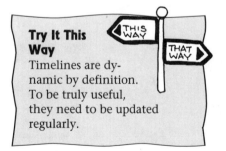

Try It This Way
Timelines are dynamic by definition. To be truly useful, they need to be updated regularly.

Nothing helps productivity like peer pressure to succeed. What makes the timeline especially powerful is that it's time-sensitive. I suggest updating your timeline daily and distributing copies of a weekly Master Timeline to your staff, showing the status of major projects. Before you know it, you'll get people thinking together, working to beat deadlines, helping each other, brainstorming, and trying to outwork each other.

An example of a timeline is shown in the following figure.

Timeline						
Project	Who	Possible Result	Probability	Expected Month		
				Jan	Feb	Mar
Sell Assets	Bob	$10,000	50%	2,500	2,500	0
Cut Overhead	Mary	$4,000	75%	1,000	1,000	1,000
Refinancer Debt	Jean	$20,000	60%	0	6,000	6,000
etc.						
etc.						
etc.						

The Least You Need to Know

➤ Leadership is motivating others to accomplish goals. It's a continual effort, not a tub-thumping speech.

➤ If you know where things are going, you can help people get there. Be a visionary—one people can understand.

➤ You have to have a style of leadership. Stay true to it.

➤ If you make heroes of your employees, they will do heroic things.

➤ Posting a timeline on the wall of your workplace will increase productivity dramatically.

Managing Your Manager

"Ah," you think as you become manager, "finally I can do it *my* way." Well…I wouldn't get your hopes up. Everyone reports to someone. Maybe for you it's the manager above you, or the president, or the board of directors. Whomever it is, you may well find yourself managing your manager as much as you manage your employees.

You probably won't agree with everything your boss says; in fact, disagreeing may be your single biggest contribution to your organization. The question is, how do you disagree without ending up on the outside looking in? After all, your boss is your boss because someone from on high figured he or she was right for the job. That means your boss has allies who are more entrenched than your allies. You need your boss.

This chapter will teach you how to manage your boss, to assess and manage your boss's expectations, and win his or her support. It will also give you some pointers on how to avoid the manager from Hell. (Yes, some managers are from there.) Managing your manager is an essential part of managing, and one key to your success. Read on to find out how it's done.

What Are Your Boss's Expectations?

People taking a new job often feel anxious and stressed. They feel like they don't have a clue, and they're probably right. When you're in this phase, it's tempting to assume that hard work will make you successful and that even harder work will make you even more successful. Don't you believe it! Instead, focus on identifying realistic expectations and meeting them.

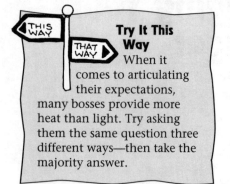

Try It This Way
When it comes to articulating their expectations, many bosses provide more heat than light. Try asking them the same question three different ways—then take the majority answer.

Rarely are managers given a clear list of expectations. Yet every boss has them, and your evaluation may well depend on how well you fulfilled them. You will probably want to sit down with your boss early on (preferably your first day) and find out what those expectations are. If you don't know what is expected, you can't very well know whether you are delivering, can you? Take the initiative. Ask questions.

How Do You Discover the Expectations?

Listen. Talk. Read. Ask questions of anyone who works for your boss—or used to. Describe how you like to do things, and ask people whether they think your way is going to work. Read the rules; study the goals of the organization. Research the market and the finances of your group. Most importantly, find out as much as you can about what is not written down. This could end up having more of an impact than you might think.

For example, does the boss believe; in formality or informality? Are hours regimented or flexible? Is there a dress code? Are there regular staff meetings, if so, what do they cover? Does your boss give performance reviews, if so, how often? Are you expected to give performance reviews?

You need to find out the specific objective of the company and for your area of responsibility. Get a number. Get a date. Find out the consequences for missing goals, and the rewards for achieving them.

What Do You Ask to Clarify Expectations?

Next, sit down with your manager and ask some direct questions. For example, you might want to ask:

➤ What is the corporate culture? Does your boss want to build it or destroy it? Where do you fit in?

➤ Did the boss want you for the job or someone else? If not you, why not?

➤ Does the boss want written or verbal reports? Is he looking for an in-depth analysis or a summary of the situation?

➤ What rules does the boss consider essential? Is she most concerned with hours? Clothing? Attitude? Timeliness? Accuracy? Quality? Commitment?

➤ What is the company's situation? Is it growing or shrinking? Is it stable or in crisis? Is it seeking change or just fine-tuning? Is it thriving or just trying to survive?

➤ What is the boss' motivation? Does he want to advance or stay in the same place? To take chances or maintain the status quo? Does she want status and power, or anonymity?

➤ What are your responsibilities?

➤ What is your compensation? What is your bonus?

➤ What constitutes a good or bad performance? How often are you evaluated? What happens as a result of reviews?

➤ What training will you receive, and from whom?

Try It This Way
Don't just listen to words. Look at body language; listen for passion. Is your boss trying to avoid certain subjects? Try and tune in to the signals.

Managing Expectations

Knowing what your boss wants is a crucial first step, but it doesn't guarantee that your life will suddenly become simple. Now you have to figure out how to manage those expectations.

Are they realistic? Can you fulfill them in the time specified and with the funds that have been budgeted? Make sure you're clear on these issues before you promise to deliver. If you can't meet expectations, you'll need to come up with your own revised expectations. What *can* you deliver? Don't promise anything unless you're pretty confident that you'll be able to come through.

The fun part, of course, is telling your boss that her expectations have been revised, that she doesn't really expect what she thought she did. Needless to say, this may not be easy. Bosses also have bosses. They may not have any flexibility, or they may not want to be flexible. They may believe that their original expectations *were* realistic; they may even *object* to having them revised.

Stressbusters
Take the measure of your environment before launching into your new position. If the group is in chaos and crisis, your boss may be pushed into an autocratic role. The opportunities can be great during a crisis, but so can the career risks. Such a situation is not for the faint of heart.

A friend of mine took over a drugstore chain that was in desperate need of a turnaround. The chairman of the board asked Allen how long it would take to turn the company around.

"Five years," Allen responded.

The chairman said, "Great. That's exactly what I told my board." Then he paused and added, "There's only one problem. I told them that two years ago. So actually you only have three years to do it."

Don't say yes unless you mean it. You're better off turning down an impossible situation than taking it on and failing.

Revising Expectations

If you need to revise your boss's expectations for a certain job or task, start by setting up small, attainable goals of your own that complement the goals of your organization. Communicate them to your boss. Now is the time to gain his confidence, so that when the time for revising expectations comes around, you won't face a credibility problem.

Do the same with long-range goals (see Chapter 10 for more details on long-range goals). If your boss is committed to your targets, you are well on the way to shaping his expectations.

If necessary, hire consultants—approved by your boss—and work with them to revise expectations. The old axiom speaks the truth—*Anyone from out of town is an expert.* Get the experts on your side.

Winning Your Boss's Support

The support of your manager is not an extra, like automatic locks or cruise control: It's a must. Your effectiveness depends on it. Here's how to get your manager on your side.

➤ Find out what is sacred to your manager and stay away from it. Don't go messing with his pet projects. Okay, so a project makes no sense. Before you eliminate it, find out whether it's the brainchild of his favorite niece. (Yikes! Aren't you glad you asked?)

➤ Find a common, non-business ground on which to relate to your boss. Sports, food, wine, music—whatever avenue you can find for relaxed, one-on-one conversations that aren't always about business. If you can find a way to get comfortable with your boss as a *friend,* you will be able to say tough things when necessary; and it will, from time to time, be necessary. You may also find out indirectly how the boss thinks about business. A conversation about sports teams, for instance, may give you an idea of how the boss wants your team to operate. Avoid controversial subjects such as office politics and religion, and don't, under any circumstances, engage in gossip about other employees. You may like someone the boss doesn't like, and vice versa.

➤ Make your ideas the boss's ideas. Include the boss in your strategy sessions and solicit her input.

➤ Have regular progress review meetings. Objectively analyze the performance of your team against preset objectives.

Try It This Way
Instead of setting huge, hard-to-accomplish goals, set small goals—baby steps—and let the boss know about them. When the boss sees you reach your goals, confidence in you will grow.

And Then There's the Boss from Hell...

Some bosses are like a gift from Heaven. And then there are others. Bad bosses come in all shapes, sizes, genders, and colors. Some just want to ruin your life. Don't let them. Stay away.

I had a boss once who underpaid people. To be able to do this, he needed a buffer between him and his employees—in other words, between him and reality. I turned out to be that buffer. The year I worked for him, he had me hand out the annual bonuses. The formula he had worked out for distribution of bonuses was quite unusual. Here's how it worked: 95 percent of the corporate bonus would go to him, and the remaining 5 percent would go to 45 other employees. Some people received bonuses of $15. I can't recall that anyone said, "Thank you."

There's only one way to deal with a boss from Hell: Stay away. Even if it means turning down a promotion. You may think that refusing a promotion will hurt you, but failure hurts much worse—and with the kind of manager we're talking about, failure is practically inevitable. It can also do serious damage to your reputation.

Stressbusters
Bosses who are doing a poor job tend to focus blame on their employees. If a boss has lost a string of managers to resignation or firing, *beware!*

Before you accept a managerial job, do some research. Find out about the boss's reputation and capabilities. If he is known as someone without a benevolent bone in his body, stay away. You won't win.

Of course, you'll need to come up with a graceful explanation of why this is not the appropriate time for a promotion. Maybe you are in the midst of something really important for the company and you just don't feel right not carrying it to completion. Perhaps a parent is ill and you are concerned that at this moment you will not be able to give the job the full effort that it needs. You may even think that the company can get along adequately without spending more money and adding more management. You'll think of something. Remember, it may be the best career move you ever make.

The key to preserving your options is to carry your refusal off gracefully. Whatever you do, don't appear antagonistic. "I won't work for him because he is a schmuck" may be factually correct, but it doesn't promote your interests. You want to appear to be thinking solely of what is best for the organization.

Bosses from Hell fall into four basic categories or afflictions:

➤ *Those with tunnel vision.* The motto with this type is, "My way or the highway." Take the highway. You'll never get to grow or implement any of your exciting new ideas. The highway is a much better option.

➤ *Those who are prejudiced.* Managers are as big as their dreams and as small as their prejudices. This prejudice can be deep. It can turn on you at any moment. If your boss thinks you're being imposed on her by the person who hired you, she'll resent you. She'll do anything to help you—fail.

➤ *Those who are credit grabbers.* When things go well, they claim credit, and when things go badly, they blame you. They rise while you sink. They give you work while they golf or take vacations. Take an extended vacation yourself from this credit grabber. Find another position.

➤ *Those who are negative.* Rewarding work is enjoyable work. Sooner or later, constant negativity will destroy your sense of self-worth. Time to move on.

Luck can be a matter of being in the right place at the right time, or it can mean not being in the wrong place at the wrong time. Be kind to yourself: Stay away from Hell.

The Least You Need to Know

➤ Finding out what your manager's expectations are is the first step to fulfilling them. The next is revising those expectations so that they're realistic.

➤ By setting small goals, letting the manager know about them, and then meeting them, you will build the manager's confidence in you.

➤ It helps to find a common, non-business ground to share with your manager. By taking some of the formality out of the relationship, you'll make future problem solving easier.

➤ If you are offered a job under a bad manager, stay away. Don't let yourself get set up for failure.

Chapter 8

Finding Your Core and Using It: You Are What You Are

In This Chapter

➤ What your "core" is—and why it is so important

➤ The questions to ask to find your core

➤ Focusing on your core

➤ Translating your organization's core into success

Your organization has an essence. It has a core that's solid and strong—something that makes your employees energize. It's there, all right, but you may not know it.

A lot of organizations try to be all things to all people, kind of like "muzak"—that schmaltzy "elevator music" that everyone tolerates but no one much likes. The successful organizations take a different tack. They focus on a unique strength or feature and make the most of it. As a manager, you can go for muzak, or you can show your style. It's your company, but if you want my advice, I say get off the elevator and play some *music*.

In this chapter you will find out how to make your own music by finding your muse—your core. Every person and every organization has one thing it does best. That one thing is where talent and opportunity and desire intersect. You will learn what a core is, how to identify the core of your business, and how to incorporate it into your plan to get maximum benefit from it. As you read, feel free to sing along. When you find your core, you can make beautiful music.

Core—What's It Mean?

Most managers, when they think "core," think of a specialization like marketing, finance, or production. Actually, the core is much deeper. It will usually manifest itself in one or more of those specialties, but the real core is inside of the people. It is the raw nerve, the answer to...*Why are we here?* It is what electrifies everyone and galvanizes their thinking into actions. It is the driving force that is the company's raison d'être.

The core is:

➤ Simple

➤ Internal

➤ An absolute truth

➤ A gut grabber

➤ A source of happiness

➤ A source of pride

Discovering Your Core

Knowledge is power. Business is clutter, and too much clutter can obscure knowledge. It's not always easy to cut through that clutter and find your essence!

In some cases, of course, it blinks at you in neon. You can't miss it; it's the one thing energizing your people.

Easy or difficult, you've got to find it. The brilliance of your success depends on it.

Press Release

When the founder of the Kresge Stores donated a building to Harvard University, he explained how a simple understanding of a core competency can lead to great things in this way: "I came to the United States. I decided people wanted to buy things cheap. That's how you got your building."

The Heartbeat of Your Business

"Core," by the way, comes from the Latin word for *heart*—as in "coronary." Your core is the heart of your business. It's what you really believe in. When you have a core, you have a focus. It eliminates a lot of the second-guessing that can slow a company down.

Peter Bolleteri, a world-famous tennis instructor, teaches stars to develop their weapon. If their best weapon is the backhand, Bolleteri says it is more important to take advantage of the advantage than to try to catch up somewhere else. Develop your weapon. If it is your serve, make it unstoppable. If it is marketing, or research and development (R&D), take it to the hilt.

When you know your real gift—the one thing that stands out above all your other skills—you can do a number of things:

➤ Clarify your mission.

➤ Reduce the personnel conflicts.

➤ Capitalize on your strengths.

➤ Focus on your passion.

➤ Ignore exciting but false directions.

➤ Add meaning to people's work.

➤ Get significantly better results.

Press Release

Stanley Marcus, the retail guru, had a friend who made perhaps the best ice cream in the world—and who would give away the recipe to anyone who asked. Marcus was appalled: How could he do that? Didn't he realize how valuable the recipe was? His friend, however, was nonchalant. "Never mind," he said. "When they find out how difficult it is to make and how much it costs to do it right, they will stop trying to copy us." His company's core was *quality*. He made ice cream that was so great no one could compete.

The idea of zeroing in on your core is to set up your organization like a living, breathing organism. You want the organization to have one thought process, one focus.

When your group has a set of core values identified and in place, everyone can get the one essential ingredient for success—a *feel* for the business. The job moves from intellect to gut. This goes for any profession. Once you know your core, the distractions and false starts that plague inefficient organizations will fall away. Instead of being paralyzed by opportunity and conflict, you will be energized by your essence.

Press Release

A Stanford Business School professor has found that visionary public companies perform 26 times better than the general market.

Locating Your Center

Your core competency is the thing you do best. What is your core, your essence? It is not what you *want* to be, but rather what you are.

Simply Stated
A *visionary public company* is a company with a clear, overriding long term agenda rather than quarter to quarter profits.

It could be sales, efficiency, research and development, brand image, quality, or any of a variety of things—whatever excites your people. If your people are excited, they are motivated for success.

But core competency runs deeper than that. You not only have to love that aspect of your business; you also have to be good at it.

Before Ray Kroc bought McDonald's, he was a vendor selling to what was then a small restaurant. He saw that the core competency of McDonald's was speed and value. He recognized fast food as a competency before anyone else did. He invested in McDonald's and never looked back.

How do you find your core competency? You find it by listening. *Listen* to the people who do the work. Listen to the people who buy the product (or service). Listen to the vendors. They all have something to tell you about your company's greatest strength.

The core is belief-driven, a philosophical wire that powers your organization. The core satisfies both economic and human needs. The core is true. The core is based on information. It's the breath of life for your operation—invisible, but real.

Of course, before you can listen, you have to ask questions. The most efficient way to do this is by way of a questionnaire. The following sample is designed to get at the key issue: How are you perceived by those inside and outside of your organization? For a complete picture, you'll want to poll your employees, your customers, and your vendors. Obviously the same questionnaire won't work for all three of these groups; this sample is a composite of what should really be three different questionnaires.

What Sets Us Apart?

Circle the number that you think is the most appropriate. (1 = disagree strongly, 2 = disagree somewhat, 3 = not sure, 4 = agree somewhat, and 5 = agree strongly).

1) What is our company's greatest strength?

Sales	1	2	3	4	5
Marketing	1	2	3	4	5
R&D	1	2	3	4	5
Cost Efficiency	1	2	3	4	5

Production	1	2	3	4	5
Quality	1	2	3	4	5
Service	1	2	3	4	5
Finance	1	2	3	4	5
Other _____	1	2	3	4	5

2) How would you rank us in comparison to our immediate competition?

Sales	1	2	3	4	5
Marketing	1	2	3	4	5
R&D	1	2	3	4	5
Cost Efficiency	1	2	3	4	5
Production	1	2	3	4	5
Quality	1	2	3	4	5
Service	1	2	3	4	5
Finance	1	2	3	4	5
Other _____	1	2	3	4	5

3) What do we talk about most in our internal informal and formal meetings?

Sales	1	2	3	4	5
Marketing	1	2	3	4	5
R&D	1	2	3	4	5
Cost Efficiency	1	2	3	4	5
Production	1	2	3	4	5
Quality	1	2	3	4	5
Service	1	2	3	4	5
Finance	1	2	3	4	5
Other _____	1	2	3	4	5

4) What activities come easiest to our company?

Sales	1	2	3	4	5
Marketing	1	2	3	4	5

continues

---

continued

R&D	1	2	3	4	5
Cost Efficiency	1	2	3	4	5
Production	1	2	3	4	5
Quality	1	2	3	4	5
Service	1	2	3	4	5
Finance	1	2	3	4	5
Other _____	1	2	3	4	5

5) What do outside articles on our company focus on most?

Sales	1	2	3	4	5
Marketing	1	2	3	4	5
R&D	1	2	3	4	5
Cost Efficiency	1	2	3	4	5
Production	1	2	3	4	5
Quality	1	2	3	4	5
Service	1	2	3	4	5
Finance	1	2	3	4	5
Other _____	1	2	3	4	5

Who Are You REALLY?

Inevitably, you will start leaning toward an essence. It's there. You may already know what it is, or you may be surprised.

Here is another method. This technique works really well, provided you get honest input. Give the graph to your key people to complete, and don't forget to complete one yourself. Stress that the answers are to be completely anonymous. Remember, no agendas. Of course, you will see differences. People have their own perspectives, their own thoughts, their own beliefs. Enjoy the diversity, but chase your essence.

On the following graph I include attributes as well as functional specialties. I think it helps if people understand that there is a relationship between the two as they cross-reference. And I want to include the literal thinkers as well as the abstract ones.

Attributes	Functions
Creative	Finance
Disciplined	Sales
Principled	Marketing
Quality-Driven	Production
Value-Oriented	Sourcing
Cost-Conscious	Distribution
Service-Oriented	Operations
Profit-Driven	
Socially Responsible	
Flexible	
Speedy	

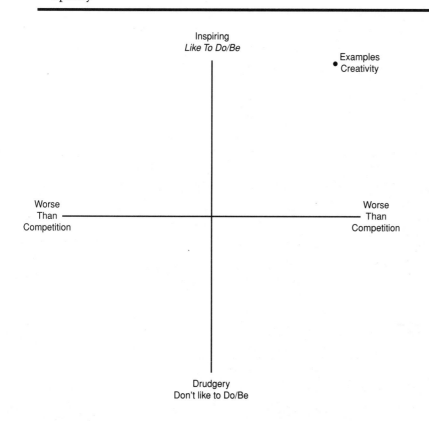

Once you have these plotted, you can identify your core (as perceived) in the upper-right quadrant. Don't expect unanimity. It will seldom be that clear, but usually a consensus

Stressbusters
When you ask internal people to name your core competency, you will find a bias. The natural tendency will be for everyone to believe their division, their job, is the most important. Be careful to take a bigger view of the company.

Simply Stated
Outsourcing is hiring individuals outside of a company to do work for the company that, in the past, was usually done by internal employees.

will occur. If it doesn't, you have a real challenge in front of you, which could also mean a great opportunity. Most challenges have the potential to be great opportunities.

Once you find your core, recognize it, discuss it, worry about it, and refine it. Then proceed forward. Structure your organization around it. No matter how attractive, don't give away your essence. Don't chase short-term trends or worry about what others are doing. Stay true to your core—be unique and stand out, and you'll be successful.

Now—Focus on It!

You've found your voice, your view, your way of doing things. You've identified your core and encouraged your people to focus on it. Your biggest job now is to get out of the employees' way and watch them succeed.

But your other job is to begin moving all your resources in that direction. This will mean making some hard decisions. Moving forward. Making certain kinds of cuts. Spinning off unnecessary internal bureaucracy. Once you begin moving in the right direction, so will your organization.

How many people in your organization are supporting other functions, functions not related to your core? If sales is your competency, you might consider *outsourcing* your accounting, shipping, and production. There are companies that specialize in those functions and are as passionate about them as you are about selling.

Any number of functions can be outsourced—warehousing and shipping, accounting, marketing. All you may really need internally is a small team focused just on the core.

Sun Microsystems, the very successful Silicon Valley company, outsources whatever they can. If it works for a wildly successful company like Sun, it might just work for you.

Build a Core Team

Americans are often tempted to assume that bigger is better. In business, this can be extended to mean that having everything under direct control is better. Experience teaches us differently. It is better to be quick and to operate as a team. It is better to avoid bureaucracy and confusion. It is better to focus on your own special competence.

Clarity is very, very important. For years, Jaguar told the world that its competence was high quality, when we all knew it was luxury. High quality? The car is known for breaking down. Now, finally, Ford is making it better. The point is, Jaguar was a company that did not know its core. You need to find yours and focus on it.

Stressbusters
Core-value-focused companies are not always warm and fuzzy places to work; people usually work harder as they compete with the competition and with themselves.

Remember, nothing—and I mean nothing—needs to be part of your company except your core. At its heart, your effort needs to be developing a team with compatible values. You want people who can automatically act in concert without being told to do so. When a team of people focus their energies on one objective, the results can be remarkable.

Keeping the Focus

There are countless ways to keep your people focused on the core. Here are a few:

➤ *Make signs and distribute them throughout the company.* IBM did this for years with the slogan "THINK."

➤ *Hold internal meetings around the core topic.* The North Face invited customers and suppliers, as well as employees, to their meetings.

➤ *Bring in speakers who are specialists on the topic.* Business schools are great places to look for speakers.

➤ *Set up specific benchmarks to measure your performance.* Discuss the progress and the standards.

➤ *Have your people write articles about your core.* The more it is written down and clarified, the more it is believed.

Plan Your Product and Your Process

It's not enough to just believe in something. You also have to make what you believe in part of your plans. Chapter 10 will take a close look at long-range planning; for now the thing to keep in mind is that your core is the starting place of all successful plans. As you think about it, you will want to incorporate three viewpoints:

➤ *Your personal core values*—determined by your own graphing, your intuition, and your passions.

➤ *Your employees' core values*—determined by their graphing, their statements, and their actions.

➤ *The core values needed to succeed in your market*—determined by questioning customers, vendors, and industry gurus.

Try It This Way
Review your core values on a regular basis and match them to the evolving environment. Markets change. People change. Your organization changes. Take this into account as you do your regular reviews.

When you synchronize these three viewpoints, you will have tuned into your core. You can now set up a plan with clear goals, a plan that encourages those who believe in it to work harder. Others might prefer to look for another place to work, and that's fine. You're in the strongest position you can be when you and your people share a common goal.

You want to be different, you want to be better—but you have to be you. It's the same way with your organization. If you want to capitalize on your core, plan around your strengths and avoid your weaknesses. If you are a risk-taking, growth-oriented sales team and you have to outsource every other part of your business (distribution, finance, sourcing, etc.), so be it.

Press Release

There are only six control dials on a Boeing 747, and the 2,000-year-old Catholic Church, spiritual home of over half of the world's Christians, continues to flourish with only five levels of authority.

Find clarity. Remember, your best chance of success is through differentiation, and you can't know what is different about your group until you know what your group does and what it *is*. Clarity of your core will move you in the direction of success.

The Least You Need to Know

➤ Your core is the heart of your business. It is what you really believe in and what your people naturally focus upon. It is not what you "want" to be, but what you are.

➤ Finding your core means asking a lot of questions of a lot of people.

➤ Your core is your advantage. You want to do everything you can to develop your advantage.

➤ Once you've identified your core, focus on it!

➤ Make your core the starting place for all your future planning.

Chapter 9

Motivating Your People: When "Good Enough" Isn't

In This Chapter

➤ How to motivate without words

➤ Why money is most easily understood

➤ Other effective ways to motive

➤ What makes a winning attitude

As a manager, you aren't on your own. You wouldn't be a manager if you were, would you? You are part of a team, and it's important to remember that your success depends on the abilities of your team members even more than on your particular talents and skills.

But wait, there's good news. As a manager, you have a *huge* influence on others. You can help them tremendously (they can help you, too). But you don't run anyone. I'll say it again for emphasis: *You don't run anyone.* No one is your slave. You can't force work—let alone *good work*. In fact, most workers operate pretty independently in today's world.

They do respond to motivation, however. This chapter explores the psychology of motivation and what the most effective approaches are in business. You'll learn how symbolism works, how money figures into the motivation equation, how to motivate without money, and why winning is the greatest motivation of all.

Symbolism Says It

The first day that Tim Kohl took over Scott, the ski pole and goggle company, he had a dumpster placed in front of the building. Then he made a single request to the employees of his company: Throw everything out.

His message was simple. The past is the past. This is a new era; all vestiges of the way things used to be done are being jettisoned. The future is now.

Tim Kohl understood that actions speak louder than words. He wanted to move forward and make his company less bureaucratic and traditional. One approach, I suppose, could have been to hold a series of meetings to try and explain that philosophy to everyone and hope that they actually listened. Instead, he brought a dumpster to the front door.

This is a dramatic example of something every manager should understand—*actions* are always noticed. Even when you don't want them to be, they are noticed. Humans are natural storytellers. Give them good stories, and before you know it, a legend will begin to take shape.

Try It This Way
The best place to hold a party is right where everyone works. If people associate that space with a fun time, they will get even more out of the message.

A celebration is another powerful way to convey a message. It could be an anniversary party for the company or a celebration of a record month. It could be a lot of things, but what it *should* be is a celebration of unity and accomplishment. Have some fun—give people a chance to let off steam. When work is fun, work is inevitably better.

Enjoyment sends a great message. Of course, so does hard work.

Magnifying Your Corporate Voice

Everything you do conveys a message. Don't expect people to "Do as I say, not as I do." Did it ever work on you? Well, it won't work for your people, either.

People will pretty much follow your lead. They will work as hard as you, take the organization as seriously as you, and believe as much as you—at least, most will. Your attitude and actions set the tone for the entire company, starting at the beginning with your level of passion.

Press Release

Employees remember stories. At Hewlett-Packard, where the philosophy is "Trust Our People," Bill Hewlett, one of the company's founders, once found a storeroom locked with a chain. Hewlett wasn't happy. He found a chain cutter, cut the chain, and left it on the department manager's desk. The storeroom was not locked again.

As a worker and manager, your actions set the tone. Be sure and align the messages so that you're presenting a consistent theme.

Here are some examples of symbolic acts:

➤ Give everyone the keys to the office and the security code numbers to the doors and computers, and you will create an atmosphere of trust.

➤ Arrive at work at 5:30 a.m. and leave after everyone is gone, and you will have a work force that goes the extra mile.

➤ Dress formally, and you will have a staff who take their jobs seriously. Dress casually, and you will attract people whose attitude is also somewhat casual.

➤ Watch your expense account closely, and others will watch theirs closely too. Spend lots of money and your employees will do the same.

➤ A 100-percent guaranty on your products tells your employees and your customers that you stand for quality.

➤ Donate time and money to local charitable causes, and your employees will know that making money is only part of your mission.

➤ Cry when you lose a sale and your employees will realize how passionate you are about winning. Hold a post-mortem and analyze what the company could have done differently.

➤ Provide extensive fringe benefits for your employees, and they will believe that they are your organization's most important asset.

Get the idea? Since everything you do sends a message, it's a good idea to concentrate on positive, energizing ones. And while we're on the subject, remember to say what you mean and to mean what you say. Don't let anyone accuse you of saying one thing and doing another.

Signs, slogans, and posters can further ratify your symbolism. These can be used inside as well as outside the company. When it comes to morale, the messages you give employees are important, but so are the messages you give to the world. Employees will be looking at both: Make sure they're in alignment.

Stressbusters
Sometimes it's best to say nothing. If you chew an employee out in public, you're sending a message to your whole work force. Remember, they're watching you. Treat employees with generosity and respect, even when you think they don't deserve it.

Show Them the Money

There are people in the world who will work hard without financial remuneration, but these tend to be limited to certain fields, such as the arts. People generally prefer to get paid for their labor, and they expect to see a correlation between how hard they work and how much they get paid. It's simple, really. The more you pay, the better the results. Pay is the ultimate symbolic act.

Pay gets everyone's attention. Money is money; it's a very specific way of measuring worth. And, yes, it motivates. Contrary to popular belief, however, people don't always aspire to the maximum. They mostly aspire to be comfortable.

Press Release

Ricardo Semler, one of the managers at the remarkably successful Brazilian company Semco, said management had to fight with employees to get them to take higher raises when the employees were allowed to set their own salaries.

Fair, Equitable, Motivating Pay

There are three ways to measure fair and equitable pay:

1. *Inside the company*. Employees want comparable pay for comparable efforts, responsibilities, and results.

2. *Outside the company*. Employees want to be paid at or about industry standards and at or about regional geographic standards.

3. *Overall*. Employees expect you to meet all legal requirements regarding minimum wage, overtime compensation, vacations, and other legal provisions intended to allow people to live with dignity and at a decent standard of living.

Get the Lowdown on Compensation

You've got to have your facts straight. Employees will know the average compensation figures across your industry and in your region, and you'd better know them, too. Don't be faced with a challenge for facts. Find out what the average pay is in your industry.

In some industries, you can even ask your competitors. For obvious reasons, information provided by your competitors may not always be reliable.

There are different places to look, depending on the job:

➤ For compensation information for *executives*, try major accounting firms. Many do compensation surveys and will sell the results.

➤ Consider industry associations. The information these provide can justify the cost of joining the group.

➤ Some consulting firms focus solely on creating better compensation programs.

➤ For *sales personnel,* industry associations are the place to get compensation information. Pay varies significantly from industry to industry, so you'll need fairly exact guidelines.

➤ Management recruiting firms—also known as "headhunters"—are a good source of information on *manager* compensation, especially if they specialize in your industry or in your category of employment.

Try It This Way
For information on executive pay, call Ernst and Young's *National Executive Survey* at 1-800-726-7339.

➤ For *staff and clerical personnel,* consider reports from local and regional government. They offer reliable guidelines for the local job market.

➤ For *union employees,* you can count on the union to keep you informed—up to a point. Unions keep records of compensation information. Of course, they have a vested interest in the numbers they present, but they are still the best place to start, since you're going to be hearing about those numbers sooner or later anyway.

How Shall I Pay Thee? Let Me Count the Ways

Dealing with employee compensation is a serious business covered by all sorts of illogical national, local, and union regulations. If you don't know them, don't wing it. You could really regret it.

Study the rules, attend classes, or hire experts. You need help. It's important to send the right message to the work force—and the message will differ depending on who the work force is.

For instance, there are four basic ways to pay:

➤ Piece rate

➤ Hourly pay

➤ Salaried pay

➤ Commissions

There are advocates of each method, and each works in different circumstances. Make sure you study the varying circumstances in your own organization before you decide which way to go.

Some companies are very open about their compensation policies. Others aren't. The ones that aren't are creating unnecessary grief for themselves.

Stressbusters
No compensation system is forever. Objectives may change with time. Be sure to review your policies to see whether they still meet your objectives and whether they fit the current environment.

If salaries are not public record, skeptical employees will assume the worst—that everyone is paid more than them. That makes them feel unappreciated.

When it comes to payment, fairness is essential. The best way to achieve it is by means of formal guidelines. As the ultimate symbolic act, compensation can and should be motivating. If it isn't motivating, it is probably de-motivating. Don't avoid the subject—you have to pay, so think it out.

As you write the guidelines, consider:

➤ How often is compensation reviewed?

➤ Who does the review and what is that person's authority?

➤ Is there equal pay for equal work?

➤ Who gets incentive pay?

Incentive pay—piece rate or commissions—allows people to earn what they deserve, penalizing the slackers. On the downside, it also disregards factors that are not under the employee's control. Opponents say it puts quantity in front of quality. I disagree. If an incentive plan is properly installed (keep reading), quality does not suffer. Sometimes it even improves.

Pay as You Grow

Times change. Pay plans that once made sense may need an overhaul. Mature organizations will approach the payment issue differently from the way they did when they were first starting out.

Small or new organizations will generally try to make expenses as variable as possible as a way of protecting themselves from uncertainty. These organizations typically try to avoid too many fixed obligations. For instance, in the case of sales reps, they may put them on a commission on a part-time basis and allow them to work for others. This gives companies access to skilled talent at a lower level.

As companies grow, however, they will begin to bring people "in-house" on fixed salaries. The idea is to make business more predictable. This can sometimes result in a lack of motivation; it can also cause problems if the business slows down.

Bonus Points

Bonuses should be exactly that—*bonuses*. In other words, they should be extra—a payment for going above and beyond the call of duty. They should never be automatic, because then they're not really bonuses. Bonuses that become automatic aren't motivating and should probably just be made part of the employee's salary.

Bonuses that truly reward performance, on the other hand, are electrifying. Best of all are bonuses whose intrinsic value transcends the dollar amount. If a retail manager offers an employee $10 to sell a particular pair of skis, it may not stimulate much response. The same amount in the form of a six-pack of imported beer might have a completely different effect.

How should bonuses be awarded? Here a different kind of fairness principle applies. I happen to believe bonuses should reward performance, not effort. If you give the same to everyone, you don't reward the peak performers. In fact, the peak performers may feel penalized and quit.

Bonuses are most effective when they are tied to organizational objectives such as growing sales, expanding profits, increasing dealers, or reduction of expenses. The more specific and measurable the goals, the more effective they will be. Feel-good bonuses, without a measurement to back them up, can leave you with a lot of people who don't feel all that good.

How should bonuses be awarded? There are two common approaches, each with its own advantages and disadvantages.

The first is to base bonuses on company profits. With this system, *everyone* thinks about and works toward a goal of increased profits. If the company does great, everyone is rewarded. The downside is that many people have only a nominal impact on profits and don't feel in control. Some may even think you are manipulating profits to their disadvantage. Furthermore, if one division does poorly but the company results were great, you are inadvertently rewarding poor performers.

The second approach is to reward individual objectives. Here the clear benefit is that people feel more in control of their own destiny—and their bonus. The downside is that you can be paying out bonuses even when the company is losing money.

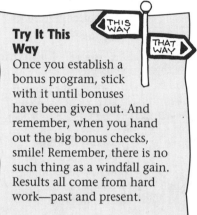

Try It This Way
Once you establish a bonus program, stick with it until bonuses have been given out. And remember, when you hand out the big bonus checks, smile! Remember, there is no such thing as a windfall gain. Results all come from hard work—past and present.

Stressbusters
If your plan has loopholes, they will be figured out. I once saw a group of sales reps do this. They knew that bonuses were based on exceeding certain limits. So, those who had no chance of reaching their quota diverted sales to those who were just short of the quota to boost them into the bonus level. This allowed some of the reps to get bonuses, and then they shared the bonuses with the reps who helped out.

All things considered, I think it's better to base bonuses on individual objectives. You're much more likely to keep your peak performers that way.

Getting People Invested: Long-Term Compensation

Long-term compensation is another tool, and a very valuable one. It serves three purposes:

➤ Employees will be less tempted to sacrifice the long term in pursuing their immediate objectives.

➤ People can be paid with future dollars, which may be less precious than dollars today, and may (because of tax laws) be able to multiply without being decimated by taxes.

➤ Corporate loyalty can be rewarded.

The further up the corporate ladder you move, the longer the perspective should be. Office and production workers think about daily output. Middle management adds in an annual perspective. Top management's job is to contribute a long-term perspective. For this reason it makes sense to reward corporate performance with long-term incentives. The best long-term incentives, in my opinion, are *options*. Options benefit the holder if the company does well, thus aligning the interests of the employees (at least in theory) with those of the owners.

Simply Stated
Options are rights to buy stock in a company at a certain price.

There are three basic kinds of options:

➤ *Qualified options.* In their simplest form, qualified options are the right to buy registered stock. Employees are under no obligation to exercise this right, but those who do buy shares become shareholders in the company as well as employees.

➤ *Non-qualified options.* These options require registration before being sold, and thus, are not as liquid as qualified options.

➤ *Phantom options.* These options are not registered with securities officials. They are simply a commitment by the company to give rights that act like shares (and thus, move up or down with the value of shares). They can later be redeemed with the company without actually having to buy or sell shares.

Hey—Thanks!

Workers need support and appreciation more often than a once-a-year bonus. They need to know that they matter.

Great managers understand that money alone cannot motivate. It takes more. Here are some ways to notice people:

➤ *Praise.* Whether verbal or written, a quick note, a formal letter of commendation, or a simple "Thanks," praise can go further than you might think.

➤ *Awards.* Plaques, certificates, trophies, key chains, pens, or anything that employees can show to others sends the message that you value their work.

➤ *Individual recognition.* There are various ways of giving public recognition. A common one is an "Employee of the Month" program, in which a photograph of the featured employee is displayed in a prominent place. Putting the employee's name on her work station is a form of recognition. You might even consider naming a product after her.

➤ *Something special.* Flowers, tickets to an event, a day off, a celebration of their anniversary with the organization, or a dinner paid for by the company are all appropriate expressions of appreciation.

➤ *Peer group prestige.* Receiving praise in front of peers, getting a chance to meet with the "big boss," an invitation to contribute ideas and suggestions, and a chance to run an internal event will make an employee feel as if her presence is valued.

➤ *Organization representation.* Giving team members a business card or corporate credit card, letting them meet people important to your business, and giving them clothing with the company's logo on it says "You're a part of this operation."

The best awards of all are spontaneous. If you are bored at your desk, think of your employees. They are probably bored too. Come up with some award and present it. Everyone, including you, will feel better about the organization.

We're Number One!

Everybody wants to be on a winning team. If you don't believe it, take a look at a sports event on TV. Unless you're watching a billiards tournament, chances are you'll see thousands of people in the stands, cheering the players who win. What are they saying? "We're number one!"

The people in your organization want to feel like winners. When your organization accomplishes a goal, celebrate it. Don't let it slide. Winning is a great motivator! Take advantage of success to build your team's collective psyche. If they feel like winners, they'll act like winners—and that means they'll win more often.

Press Release

The day Greg LeMond won the Tour de France, Giro Sport, the bicycle helmet manufacturer, tracked down everyone at the company who had worked on LeMond's helmet and held a big celebration. Each employee was given a helmet similar to the one Greg LeMond was wearing when he crossed the finish line. Giro employees went home feeling as if they owned a small part of the world's most prestigious bicycle racing victory.

Even more important than celebrating your people as winners is keeping them from feeling like losers. The moment they start to do that it will become a self-fulfilling prophecy. If your people are afraid to make a mistake, they won't do anything.

Winners take chances. Winners are not afraid to fail, as long as they learn from failure. Don't paralyze your people with fear of losing—inspire them with visions of winning. And when they win, acknowledge it.

The Least You Need to Know

➤ People remember stories more than words, so give your people stories that capture your message.

➤ Money motivates—when you do it right. Learn what the standard pay is in your industry and structure your compensation accordingly.

➤ Bonuses are most effective when they're driven by objectives. Standard or subjective bonuses are not terribly motivating.

➤ Employees need more than money to get motivated. They need to know that they matter.

➤ When employees feel like they're on a winning team, they'll work like winners.

Goal Setting—Setting the Bar and Raising It a Notch or Two

Picture it: You're standing at the podium. A silent, spellbound audience is hanging on your every word. You have a plan, and they want to hear it.

Does this sound like the way things get done in your office? Not very likely.

Reality is probably more like a bazaar in *Casablanca*—12 million things happening at once, with a lot of shouting and dissonance. You want to get everyone focused and working together, but how are you going to do that when there's so much going on?

This chapter is going to tell you. I'm going to talk about goal setting, long-range planning, and budgeting, three essential management tools. Ignore them at your peril! Make them work for you, and you can accomplish great things.

Expectations = Results

What do you want?

What do you REALLY want? Do you know?

This is what goal setting addresses. Sometimes it's hard to know what we're really going for. Goal setting is a formal process for separating the "must do's" from the "want to's." When you set goals, you take control of your destiny and the destiny of your organization. You move beyond simply dreaming.

This is the time for specifics. Don't let yourself be hazy. Hazy goals produce hazy results. So let me ask you again: *What the heck do you want?*

The Long-Range Plan

Stressbusters
Dun and Bradstreet reports that 50 percent of all new businesses fail in their first year, only 33 percent see their fourth birthday, and only 20 percent see a tenth birthday. The primary culprits: inadequate plans and information.

You can call it anything you want, but you've got to do it. You've got to plan. I like the name "Long-Range Plan." Others prefer "Strategic Plan." Call it "Fred" if it makes you happy; just do something about it!

As James L. Hayes of the American Management Association puts it, "Effective managers live in the present but concentrate on the future."

The objective is setting a course for your business. Long-range plans define the boundaries; then employees figure out the best way to do the job within those boundaries.

Common Pitfalls

But sometimes, plans fail. Here are some common reasons:

➤ The plan is finished and put away—never seen again.

➤ The plan is too rigid.

➤ Employees are given responsibility but not authority.

➤ The plan has bad input, leading to bad output.

➤ Key employees are excluded during the plan's development.

➤ The plan fails to anticipate change.

➤ The plan is forgotten amid the excitement of new opportunities.

The key to any long-range plan is to make it long-term enough (say, three to five years) that you can make decisions with perspective. You don't want to fall into the trap of basing your business "strategy" on short-term reactions to day-to-day situations.

Revisit the plan every year or so. How has the external environment changed, and how should you respond? What changes need to be made to your plan? A long-range plan must be an alive and vital document that inspires as well as brings focus.

Finally, your plan needs to involve others. Without getting trapped in the committee syndrome of too many opinions rendering the plan meaningless, you want to make sure your employees have some input. After all, they're going to implement whatever you come up with.

Involve Others

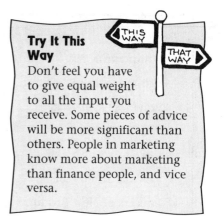

Try It This Way
Don't feel you have to give equal weight to all the input you receive. Some pieces of advice will be more significant than others. People in marketing know more about marketing than finance people, and vice versa.

If you think of long-range planning as a process as well as a product, you'll probably get a lot more out of the exercise. Just getting people together to think about this stuff is worthwhile. The more you involve your team, the more you will get from them—and the more they will get. Best of all, the results will show.

The process allows everyone to work together and learn more about one another. That's important, because they're going to be counting on each other.

One way to formalize the process and to organize the input into a manageable form is to come up with a questionnaire. Plan to distribute it to your strategic partners (customers and suppliers) as well as to your middle and upper management. By asking the same questions of insiders and outsiders, you can test the accuracy of some of your internal assumptions.

A sample questionnaire follows.

Long-Range Questionnaire

Circle the number that most clearly represents your opinion, from 1 (poor) to 5 (excellent).

PRODUCTS/SERVICES

Quality

| Current year | 1 | 2 | 3 | 4 | 5 |
| Previous three years | 1 | 2 | 3 | 4 | 5 |

DESIGN

Innovation

| Current year | 1 | 2 | 3 | 4 | 5 |
| Previous three years | 1 | 2 | 3 | 4 | 5 |

continues

---

continued

Uniqueness

Current year	1	2	3	4	5
Previous three years	1	2	3	4	5

Color Selection

Current year	1	2	3	4	5
Previous three years	1	2	3	4	5

Success of New Products

Current year	1	2	3	4	5
Previous three years	1	2	3	4	5

Sensitivity to Market

Current year	1	2	3	4	5
Previous three years	1	2	3	4	5

Please comment on the design areas you think the company needs to improve.

FOCUS

What one thing do you feel each of the following divisions should focus on during the next two years to significantly improve company profits and success?

Manufacturing/Sourcing

Sales, Marketing & Design

Finance & Operations

GENERAL ASSESSMENT

What are our greatest strengths in relation to our competitors?

1)
2)
3)

What are our greatest weaknesses in relation to our competitors?

1)
2)
3)

Who are our major competitors?

What are the major problems we face in the short term (one year)?

1)

2)

3)

What are the major problems we face in the long term (five years)?

1)

2)

3)

WHAT SHOULD OUR COMPANY'S OBJECTIVES BE?

	Sales	Gross Profit (%)	Pre-Tax Profit (%)
Year 1			
Year 2			
Year 3			
Year 4			

This kind of questionnaire can help you get a feel for what people inside and outside your company believe will make the company better. Take this information and work with it. Now you can begin the development of a long-range plan.

Creating the Plan

Before I tell you how I go about creating a long-range plan, I should mention, in the interest of full disclosure, that there are now software programs to help you do this. I happen to have mixed feelings about them. On the one hand, I think a template can be extremely helpful. On the other hand, there's a danger that people will simply plug in information without really thinking about it or knowing what it all means. The software-guided plan ends up with a paint-by-numbers feeling to it—it's correct, but lifeless. Long-range planning requires more serious brain work, coupled with regular reality checks.

Do get your plan in writing, however, and do make sure to include these four elements:

1. Mission Statement = Why
2. Goals = What & When

3. Strategies = How

4. Policies = The Method of Execution

Your Mission Statement: Who Cares?

Most mission statements are put together by a committee and read like it. It often seems as if one word is put in by each participant. There is little unity and even less clarity. As for actual meaning that folks can grab onto—well, forget it.

So what is a good mission statement and how do you get it to mean something?

Well, for one thing, I prefer the term "vision statement." Visions are something people follow. The statement should be a driving force. Nothing starts without a vision or can be sustained without one. Vision is your reason for existing as a business. Believe it and live it. It's the truth.

To give you an idea of the range of possibilities, here are two of my favorite vision statements. The first belongs to a local hotel chain. The statement is simply "Service." It's clear. Everyone working for the chain understands. The statement is tailored to the organization.

The second statement belongs to a well-known outdoor clothing company, Royal Robbins. It's lengthier and more philosophical. The statement reads: "To prove through integrity, service, fair play, and a passion for adventure that success in business, as in life, comes through the triumph of principles." Again, it's clear, and it's tailored to the organization.

Check your vision statement against these four criteria:

1. Is it clear?

2. Is it memorable?

3. Is it inspiring?

4. Is it tailored to your organization?

If it's weak in any of these areas, it needs more work.

No Top Line, No Bottom Line

Goals are essential if you don't want to drift aimlessly from one good idea to another. Goals lead to accomplishments.

Every company should have two kinds of goals: *qualitative* and *quantitative*.

An old corporate axiom says, "Give a number or give a date, but never give both." That axiom is absolutely contrary to success. Give both! Be specific and then do it.

Examples of *quantitative goals* are sales, margins, profits, return on investment, and market share. There are lots of others. Anything that is measurable can be turned into a quantitative goal.

Qualitative goals are more subjective but just as important. Building the brand image, nurturing a creative environment, and adapting the company to leading-edge technologies are all examples of qualitative goals.

> **Simply Stated**
> *Quantitative goals* are measurable: "Such-and-such an amount by such-and-such a date." *Qualitative goals* are more subjective. They address intangibles like quality and creativity.

The thing to avoid, as you're drawing up your list, is having too many goals. Too many goals is the same thing as no goals at all. When in doubt, simplify and focus. And wherever possible, make the goals specific. It will eliminate a lot of excuses.

Strategize!

Strategies are the blueprint to get to your goals. They can be general or specific, but they are usually more concerned with concepts than with numbers. Here are some examples of strategies:

➤ Decrease costs by increasing volume and keeping costs fixed.

➤ Increase profits by increasing market share.

➤ Segment the customers according to their potential.

Or you might prefer a more targeted strategy:

➤ Win market share by underpricing competitors.

➤ Reduce overhead by 20 percent.

➤ Expand sales globally to add new customers.

➤ Have the best service in the business.

As with goals, the key to strategies is simplification. You don't have to do everything now. You can always institute new, additional strategies later.

> **Press Release**
>
> The guiding strategy for Nike was CEO Phil Knight's business plan. He developed this plan while he was a student at Stanford Business School and with some help from his old track coach, Bob Bowerman. Obviously, over time, the concept evolved, but it all starts with a plan. Since then, he's hit the ground running.

Set Policy

You don't want to come up with the most elaborate plan in the world, only the most effective.

Policies are what give personality to your approach. The possibilities are almost limitless. Just keep it simple.

Simply Stated
Policies are day-to-day tactics. They provide rules for you as a manager to implement.

Policies are the way you do business. They support your strategies while personalizing them to your organization. Two companies could have the same strategy—say, increasing market share by 20 percent. But one could choose to do it through heavy advertising while the other could do it by increased investment in product development.

Although you will have many policies, some are clearly going to be more important than others. I find that it's helpful to rank them. Settle on the most important and leave the rest out of the plan.

Here are some questions you might ask to help you develop policies. You'll probably be able to come up with others, depending on your particular needs.

Financial

> How fast do you pay your bills?

> What terms do you extend?

> Do you leverage your company or play conservatively?

> Do you show your numbers to people or keep them hidden?

> Do you buy equipment or lease it?

> Do you use banks or factors?

Personnel

> Do you have pension and retirement plans?

> Do you have bonus plans, and if so, who is included?

> Do you reward longevity?

> Do you give non-monetary rewards?

> What holidays do you celebrate?

> Do you have one facility or many?

Marketing

Do you promote to the ultimate consumer or to an intermediary purchaser?

Do you use electronic marketing or more traditional channels?

Do you use payment terms as a selling tool?

Do you have in-house salespeople or commissioned agents?

Do you hold back-up inventory or only supply to order?

Product

Do you have high quality/high price or lower quality/low price?

Do you have a broad or narrow product line?

Do you produce your product or buy elsewhere?

Do you use proprietary materials or generic?

Do you offer fashion or function?

Policies are indispensable. Whichever you put in place, be sure you align them into a cohesive, single-focus plan. If you do your job right, you'll be ahead of most of the competition from the word Go.

Budgeting—The Clearest Goal of All

You've got your long-range planning done. Great! Good going! But don't go forgetting about your short-term goals, or you won't be around to see your long-range plan succeed. This is where budgeting comes in.

You're going to need financial projections broken out by month, in a consistent fashion, and you need them to be tied to the long-range plan.

Budgeting is a delicate process. If you have too few line items, you may not be able to pinpoint what works and what doesn't. Too many and you'll be swamped. Here are some simple suggestions that may help:

➤ Use as much historical data as possible. Data from the past is one of the best indicators of what the future looks like.

➤ Have only as many lines as you can make sense of.

➤ Break things out in monthly increments so you can regularly measure.

➤ Compare your budget to your long-range plan to make sure the two tie to one another.

➤ Have the people who are involved in carrying out the budget help develop it. This will give more accurate input and acceptance.

➤ Tie your budget directly into your accounting system.

Financial Checkpoints

You've got your long-range plan, your mission statement, your policies, and your budget all set up. How do you find out how you're doing?

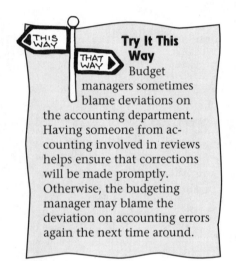

Try It This Way
Budget managers sometimes blame deviations on the accounting department. Having someone from accounting involved in reviews helps ensure that corrections will be made promptly. Otherwise, the budgeting manager may blame the deviation on accounting errors again the next time around.

The answer is, review. On a regular basis, take time to check your performance against the budget and take corrective action, if necessary.

A review, by definition, is an after-the-fact analysis. The closer the review is to the period in which things happened, the better. People will remember the situation more accurately and do a better job correcting it. Don't let sluggish accounting slow down this process. Take charge.

Sit down with your people and go through the line items one at a time with those people responsible for each item. Make sure you both understand what is happening.

When you find significant deviations between actual results and the budgeted amount, it's important to act promptly to investigate and fix the problem. Whatever you decide, put it in writing and then follow up during the next review period. Be specific with numbers and dates.

Rewards and Sanctions—Where the Rubber Meets the Road

The purpose of planning is to create a path to success and then follow that path. Inevitably, some people will do better than others in following the path.

The only way to deal with this is to reward the performers and discourage the slackers. If you don't, you may find yourself being taken advantage of by the slackers, while the performers begin to suspect that you don't care.

The rewards should be economic and non-economic, and they should be clearly stated ahead of time so that everyone knows about them. Rewards and sanctions are a major part of the execution of a good plan. After all, without execution, the plan is simply wasted paper, isn't it?

The Least You Need to Know

➤ A long-range plan consists of a mission statement, goals, strategies, and policies.

➤ Budgeting gives you a precise track throughout the year to help you reach your projections.

➤ Financial reviews are checkpoints for budgets. Look for deviations in performance and correct them with a specific plan.

➤ Use rewards and sanctions to keep your people focused on goals and to send the message of your expectations.

Part 3
Organizing Your Team

It's now time to pull it together. Either it meshes and you get it to work like a finely oiled machine, or you learn to say, "Would you like fries with that?"

This part of the book is about the nuts and bolts of getting your team to work together. I'll talk about getting the various parts of your team lined up, and then I'll focus on employees—the essential part of any organization. I will discuss how to hire them, when to fire them, and how to get everyone to work together toward a common goal. In these chapters, you'll learn how to get the motor humming.

Chapter 11

Aligning Your Team and Minimizing Friction (So You Can Sleep at Night)

Organizations are people. Sure, they are about numbers and results and all the *stuff* that seems so important to all the money folks. But it all comes down to people, and people are individuals. As their manager, you need to figure out how you're all going to work together.

Growth brings change, change brings movement, movement brings about friction, and friction causes heat. In business, "heat" means controversy. In this chapter I'll talk about who you are trying to align, and what you can do to get your employees, owners, and customers to understand your mission and help you work toward your goals. So join the team and read this chapter.

Decisions, Decisions, Decisions

Employees, owners, and customers all hold a stake in your success. They have a vested interest in you doing well. If you treat your fellow stakeholders as partners, you will find that they will help you out. Everybody wins.

The goals we address in this chapter are team decision making and smooth implementation of decisions. Not surprisingly, these turn out to be integrally linked.

There are two ways of passing down decisions:

> ➤ *The Western Way*. An individual consults a few people and makes a decision. People hear of it and challenge it, and it gets tweaked in a stall-and-proceed mode. The result is herky-jerky execution as it proceeds through the various levels of the organization.

> ➤ *The Japanese Way*. Everyone in the company is consulted before a decision is made. The system, called the Ringi system, is based on a ring. All decisions run through the entire company (around the ring) to be discussed and agreed upon prior to any decision. Things move slowly in the decision phase, but once the decision is made, the execution is smooth.

Coordinating with Customers

The best way to work with customers is by treating them with complete honesty. Let them know what's up. Don't go for the we-they philosophy. Go for *we-us*.

Try It This Way Start with a tour. Bring your customers into your facility and let them meet your people. Humanize the relationship.

Sam Walton, creator of Wal-Mart, knew he didn't have all the answers. So he started out listening, and he grew quite a company.

At Wal-Mart, customers are greeted and welcomed into the store. When they are hunting for an item, they are not just told where to look; they are shown. When a customer signs a check at Wal-Mart, he or she is thanked by name. Walton says, "The nicest sounding word to any person is his own name."

Customers aren't the only ones who are treated with respect. Recognizing from the start that the company is only as good as its employees, Walton has made a point of encouraging opinions. He has given his employees permission to change and innovate daily, and declared bureaucracy and complacency his enemy.

There are lots of ways to bring your customers (and employees) into your camp, even if you don't have a chain of retail stores. Just don't take them for granted, and don't ever treat them like the enemy. Help your customers out. Here are some ideas:

➤ Involve them in your long-range plan (see Chapter 10).

➤ Invite them to your facilities to assess your new products or ideas before you roll them out to the whole market.

➤ Send a cross-disciplined team of your people out to visit them and find out their needs.

➤ Hold joint seminars and meetings on topics of common interest.

➤ Make them part of an advisory council.

➤ Make them thrilled, not just satisfied, with your service.

➤ Value them and show it.

Remember, customers pay your bills—and your salary!

Coordinating with Owners

Your owners (stockholders, partners, or board members) need to use and see your product or your service. They need more than financial reports; they need materials. They need to see what you do. If this means giving them a discount, it is probably cheap. The more involved they are with what you do, the better.

Press Release

The Jan Sport Company, which makes backpacks, holds a climb on Mt. Ranier every summer. The climb is headed by a guru in the mountain climbing world, Lou Whitaker, and is well attended by retailers, sales reps, industry magazines, employees, and owners. The experience personalizes relationships, and everyone knows everyone better by the end.

Letting People Be Human

It's an amazing thing about most people: They are human. I have found the overwhelming majority of people that I have met were human. In fact, some I originally thought weren't human actually turned out to be human. Even people who work for you are human.

Imagine that.

So, what do you do with these humans? They're more than just hard wiring. They have emotions and stuff. They have different ideas. Some of them are good ideas. Some of them are great ideas. Some of them are just ideas, but they all come from humans. And humans need to be treated like humans.

They will have emotional ups and downs, and they will change over time. They won't always just follow directions. They will ask, "Why?"

They will all have human strengths and weaknesses, no matter what role they play in your life. Customers, employees, owners—they are all people.

Smart managers capitalize on the strengths of others and they laugh (at least to themselves) at the weaknesses.

Press Release

Stanley Marcus, founder of Neiman Marcus, once said, "You train bears and dogs, but you educate people. This means that your goal is to teach people how to think, not what to think. This will result in their self-sufficiency.

Certain kinds of people problems are predictable.

For instance, many managers report that in meetings, people will discuss an issue—a long-range plan, say—and reach complete agreement. But it doesn't last. People drift in different directions; customers, markets, personnel, and finances gradually change.

People's perceptions become altered by the new reality. Suddenly, the plan is no longer 100 percent acceptable. There are new circumstances, new perspectives. Steadily, bit by bit, divergence creeps in. The deviations may not be major at first. As long as they stay within a preestablished comfort zone, you don't have to worry.

But they don't always stay in that safe range. When things seem like they're starting to fall apart, your only choice is to take control. Regroup. Reassess. Revamp your long-range plan to match the new circumstances. And remember that people are your greatest asset.

After all, machines can only produce so many widgets a day, and materials can only be fashioned into so many products. Real people, on the other hand…Real people can imagine anything.

Holding People (Like Yourself) Responsible

It is one thing to talk the talk. But you also have to walk the walk, and make sure that everyone else does too.

Holding people accountable is your job, and it begins with holding yourself accountable. This means you measure performance against commitments.

If there are problems, first try to help. But if the problems continue, it may be because someone is just trying to get your attention. If that is true, you may have to terminate that person. Devoting your energy and time to those who won't or can't reciprocate is a fruitless endeavor, not to mention a very bad example for everyone else. Keep yourself positive. Keep moving forward. Devote your time, energy, and talents to those who are getting results, thereby nullifying the results of your efforts.

Accountablility is about setting standards of performance and having people accept those standards. It leads into having your employees hold themselves accountable for the results. It is about getting people to be self starters and seeking results on their own, without constant prodding from above.

Attention getting (for status, security, and ego needs) on the part of employees is no different than it is with children. Some need constant recognition and if they can't get enough from normal feedback they will seek other ways to get recognition—acting up, demanding attention, or even intentionally screwing up their work.

Once you have the standards, ask for a number of evaluations and compare. Ask for their own. Ask for their peer's evaluation. And make an evaluation yourself.

Then take action.

Reward those who perform. Don't make fools of hard workers and peak performers by treating them like everyone else. Treat them specially.

If you really want to take accountability seriously, ask your employees to evaluate you. If you are a great manager, you are probably setting high standards for yourself already. You may be setting them higher than most of your people ever would for themselves. That's good. That's a sign of a driven leader. Don't be afraid of being evaluated. What you learn could be of tremendous benefit. After all, you're modeling for everyone. Hard work and excellence start with you.

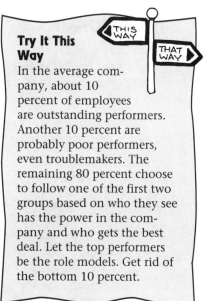

Try It This Way
In the average company, about 10 percent of employees are outstanding performers. Another 10 percent are probably poor performers, even troublemakers. The remaining 80 percent choose to follow one of the first two groups based on who they see has the power in the company and who gets the best deal. Let the top performers be the role models. Get rid of the bottom 10 percent.

Suppliers—Friend or Foe?

Suppliers tend to get treated like mushrooms—kept in the dark and covered with manure. You may think they're your adversaries, but they're an integral part of your team; indeed, your success often depends on them. Suppliers can offer a variety of things that you need:

➤ *Research and development.* Suppliers may cooperate to augment your R&D investment.

➤ *On-time delivery of goods.* An essential!

➤ *Credit and financing.* Suppliers are often the cheapest and most dependable source of financing that you can find. After all, they have a vested interest in your success.

➤ *Cooperative advertising.* Suppliers can help get your message to a wider group of customers.

Press Release

YKK, the largest zipper manufacturer in the world, has a philosophy called "The Cycle Of Goodness." One-third of their profits go to investors in YKK. One-third goes to investment in R&D. And one-third goes to helping customers grow and prosper.

Small World!

Yup. The world is shrinking. The market is growing. Companies and their suppliers and customers are expanding all over the globe. This can make it difficult to put together a solid team—and yet teamwork is more and more crucial if a company is going to be competitive. The world is closer together, yet your partners are farther apart. Life is weird.

Distance and differences in culture can lead to misunderstandings. The further apart the parties are geographically, the more chance there is for errors of interpretation.

The only way to counter this is with diligence. All sides have to work extra hard to make relationships succeed.

Here are a few suggestions for improving far-flung business relationships:

Stressbusters
Sometimes salespeople try to keep others in the company away from customers, out of the fear that their importance will be diminished or that others in the company will be insensitive to customers' needs. The best way to handle this is to include the salesperson in the team you send the customer. This gets others involved while allowing the salesperson to feel in control.

➤ Invest in communications technology. Faxes, e-mail, and video conferencing all improve communication

➤ Arrange regular exchanges of personnel from one site to another. Don't rely on visits from sales staff. Do what you can to see that all the people involved in the relationship meet. Familiarity overcomes doubts. Do this inside your own operation as well.

➤ Include people in your planning process. When people know they are appreciated, they open up and contribute and treat you in a much better way.

➤ Share information with people. If you treat them like insiders, they will be more supportive, offering more help and more accurate feedback. Paranoia, on the other hand, breeds more paranoia.

➤ Be loyal. If you stick with people, they will stick with you. Every company has peaks and valleys. But if you make it clear that you're not trying to exploit people, that you will be with them for the long haul, people will most likely be there for you, too.

➤ Give awards and recognition to team members. Don't take them for granted. Everyone and every company likes praise and recognition.

The Story of Ralph

No matter how you do it or what situation you face, you will have to get everyone involved if you want it all to succeed. You need motion. You need win-win.

Take my friend Ralph Keeney.

Ralph was on the teaching faculty of a West Coast university that was facing severe budget cuts. His whole department was going to have to be eliminated, and other departments were being cut back. Ralph was anxious to continue his work, even if it had to be through other departments. None of them, however, seemed to have the money to pay him or to pay for his research.

Ralph knew he was due severance pay. Moreover, his research money hadn't officially ended yet, although it was clearly going to. He was still funded. Ralph had an idea.

First he said he would waive his severance pay from his old department as long as the money was given to his new department to help pay his salary. They gladly complied.

Then he asked the people funding the research to transfer the funding to his new department. They gladly complied.

"I want a raise too," he said next. "I deserve it for finding all this money for you." They gladly complied.

Win-win.

He had aligned his team.

The Least You Need to Know

➤ Customers are not lower than you. They are part of the team.

➤ Getting your owners on board requires that you treat them as special. They are special.

➤ Relationships involve complex human beings whose evolving needs must always be taken into account.

➤ Aligning everyone in a global way is essential but difficult. The key is an ongoing attitude of openness and honesty.

Creating Successful Employees: If They Are Successful, You Will Be Too

In This Chapter

➤ Fostering your employees' success

➤ Long-term security programs: 401(k)s and ESOPs

➤ Approaches to encouragement

➤ Addressing employees' personal problems

Organizations are the sum total of their employees. To push the metaphor a bit further, employees are a little like numbers. Some are positive, some are negative. No matter how outstanding the positive employees are, the negative ones are going to subtract from their performance. Your job, as manager, is to keep the team total as high as possible.

Everyone wants to succeed, and you're there to help. The more time you spend helping your employees grow into success, the less time you'll have to spend searching for new employees.

In this chapter I'll focus on creating employees who create success. Why is a non-threatening environment essential, and how do you achieve it? What do I mean when I say you need to liberate your employees? What's the difference between attainable goals and unattainable ones? We'll be looking at the role of interactive management and the art of communication. Finally, we'll venture into the thicket of employee problems and consider what effect your reactions to problems has on results. Let's do it!

At Ease

In an ideal work environment, employees can put their best efforts into an organization and still feel comfortable. Succeed in making employees comfortable, and you will be rewarded with 100 percent of their time and 200 percent of their commitment. Remember, your employees are your most important asset.

Employees are not machines. It's a waste of time to treat them as if they were, because they don't work that way and never will. You MUST establish a personal relationship with each of your employees. You don't have to become friends with each one, although there's nothing wrong with developing such friendships. Many managers feel uncomfortable being friends with someone who works for them, and that's understandable.

You just need to understand each other. That comes from a foundation of mutual empathy—a personal relationship in which both sides are aware of each other's perspective.

> **Stressbusters**
> Tyrants don't usually make great managers. Screaming and yelling may bring short-term results, but they will invariably undermine your influence.

As you get to know your people as human beings, you'll begin to understand what makes them tick. What are their wants and needs? What are their dreams and fears? Let your insights about these questions guide you in creating a positive, constructive environment.

Threatening environments create paralysis and high turnover. You have to do everything you can to avoid this.

To start with, there are rules—federal laws, state laws, securities regulations, and insurance regulations to name just a few. Not your rules—*the* rules. You may think you can get around them. A lot of people try. Let me tell you, that's *not* the way you want to go, not unless you want to get in a whole bunch of trouble.

> **Stressbusters**
> If you discover an employee violating the law, whether through sexual harassment, theft, failure to meet legal standards, or whatever, don't hesitate. Suspend them or dismiss them. If you don't, things will quickly get out of control.

If you wink at the rules, employees won't know your definition of right or wrong. They may think you don't care about rules. They may think that you think that it's okay to operate outside the rules. They'll start to follow your example. BIG mistake.

Employees are looking to you for guidance. Don't be the wrong kind of role model.

Let Your People Go

No, I don't mean fire them. I mean give them some freedom. Sometimes you have to cede control over certain things in order to get control of what really counts—results. Managers can't do everything themselves. Let your employees feel some power in the company. Let them take some control, with your guidance.

There are four ways of doing this, as discussed in the following sections.

Management by Exception

With management by exception, you set up the standards you want met, then you state what you consider an acceptable variance (for example, 5 percent). Anything that comes within the allowed variance is considered normal. Your job is to look closely at everything else.

Management by Objective

Management by objective is similar to management by exception. You set up objectives for subordinates, then step back and resist the temptation to micro-manage. Micromanagement undercuts an employee's sense of authority and decreases motivation. Remember, what you care about is *results*.

Make sure you're all clear about what you want done and what the general approach should be; then let your team alone. If they succeed, reward them. If they stumble, take corrective action. Remember the R-word—Results.

> **Stressbusters**
> Assign responsibility to one person for one task. Assigning responsibility to two is like assigning it to none. The probable results: confusion, animosity, and missed goals.

Allow Mistakes

Permitting mistakes is a difficult thing for a manager. I'm recommending that you allow someone to fail even when you know in advance that they will fail. Failure is an essential part of the learning process.

Managers can't make all the decisions. By allowing people to make mistakes and learn from them, you teach them to think for themselves. Parents do this with their children, if they're wise, and you can do it with your team. If you practice this judiciously, you will grow yourself a great employee.

Of course, this doesn't mean you should be reckless. But you know that already.

Possibility Thinking

Possibility thinking works well in meetings. I like to start meetings this way. I encourage employees to come up with what might seem like outlandish ideas: "What if...?"

"What if" is a great tool for overcoming limits. I don't know what your experience has been, but I've found that the resident "experts" are great at finding reasons why something won't work. They can strike fear into uncertain employees and scuttle novel ideas before they get a fair hearing. But what if the experts are wrong?

That's why I use possibility thinking at the beginning of meetings. Of course, at the end we have to deal with reality (and the experts). But in the meantime we've come up with some great ideas. Try it!

Give 'Em What They Need

People need adequate compensation. If they are always feeling at risk in their job, they will not be very productive.

You need to know the needs of your employees. It's probably unrealistic to try and individualize every pay package, but some flexibility is important when you're putting together your compensation packages. Different employees have different wants and needs.

Of course, with the IRS keeping an eagle eye on things, too much creativity with pay packages can also get you into trouble. On-site health club benefits can't be taxed, for example, but an allowance to buy a membership in outside clubs can. Check with your accountant to be sure.

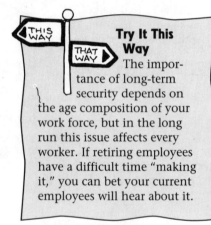

Try It This Way The importance of long-term security depends on the age composition of your work force, but in the long run this issue affects every worker. If retiring employees have a difficult time "making it," you can bet your current employees will hear about it.

Get Me Security!

Your employees are probably not banking on Social Security to take care of them in their golden years. They are probably hoping that you, or your organization, will be helping to keep them above the poverty level when the time comes to rest from their labors. If you also show some interest in this issue, they will be able to approach work with one less distraction.

Get programs in place that will help employees, if you haven't done so already. Options and bonuses work well for managers, but most employees will need something that's more systematized.

401(k) Plans

A 401(k) is a retirement account into which employees regularly deposit funds. The money is put in pretax, where it accumulates and compounds over the years, untaxed, until the time comes for the funds to be distributed. The company can choose to match a portion of the funds, also without taxation to the employees until distribution.

Because of corporate matching and the ability to defer taxation, a 401(k) can function as a form of long-term motivation. Although there are some restrictions in place to ensure equitable treatment of all participants, the matching contribution can be based on a percentage of each employee's income, allowing those who make more money to put more away, tax free, while having it matched by the company.

Employee Stock Option Programs (ESOPs)

An ESOP program allows all employees to have ownership in their own company. First, the company buys back its shares from existing owners; then it resells them to employees, either immediately or over time. The stock is all held together in one lump sum and is managed by an outside administrator. The stock purchase can come out of salary, bonuses, or the employee's own pocket.

ESOP programs have several benefits:

➤ They provide liquidity for existing shareholders, which can be quite important in a private company and may save the shareholders from having to sell out to outsiders.

➤ It makes owners out of employees. Making owners out of employees helps synchronize goals. When employees own stock, they care more about organizational goals; and owners care more about treatment of workers.

➤ The company, acting as the financing agent for stock purchases, has the flexibility to decide whether and how much stock will be purchased each year.

➤ The company can borrow money to buy stock from banks, which are authorized to give a favorable loan rate based on government guarantees.

➤ Employees are motivated by their ownership of stock, to work in the best long-term interests of the company.

ESOP programs also have some drawbacks:

➤ The repurchase of shares from owners has to be prorated to ownership. These programs are hard to use in a targeted buyout of one or two partial owners of the company who wish to sell.

➤ The value of the stock must be appraised each year, and an outside administrator must be hired to manage the shares. Each of these requirements has a cost associated with it.

➤ An employee who desires cash instead of stock may have no say in the matter.

Attainable Goals

Goals motivate people. They provide direction and focus and increase confidence. Unless, of course, they're out of reach. Then, sad to say, they have exactly the opposite effect. The employee feels set up for failure, and in a way, he's right. "I can't succeed at this," he thinks, "so why bother to try?"

Different managers set different goals for different reasons. Some set high standards to motivate and challenge. Others set lower standards to be sure goals are met. This helps them look good in performance reviews. Still others set goals based on what their superiors have asked of them.

Whatever is behind the particular goal you're setting, think carefully about what you're asking for and how much time you're providing. Does the time frame of the goal match the focus of the employee? If this is someone who's charged with daily output, don't

overwhelm her with annual goals. Keep expectations realistic.

A final point about goals: You need to know—and employees need to know—where they are in relation to their goal. Progress reports help keep people inspired, and allow them to make whatever adjustments may be necessary.

Some managers are stuck in a culture that guards its information like state secrets, even from employees. Others are dominated by accountants who insist on precision at the expense of timeliness. In such situations, you'll have to work hard to defend the importance of progress reports. It's up to you to fight for your employees' right to information.

Create Interactive Management

Don't tell me; let me try and read your mind. You don't have to talk to your team members because you already know what they're thinking, right?

If you want to be effective, you have to communicate. Clearly. Precisely. Say it better. Write it better. Listen better and demand the same from your employees.

You need to be interactive—meaning that you delegate to people, talk to people, give them access to what they need to know, and that you are responsive when it is required. They need to understand what you want and to know that you are supporting them and believe in their abilities.

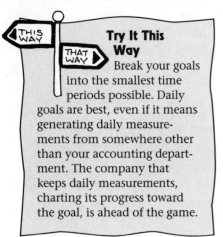

Try It This Way
Stick to reality when setting goals. Even if it isn't what your boss wants. Even if your boss is glaring at you. You can't force the impossible, not even to please your superiors. Stand firm against temptation today, so that you don't end up displeasing the boss for the next 364 days.

Try It This Way
Break your goals into the smallest time periods possible. Daily goals are best, even if it means generating daily measurements from somewhere other than your accounting department. The company that keeps daily measurements, charting its progress toward the goal, is ahead of the game.

Making Yourself Understood

The success of delegation depends on clear communication, so that the people you are delegating to understand just what you want them to accomplish. Communication is a skill that requires constant upkeep and refinement. It is also a two-way street.

Press Release

Even the best communicators face obstacles in trying to get their point across. Experts report that only 30 percent of what is spoken is retained by the listener—that is, remembered later—no matter how skillful the speaker.

Enthusiasm is a great beginning, but more is needed. How are your communication skills? Some people are born communicators; others have to learn. Fortunately, that's not such a daunting task. Your local community college probably offers writing classes from time to time. Organizations such as Toastmasters and the National Speakers Association have many local bureaus for those interested in honing their speaking skills.

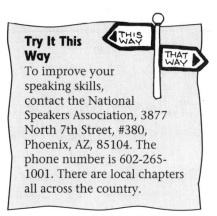

Try It This Way

To improve your speaking skills, contact the National Speakers Association, 3877 North 7th Street, #380, Phoenix, AZ, 85104. The phone number is 602-265-1001. There are local chapters all across the country.

This is the age of electronic communication—e-mail, faxing, and video conferencing. Some folks even fall back on the telephone now and then! Yet none of these technological marvels beats a face-to-face meeting. They may make communicating easier, but they don't necessarily do a better job getting the message across. Believe it or not, there's still a lot to be said for seeing the person to whom you're talking. For one thing, it makes listening a heck of a lot easier.

Say what? That's right, you have to listen in order to communicate.

Start from the basic assumption that many people don't have a clue what you're talking about. That's because their underlying concerns and assumptions may, unknown to all concerned, be completely different from yours. Not *wrong,* just different. If you want people to listen, and you want to be able to listen, it helps to try and meet face to face as often as possible. Sure, it's expensive to fly people to meetings. Often, however, expensive is cheap and cheap is expensive.

Besides, how else can you know for sure whether people are reading *The Wall Street Journal* or today's "Dilbert" cartoon strip while they are "listening" to you? If you see them, you oblige them to see you.

Studying Body Language

"Do you follow what I'm saying?"

"Absolutely."

But does he? Don't just rely on his verbal assurance. What is his body language telling you? The way people sit tells as much or more about what they think of your message than anything they say out loud.

Body language. Volumes have been written about it, but here are a few simple clues to get you started:

➤ When someone's arms are crossed like a pretzel, it's a signal that she's not very willing to listen to your ideas. She's closing you out.

➤ When someone leans toward you, she's receptive.

➤ When someone rubs his chin or face, he's not understanding your message.

➤ When someone has a foot crossed over a knee, and he's holding the foot, he's thinking about kicking you.

Tailoring Your Approach to Your Market

If you look around, you will probably observe that people are different. Not just their looks, but also their approach to life and business.

To be effective you need to take this into consideration. There are lots and lots of ways you can do this. For example:

➤ Some people are *aural*—they say, "I heard what you're saying." They are not impressed by charts and graphs. They want to hear your explanation, ask questions, and get answers. Even adding audio tracks to your presentations, like background music, or sounds helps these people understand what you're saying.

➤ Some people are *visual*—they say things like, "I see what you mean." Show them the charts and graphs.

➤ Some people are *emotional*—they say, "That feels right to me." They like non-quantitative logic. Explain benefits, not features.

How Are We Doing?

You've got to talk about what is expected and what you think is happening with your employees. Most of the time, if you are clear, you will find that you and your employees think alike—and both understand the goals and the way to get to the goals.

But not always.

It's important to hold regular reviews to make sure that progress is being made. In these meetings you should do the following:

➤ Review the objectives.

➤ Review your progress toward objectives.

➤ Analyze the costs incurred relative to the budget.

➤ Discuss the problem areas.

➤ Develop a short-term plan to ensure reaching the objective.

Helping Employees with Personal Problems

If you are in business for any time at all, you're going to be confronted by employees' personal problems. Drugs, alcohol, sex, bankruptcy, illness, family problems—hang in there for a while and you will see it all. And then you'll see more.

There are two basic schools of thought on employee problems. Neither one says to ignore them and they'll go away.

The first school says that employees are adults and should be able to take care of themselves. This approach calls for having comprehensive insurance plans in place that will solve most of the issues without your input. If you get involved in people's lives, this argument goes, your attention will be diverted from your business, and your judgment will be affected.

The second school is more paternalistic. It believes you should help people in troubled times. If you do, goes the thinking, not only will those you help be more loyal to you, others also will come to see you as someone who cares for those who need help. Employees do talk to each other, although managers sometimes forget this. It doesn't mean you should always deal with problems personally, but you can direct people to professional help.

As you can probably tell, I lean toward the second school. One word of caution, though: If problems show up on a regular basis with the same employee, you may have a bigger problem on your hands than you think. You may have to abandon the paternalism. Sometimes, frankly, tough problems require a tough approach. But try compassion first. You never know when it might come back to you, and in ways you might not expect.

The Least You Need to Know

➤ Failure that leads to learning can turn into great success.

➤ Providing employees with long-term security plans such as 401(k)s and ESOPs give them one less thing to distract them from their jobs.

➤ Good communication is based on a range of skills, including listening, understanding body language, and regular reviews to chart progress.

➤ When employees have personal problems, ignoring them is not an option. Let your insurance handle it, or become personally involved.

Chapter 13

Building the Right Team—Go Hire and Hire

> ## In This Chapter
>
> ➤ Writing the job description
>
> ➤ Where to look for the right people
>
> ➤ What to concentrate on in the interview
>
> ➤ Reaching a decision
>
> ➤ What happens after you hire

When you want to make a good hire, there's no substitute for spending time on it. And if you want to run a great company, you need great people. Ergo, be prepared to spend time assembling your team. It is not just in your line of work. It *is* your work.

Each time that you're called upon to hire someone represents a unique opportunity. Don't just replace people. Upgrade. Find someone who *adds* to your team.

This chapter is about how to assemble your team: where to look, how to look, and then how to make the right decision. I'll also give you some rules for dealing with new people, an important area that business advisors often miss. Don't hire someone else to read this chapter. You're going to have to do it yourself.

Can You Describe It?

If you don't know what you want, how are you going to find it? Sure, you might get lucky. But you probably won't. On the whole, it's better to make your own luck.

Besides, you want to be fair to the prospective employee. How can she know whether the job is for her unless you tell her exactly what is expected? Again, you might get lucky. But again, you probably won't.

You need job descriptions, and accurate ones, at that. That could mean updating or rewriting some existing job descriptions. Things change, roles change. Some people are just bad writers.

A job description is a snapshot of how you see the job at the time. It is almost a contract: *This is what we expect, and this is what you get.*

The first step in writing a job description is to read the existing job descriptions and make whatever revisions you think are necessary. Put a high premium on accuracy. Here are some suggestions for what to include in job descriptions:

➤ A description of the physical tasks, including whatever skills and knowledge you believe to be essential.

➤ A list of the training you provide, including any support for outside education or time off for an employees pursuit of outside education.

➤ A clear explanation of the authority and responsibility of the job, including personnel oversight, signing authority, and so on.

➤ The goals and objectives of the job, complete with timelines, measurement points, and performance standards.

➤ A clear identification of the person to whom the applicant will report, as well as those who will report to the applicant. Who the employee can go to when they have questions?

➤ An account of the pay scale, fringe benefits, and perquisites, with salary review timetables, advancement criteria, and company policies.

Job descriptions can be lengthy or concise. Most people prefer the latter.

Simplify your task. Take the existing job description, if there is one, and use as much of it as possible. If one doesn't exist, use some other job description as a template. It can even be from another company. As a last resort, use your creative writing abilities.

Use the job description to your advantage by making sure the applicant understands it. Don't be an optimist on this.

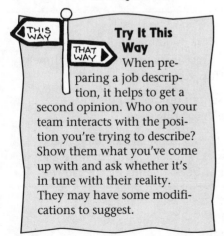

Try It This Way When preparing a job description, it helps to get a second opinion. Who on your team interacts with the position you're trying to describe? Show them what you've come up with and ask whether it's in tune with their reality. They may have some modifications to suggest.

After she reads it, explain it, following the ancient wisdom tradition: *Tell them what you are going to tell them, then tell them, and then tell them what you told them.*

Good Form!

Unless your organization has a terrible reputation (and if it does, why are *you* working there?), you'll probably receive a lot of résumés. Some may be solicited. Most won't be. None will be in the same format. They'll cover all sorts of topics that may or may not be relevant.

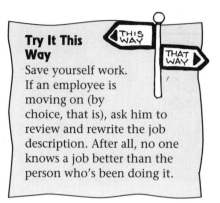

Try It This Way
Save yourself work. If an employee is moving on (by choice, that is), ask him to review and rewrite the job description. After all, no one knows a job better than the person who's been doing it.

All of this makes the job of evaluating them virtually impossible. Take charge. Come up with your own form that defines what *you* want. That way you'll have some basis for comparison. The form should be as short and simple as practical. Once you get serious about candidates, you can ask more questions or even provide other forms if you choose.

A word or two about the law. As you probably know, the law is fairly zealous in pursuing discrimination violations, so be careful what you ask an applicant. There are a few basic no-no's. Don't ask about:

➤ Age or date of birth.

➤ Marital status or child care responsibilities. Employers may not make inferences as to a prospective employee's obligations or availability. Don't comment on a wedding ring, if you happen to see one; it's illegal.

➤ Arrest records. You can ask about previous convictions for felonies, but not about unproved allegations.

➤ The candidate's gender. Usually you can observe this in your interview. If by chance you can't, don't ask. It's not a legitimate reason for not hiring.

➤ Religion.

➤ Whether they are a citizen or have a green card. This can only be asked after someone has been hired.

➤ Nationality, disabilities, or anything that can in any way be construed as discrimination.

Finding the Right People

People are everywhere, and you need some. Where do you begin?

In most companies the personnel department handles all the initial stages. Some companies are lucky enough not to have a personnel department—and I mean that in the nicest

Stressbusters
It's tough to get great people through a personnel department. Many great people have idiosyncrasies that may not get past a generic screening process. If you can, review all applications.

Try It This Way
To ensure a manageable timeline, set a deadline for all applications. You don't want the job search to stop too soon or to go on forever. Set a strict schedule for interviewing and hiring, and stick to it.

way. No matter where it starts, the format should be clear. Look where you can find good people.

An Inside Job

If you can, promote someone from within the company. It does wonders for team morale. Sure, an occasional person will be jealous, but I think most people are happy to see one of their own promoted. It gives everyone hope: *Do well here and you will be rewarded* is the message you're sending.

Post the job in-house; if you have the luxury of a company newsletter, publish the description there. Make the announcement at staff meetings. Get the word out. Great people work at your company; maybe you even hired some of them. If good jobs start going to people outside the company, many could become disgruntled. So think of your insiders first.

Here's my rule of thumb; you may find it helpful. If an internal employee is only five percent less qualified than an outsider, I'll stay with what I know and with the people that I know. The extra I gain from the symbolism of the move more than makes up for the five percent shortfall.

Broadening the Search

You won't always be able to find a great job candidate from within your company. The operative word here is *great*. In this case, by all means look outside the organization.

Perhaps you need technical skills that your current employees don't have. Perhaps someone outside your company is simply exceptional. Maybe this is one of those times when you need an outsider's perspective. If an outside candidate has something significant to offer, go for it.

Tune in to Your Network

A network is a group of people you know well, and who know you. A network can be a great source for identifying prospective employees; it can also provide a valuable screening process for you *and* for the applicant. You can expect the network member to be brutally honest with both of you about each other. This is a good thing; it avoids false expectations.

The best thing about network recommendations is that the person being recommended is more likely than not to be of similar character and drive as the person doing the recommending. Birds of a feather flock together. If James is part of *your* network, the people in James's network are probably okay. Right? Usually so.

Headhunters and Other Specialists

Lots of folks have made a career of helping employers and employees find each other. Headhunters and employment agencies cost money, but they often know just the person to fill your vacant position, someone who's either already available or looking to jump to a better opportunity.

Employment specialists can offer other kinds of expert help, too. For example, they can help refine a job description and let you know how the compensation you're offering stacks up against the rest of the industry.

Remember, though, before you hire a professional recruiter, do some research—particularly if the recruiter wants some kind of guarantee or exclusive. Spend time with the person. Talk with employers who have dealt with him. To get the best applicants around, it helps to be involved in the process.

> **Stressbusters**
> If you are using employment agencies, be sure they are reputable. If not, you may find the people who are shopping for employees for you are also shopping your existing employees around.

Interviewing: The Facts Behind the Face

So you found some people. People you really like. Now what? How do you narrow down the field? The process usually begins with an interview.

Interviewing is an art. Reams have been written about it. If you are going to be doing a lot of it, you may want to pick up a specialty book or two on this topic. I'll tell you what works for me, however.

My first rule is very simple: Look people in the eye. This is the most important reason to schedule face-to-face interviews with applicants. You're looking for candor, conviction, energy, and honesty. You're also looking for a commitment to excellence, a commitment to your vision and mission. It isn't definitive, but it is a darn good start and it certainly will eliminate those who clearly don't qualify.

The following section lists some sample interview questions. Some are aimed at the obvious, such as education and experience. Does the applicant have the background needed to do the job? If not, how much training would she need? Others are aimed at intangibles like personality, attitude, and interpersonal skills. Does the applicant get along with people? Can she contribute and make a team better?

Walk into the interview prepared. The topics should start with the most specific and work down to the abstract. This gives you time to become comfortable with the facts before you probe deeper.

The Questions

Background

➤ What is your education and professional training?

➤ How have you applied your education and training in past jobs?

➤ How might you apply it in this job?

➤ What is your work experience?

➤ What did you like about your previous jobs?

➤ What didn't you like?

➤ What is your present job and how does it relate to our opening?

➤ What are some specific examples of your accomplishments in your present job?

➤ What is the most difficult task you ever encountered?

➤ How did you handle it?

➤ What was your most enjoyable task ever?

➤ Do you prefer teamwork or single assignments? Why?

Why are you interested in the job?

➤ How did you hear about the job?

➤ Why are you applying?

➤ What skills do you bring to the job?

➤ What unique gifts and perspectives do you bring to the job?

➤ What do you think of the pay?

➤ Do you know other people who will be co-workers? What do you think of them?

What about the big picture?

➤ What is your long-term goal?

➤ How does this job fit your long-term goal?

➤ Why do you want to leave your existing job?

➤ What is the best part of your existing job?

➤ What part of your existing job do you like the least?

➤ In the ideal world, what would be your ideal job?

These are fairly straightforward questions, but of course you want more than a yes-no answer. Your goal is to get a feeling for the employee and that employee's chances of success. For those who like neat, orderly categories, this intuition thing can be a challenge. Still, life is like that. Success is largely a matter of intangibles.

The interview, then, is more than a fact-finding mission: It's a first impression. For this reason, I think it's important to make the process as comfortable as you can. You're going to have to deal with your new employee on a daily basis, so try and make sure that the first impression is an accurate one. As the twig is bent, so grows the tree.

Remember to listen and let applicants have their say, and the screening process will happen naturally.

Here are a few tips for drawing people out:

➤ *Ask probing questions.* Avoid those that can be answered with a simple "yes" or "no."

➤ *Ask for opinions.* Get beyond facts and into how people feel about things.

➤ *Leave pregnant pauses.* Silence is a great tool. People will say something. Listen.

Tricks of the Trade

Some firms use stress interviews, in which the interviewer will ask rapid-fire complex questions to see how a prospective employee reacts to stress. Others will develop a whole ruse. They may put a prospect in a room alone and then have the phone ring just to see how the employee reacts. Or they may give them an hour's worth of work to see how they do.

I am not a fan of these techniques. If you're hiring someone to fly jets, a stress interview may be quite appropriate. Otherwise, what do you gain? Remember, everything you do sends a message. Even as the candidate does her best to impress you at the interview, she is forming an opinion of you as a prospective employer.

Check References

References help. They are not a sure-fire science, but you can learn enough almost every time to make the phone call worthwhile. Sometimes what you learn is good, and sometimes what you learn is this candidate could be a major headache. Don't skip this step: You may end up being surprised by what comes out.

Recruiters check references too, but you're better off making sure on your own. Finding a great employee is worth the effort.

> **Stressbusters**
> Hate checking those references? One applicant I got fabricated his entire work history to fit our job description. It was brilliant. His past employer was the one who tipped me off.

This Is Only a Test

No one wants to work for Big Brother. Okay, most people don't. Still, if there's a good reason for requiring applicants to take a certain kind of test, they'll understand. If there isn't a really good reason, then forget about it. It's not worth the hassle.

Stressbusters
The Americans With Disability Act (ADA) says that medical tests can only be given after a decision to hire has been made. If you ask for a medical test beforehand and then you don't hire the person, you could face a discrimination suit.

A variety of tests are routinely included in the application process—medical tests, mental tests, dexterity tests, IQ tests, even lie detector tests. My advice is, use these sparingly. A lie detector test for a receptionist could be overkill. For a CIA agent, it's probably essential.

One of the most common pre-employment tests is a drug test. If you choose this method of testing, be very careful because in some cases it can be illegal. The best thing to do is to contact your company's labor lawyer before beginning to administer this type of test.

The Moment of Truth

Or at least the moment of decision. Either way, you've got to grasp it. Take a deep breath, and—as Tom Peters says—"Ready, Fire, Aim."

Hey, you're going to be either right or wrong. Nobody is right all the time. Your employees depend on you to take action, so check the Prince Hamlet routine at the door and get on with it. It's time to choose.

Start with an intellectual assessment of the applicants. Then move on to attributes. Here's the checklist that I use after the interview is over and I'm summarizing my thoughts. I find that trying to do this during the interview often undermines the spontaneity and chemistry of the interview.

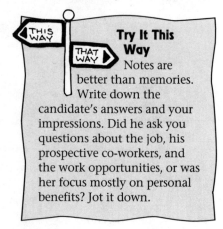

Try It This Way
Notes are better than memories. Write down the candidate's answers and your impressions. Did he ask you questions about the job, his prospective co-workers, and the work opportunities, or was her focus mostly on personal benefits? Jot it down.

❑ Can you trust him?

❑ Do you think you can count on her?

❑ Does he have a good character?

❑ Will she be a joy at work?

❑ Is he flexible and creative?

❑ Is she eager to learn and grow?

❑ Is he confident? *If he's not, I'm not.*

When candidates are equally qualified in terms of their skills and experience, you can begin to assess their motivations and desire. I compare their passion, their dedication, their sense of urgency, their sense of humor, and their tenacity.

If, after all of this, you still cannot make a decision—you are in trouble. So make an offer.

The Offer Sheet

It is nice to smile and shake hands. Don't omit that step, it's important! But then get it all in writing.

The written offer should include:

➤ A welcome to the company

➤ A job description and title

➤ A starting date

➤ The starting salary and the length of the review period

➤ A clear explanation of the compensation package—including vacations, benefits, and incentive compensation

➤ An organizational chart with all the names spelled correctly

➤ A deadline for accepting or rejecting the job offer

Don't be too shocked if your first offer is not accepted. You may need to negotiate. If the candidate is currently employed, her boss may well counter your offer. Anticipate this and prepare for it. For example, you may want to tell the candidate in advance that her current company can be expected to say: "We can't afford to lose you. Whatever they offered, we will match." Having made this prediction, you can go on to use one or all of the following counterarguments (all right, don't overdo it!):

➤ "If the only way you can get a raise is to offer to quit, is that any place you want to work?"

➤ "Is the counteroffer a true increase or just an acceleration of what you would get later?"

➤ "Once you have said you are planning on quitting, you have prejudiced yourself in the eyes of your old employer."

➤ "Isn't it time for a change?"

Some organizations don't offer much flexibility on hiring procedures. If at all possible, however, please remember the following three points:

1. *Make the pay consistent with your existing pay scale.* It's tempting to ignore your internal scale when you hire outside people, especially if you see a new employee bringing great benefits to your group. As soon as you ignore the scale, however, you affect the scale. Remember, they have to fit *here*. If you fudge on paying fairly, trust me, it'll get around.

2. *Hire people on three months' probation.* Your instincts are good, but they're probably not infallible. You can and almost certainly will make mistakes. Protect yourself and your employees (sometimes they may *want* to leave) by putting them on three

127

months' probation before they become full-time employees. This only applies to an outside hire, of course—not an internal promotion.

3. *Avoid employment contracts.* These generally favor the employee. If you must use one, have a lawyer draw it up and use a "restrictive covenant," which prevents the employee from taking a job with a competitor for certain period of time.

New Kid on the Block

Great. You've hired someone. Now what?

I'll tell you what—nurture him. Assist him. Help him grow. Cheer for him. Allow him to succeed. Remember, if he succeeds, you succeed. Here are some other things you should do:

➤ Take her around yourself and introduce her to the rest of the team.

➤ Assign him a mentor.

➤ Give her a few days of real experience in jobs in your department that are related to her own.

➤ Have an end-of-week meeting with him for his first few weeks on the job. Review how things are going and answer questions.

The Least You Need to Know

➤ Hiring a great employee begins with an accurate job description.

➤ Start your search inside your company; then if you need to, expand your search via your own network of contacts.

➤ Headhunters and other employment experts can provide a valuable service.

➤ The art of interviewing involves asking probing questions, to try to identify motivations as well as skills.

➤ In the end, go with your gut: Does the person want to be excellent? Once you decide, extend a formal, written offer.

➤ New employees need guidance and support in order to succeed.

AND YOU NEVER STUCK TO THE DRESS CODE...

Chapter 14

Some People Will Quit, Others Need to Be Fired

In This Chapter

➤ How not to overreact

➤ Progressive discipline

➤ The difference between a resignation and a termination

➤ Learning from employees who quit

➤ The right way to terminate employees

In business, as in life, mistakes happen. Sometimes—trust me on this one—sometimes, *you* are going to be the cause of mistakes. Hey, there's nothing wrong with being wrong. Being wrong is a sign of your willingness to be right. For a manager, that's a good sign.

When it comes to being wrong, the important thing is to admit it. And the place where most managers make wrong decisions is in the hiring of employees. Don't pretend the hire wasn't a mistake. Admit it and move to correct it. Otherwise the damage will only spread.

This chapter is about what to do when the wrong person is in the job. I'll talk about how to correct the problems that arise, and then, if all else fails, what the proper legal steps are for termination. I'll also cover the difference between firing and quitting…because as far as I'm concerned, you can't fire me. If you don't read this chapter, I quit.

Whoa! Slow Down!

C'mon. Who hired this person, anyway? What the heck was I thinking?

Don't waste time kicking yourself. You need to take steps to resolve the situation, or the person's co-workers will either revolt or start following his example. This is no time for timidity. It's time to be extremely careful—and smart.

Sure, you're upset, and no wonder. Personnel conflicts are among the hardest business problems you'll ever have to deal with. Getting emotional won't help, though, so why don't you go into your office, close the door, take a deep breath, and count to 40,000. Please don't fly off the handle and start issuing spontaneous dismissals.

Simply Stated

A *spontaneous dismissal* is an immediate dismissal for *cause*. Cause covers fraud, theft, and dishonesty, but not much else.

Remember, if you fire someone on the spot without cause, you may find yourself in hot water legally. Very few offenses meet the test for a *spontaneous dismissal*. Check with your labor lawyer before you start to get "spontaneous."

Of course, even if there aren't legal complications, replacing employees tends to be very expensive.

Progressive Discipline

Your first response to trouble, then, should be to try and get people back on track. Follow the steps outlined in this section. They serve a double function: If they don't succeed in bringing about the desired changes in behavior, at least they'll cover you if you need to take drastic action. Oscar Wilde said, "Believe in the best: You'll be surprised at how often you get it." This is the right attitude for a manager to start with in dealing with poor performance.

First Step: The Verbal Warning

Trouble usually takes the form of small but important infractions—bending company rules, not following directions, or creating conflicts with other employees.

Sometimes the people involved are actually your best people, the rebels. They're smart, they're creative—and they're easily bored. Others, however, are just not up for the job. How you approach someone's misbehavior will depend on what seems to be going on. Your job is to offer help and opportunity. Their job is to act on it.

Perhaps the employee is disregarding the regular hours of the organization. Maybe she's just plain sloppy. It's not a big deal, but it's a big enough deal. Take her aside, *casually,* and point out the problems. Let her know that you have higher standards, and suggest a specific change.

Even though this verbal warning is casual, it's extremely important that you *make a note of it in the employee's personnel file.* Be as exact as you can: What did you say, and what did she say? Keep a record of every disciplinary action taken. You may need it later to show that you followed proper procedure.

Second Step: The Disciplinary Warning

If the employee does not improve after a casual verbal warning, the next step is to issue a formal disciplinary warning. This also is verbal, but it should take place in an office setting in the form of a *word to the wise* discussion.

You want very much to keep this meeting positive. Your goal is to save the employee—not to mention the costs associated with firing and hiring. So don't just lecture—come up with an action plan to correct the situation.

And listen to the other side. The employee probably has a point, even if it's a flawed point. Your hope is to achieve a meeting of the minds, so you can move forward.

Here's another tip: Always include one other person, preferably someone from your Human Resources department, at a disciplinary warning meeting. The other person's presence there will underscore the importance of the meeting and corroborate what you have to say.

Finally, remember to take notes and write up an account of the meeting afterward. It should go in the employee's personnel file, along with the previous report.

Third Step: The Written Warning

Sometimes things deteriorate. Some employees will never get it; but you have to keep trying, because you may open your company up to lawsuits if you don't.

Trying doesn't mean accepting the bad behavior; it simply means you can and should continue to take steps. At this point, your next move is to issue a formal, written warning.

By this time, of course, there's a good chance that you're feeling pretty angry. This is a signal that you

Try It This Way

If an employee's behavior is bad enough to warrant a spontaneous dismissal, act promptly. All of your other employees are watching. The employee will have an excuse; they all do. But if you have cause and you know it has to be done, don't show indecision. Say good-bye.

Stressbusters

When issuing a verbal warning, avoid the three As of **agitation**, **aggression**, and **alienation**.

Stressbusters

Expect litigation. Keep complete records from the first moment you suspect a problem. Rigidly adhere to company policies, and follow the letter of the law. Ask a second person to sit in on meetings whenever possible.

need to back away. Give your frustrations time to subside; reason needs to win out over emotion in this one.

Granted, the possibility of improvement at this stage is not high. There's a good chance that the written warning will just antagonize your employee further. But you have to act with some degree of faith. Miracles do happen. The law is counting on it, even if you are not. Issue a warning in the most professional way possible. Document the warning and a corrective action plan using a standard form that both you and the employee sign.

The new written action plan may or may not be the same one that was presented before. New offenses may need to be detailed. Either way, make sure you refer to the old plan in preparing your written warning. Make a copy of everything and place the copy in the employee's personnel file.

Fourth Step: Suspension

Still no progress? The next step is suspension. This means you dismiss the employee from work for a certain number of days. Mind you, the chances that he will bounce back from suspension to become a model employee are pretty slim. His attitude is probably hardened against you, or suspension wouldn't be necessary. So suspension is usually preliminary to firing, unless he resigns first.

After all, suspension has a certain amount of stigma attached to it. It won't be easy for him to face the other employees after that. If the suspension is for longer than a week or two, economic factors will begin to loom as well.

It would be easier to bypass the suspension and simply fire the employee, and many employers do just that. Legally, you're safer suspending first. But you will need to make up your own mind about that.

Press Release

"Employment at will" is a legal term that greatly simplifies the firing process. It states that an employee has no employment contract. He's free to resign (or be terminated) at any time. It's a good idea to include this term in all employee communications, including the application form, the welcome letter, and all personnel manuals.

Fifth Step: Termination

You warned her. You called her into your office. You sent her a written warning. You suspended her. She's still not doing her job. I'm afraid this is good-bye.

Some people would rather quit than be fired. They think that it looks better on their résumé, not thinking about the fact that it looks worse at the unemployment line. When you quit, you're not eligible for unemployment benefits. When you're fired, you are. It doesn't take a rocket scientist to realize being fired has its advantages.

That's why it's not unusual for someone to quit and then later claim she was fired in order to collect unemployment benefits. Then, like a fool, you'll find yourself spending money on a labor lawyer when you should have just fired the slacker in the first place. When someone quits, get a letter, signed by both you and the employee, stating that she quit voluntarily. Put it in her file.

> **Stressbusters**
> Don't try to force the employee to quit of his own accord by making his life uncomfortable. Courts have called this "constructive discharge" and have awarded employees back wages *and* their job back.

Oh, Yeah? I'll Show You!

Fired employees are rarely happy people. Many seek retribution—for economic reasons, for ego reasons, or just to make you squirm.

As with all the preceding steps, a termination should be done in a formal atmosphere with a witness. The results should be documented and entered into a file.

Human nature being what it is (and the American legal system being what *it* is), you need to act as if you anticipate a lawsuit. The more prepared you are, the less likely a disgruntled employee will be to sue—whereas, if you seem like an easy target, you'll be one. You will probably face a lawsuit on occasion anyway, but if you've done your legal homework, you'll have a better chance of prevailing.

Never keep a bad employee just because you are afraid of being sued. Employees can sense this kind of fear, and they'll lose respect for you. They'll treat you the way kids treat a substitute teacher at school. Scary thought, huh?

Here are some guidelines for dismissing someone:

➤ Review all the files and have them on hand for the meeting.

➤ Have a second person (preferably someone from Human Resources) check your records and attend the meeting.

➤ Invite the union representative, if the union calls for it.

➤ Review any financial claims due to the employee.

➤ Review all financial claims by the company against the employee (such as monetary advances).

➤ Review, in detail, the documented problems and warnings that led to the dismissal.

> **Stressbusters**
> Pay your employee whatever she is owed on the day she leaves. Until you pay in full, you'll have to keep paying her full compensation, whether she works or not.

Simply Stated
The *Consolidated Omnibus Reconciliation Act (COBRA)* is a federal law that mandates that companies with more than 20 employees must be allowed to keep their health insurance benefits for 18 months after they leave the company. Their payment must remain the same as when they were with the company.

➤ Be brief, firm, and calm.

➤ Answer any questions, but be brief. No one is changing your mind.

➤ Give the total paycheck on the day they leave.

➤ If separation pay or vacation pay is due, it must be paid on the spot. The employee is also entitled to continuation of certain benefits under the *Consolidated Omnibus Reconciliation Act (COBRA)*.

➤ Reach an agreement on all expenses and advances, and have everyone sign it.

➤ See that the employee returns all company property, including keys, access cards, security codes, equipment, and so on.

➤ Clearly state when you would like the employee to clean out her office, desk, and work area. Make sure someone supervises.

➤ Agree to a method for handling ongoing mail and messages.

➤ Let the employee leave with dignity.

A Valuable Learning Experience

Sometimes people will just quit—good people. For their own mysterious reasons, they will decide that they'd be better off not working for you. Your job is to find out why.

You don't want to change minds, but you may want to change how you do things. At the very least, you want to listen.

Conduct an exit interview. People leave for a variety of reasons, not always because they're not satisfied with their job. Don't assume you're reading someone's mind. Find out the truth.

An employee's departure offers an opportunity to gather crucial information. Some of it may smack of sour grapes, but even those will contain some seeds of truth. What if you are the reason the employee is leaving? You'd rather it weren't so, but still, better you hear about it than the Human Resources department, right? You don't really want *them* in the middle of the mess.

Don't just ask, "Why are you leaving?" That probably won't get you the answer you want—which is the truth. Try to get at the heart of the matter with questions like:

➤ "If you were in my shoes, what would you do differently?"

➤ "What did you like least about your job here?"

➤ "What did you like most?"

➤ "What sort of additional support would you have appreciated in your old role?"

➤ "How did you get along with your supervisors?"

➤ "How did you get along with your peers?"

The Least You Need to Know

➤ Before you fire anyone, try and help him improve and succeed in his job. Saving him will save your organization money.

➤ Terminations for poor performance must be in accordance with proper procedure, officially known as progressive discipline.

➤ Employees who quit cannot receive unemployment benefits, but those who are fired can.

➤ Everything associated with the firing process should be written down, attested to by someone else, and, whenever possible, signed by the employee.

Chapter 15

A Place for Everyone and Everyone in Their Place

In This Chapter

➤ Two ways to organize: pyramid and flat organizations

➤ The importance of organizational flexibility to meet changing market conditions

➤ How to deal with consultants and technology

➤ Making resources mesh to expedite results

➤ Your management, how do you know when it's time to revise?

In theory, it all fits together. Theories are great. Reality, however, is another story and that's the one you have to face. You may think that just because your theory is sound, you will succeed. You may think that, but you would be wrong.

First of all, your dream of having the best people and keeping them together is a pipe dream. You are going to have to work with what you get. Maximizing the capabilities of those people should be your goal. But, even if you do, you have to make sure it all meshes together. In my experience, more companies have failed because of their inability to carry out plans than from anything their competitors have done.

This is a chapter about getting the gears to mesh. This is more than a management challenge—it's essential for good business. In this chapter, you'll learn about organizing employees, when to use consultants, why the high-tech world gives you new challenges and opportunities, allocating resources, and whether to stick to your plan or go beyond it. You'll see how all these pieces fit together.

Organizing Your Employees—Your Most Important Asset

Folks like to know what is expected of them. They want people to get out of their way and let them do their job, and they want help when they need it and when it should be given. Sometimes, the organization gets in their way.

Many organizations think that they are organized because they have developed an organizational chart.

Simply Stated

An *organizational chart* is a graphic that shows who reports to whom in an organization.

Still, without an *organizational chart*, people may not know what they are supposed to do or who reports to whom. The truth is that the organizational chart is merely a start. The important part of an organization and the way it really works is the hand-off—what happens in the crevices of the organization. Often, the organizational chart isn't organized around the tasks that need to be accomplished. It is merely a piece of paper.

Besides that, organizations change. They grow. People move and tasks evolve. Sometimes, whole new layers evolve as the company grows. Sometimes a rigid organizational chart dictates all the lines of communication—and those lines are just too slow to operate in today's fast-paced business world. These are just a few of the reasons why an organizational chart, if not properly constructed, can be a hindrance rather than a help.

Some companies will grow into a pyramid format, yet others will transform into more of a "flat" organization. There are benefits to both approaches, as discussed in the following sections.

Life on a Pyramid

Stressbusters

No one person can keep track of everything. Smart companies encourage extensive use of tools such as e-mail, retreats, and team-building exercises to encourage communication across functional boundaries.

Most companies are organized around a traditional pyramid. In the pyramid format, the chief executive officer (CEO) is at the top, and spread out below is the rest of the organization, broken down by functional divisions. The pyramid format originated in the military.

The pyramid approach appears most often in large companies where many people need to be organized and where significant amounts of specific expertise are required to get a job done. In a pyramid, there is a need to clarify authority and the specific responsibilities of a number of people.

How Flat Is Flat?

Some companies say that "No organization is the best organization." These companies want to be fast, agile, and flexible. Often, but not always, they are smaller and thrive on constant reorganization. They are held together primarily by a commonly held vision, not an organizational chart. Much of the work is done by teams of cross-functional employees that disband after a project is completed.

Press Release

Opticon, the $160-million-dollar Danish company, reputed to be the fastest growing hearing-aid company in the world, attributes its success to having no organizational chart. The company's employees have no permanent desks, but instead work at mobile work stations. Everybody works on projects, not just parts of projects. This system works for them.

Some companies are trying to reinvent the concept of organization, to arrive at a more collaborative form of management. Often, these are new companies. They don't have to break down entrenched fiefdoms or ones where new products and new directions are a common occurrence.

W.L. Gore and Associates, a 4,000-person company that makes and markets such diverse products as Gore-Tex fabric, medical products, and electronic products, has a different philosophy. They have what they call "Lattice Work Management," in which everyone is equal. Employees are organized in divisions around product lines. These divisions are never allowed to have more than 150 people—the maximum number that they feel any one person can know well. They believe you can't manage people unless you know them on a personal basis.

In Lattice Work Management, any individual can make a decision, unless it threatens the existence of the company. In cases where the company could be threatened by a bad move (called a "water line decision"), groups make the decisions.

The Benefits of Pyramid and Flat Organizations

The benefits of a pyramid include:

➤ Clear delineation of authority and responsibility

➤ Natural progression for employees up the corporate ladder

➤ Specialization of labor—increasing individual productivity

➤ Individualizing objectives for analysis and feedback

➤ Elimination, in theory, of chaos

The benefits of a flat organization include:

➤ Greater speed and flexibility in responding to market changes

➤ More efficient communication—especially in global companies

➤ Frees more talented contributors to advance without passing over people and alienating them

➤ More team efforts, less divisional rivalries

"It's Not My Department"

This claim is from the Excuses Hall of Fame. "It's not my department" emanates from the concept of an organizational chart. People believe or choose to act as if they believe that their responsibilities stop at the boundary of their job description.

Yet, it comes back to the hand-off or passing of information and decisions from one person to another in an organization. Unless everyone takes responsibility for hand-offs, things start falling through the cracks. Smart managers understand and make sure their people understand.

Keeping the Organization Dynamic and Flexible

The only constant in the world is change. No matter how things are, it's going to change. Count on it.

So, in this world where no product lasts forever, no market stays the same forever, and no economy is consistent, should your organization stay the same forever?

No.

The key is to keep your organizational change consistent with the changing environment around you. Not too fast. Not too slow. Try to follow along parallel with the outside world while you still try to get past it. Keep your finger on the pulse—of the world and of your organization.

Integrating New Employees

When someone joins your organization, your organization changes. There is a shift. Whether the new person replaces an employee who is leaving or he comes into a new job, he is a new element. New employees bring a unique set of skills, knowledge, and experience to the company. The quicker you ease them into the job, the sooner you'll see results. As manager, it's in your best interest to help the person succeed. If you throw him into the job in a sink-or-swim proposition, you may save some time, but it also may just sink you.

Press Release

An informed survey that my consulting company did showed the average job tenure for students just out of college from 1980 to 1997 is 3.2 years. People don't stick around for decades anymore. The descriptions of a job history is shifting from life time employment to a series of mini careers. It is a result of many things: a desire for more income, a frustration with the pace of acceleration and the fact that many companies don't change rapidly enough to thrive in the changing environment. It requires continued re-evaluation, but adds immeasurably to the excitement and feeling of progress.

Here are some suggestions on how to integrate new people into your organization:

➤ Introduce them to their co-workers. If you personally do this, it will underscore to the new employee and to others the importance that you attach to this hire.

➤ Give them a mentor. They should have someone to turn to when they have questions. It should preferably be someone who is not their boss. You don't want them to be afraid to show ignorance. You want them to learn their way past it.

➤ Give them written explanations of your expectations for the short term. Meet with them at the end of this predetermined short term and give them an honest evaluation of their progress.

➤ Give them an organizational chart, the tools they need, and a copy of your long-term plan. The more they know, the more they will contribute.

How and Where to Use Consultants

There are almost as many consultant jokes making the rounds as there are lawyer jokes: "Those that can't do, consult." Or, "A *consultant* is someone who borrows your watch and then tells you what time it is." I know 'em all. I *am* a consultant.

The jokes can be appropriate, yet there are enough of us out here making a successful living as consultants to make you think that maybe we offer something. Consultants can greatly improve your success if used properly. The operative word is *properly*.

Simply Stated

Consultants are people outside an organization that are employed to analyze and solve corporate problems. They range from small, one person operations to huge, international organizations.

Here is a list of some times when you should consider using consultants:

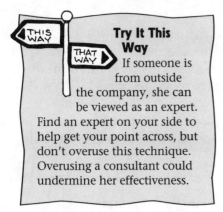

Try It This Way
If someone is from outside the company, she can be viewed as an expert. Find an expert on your side to help get your point across, but don't overuse this technique. Overusing a consultant could undermine her effectiveness.

➤ For the short term—if you need specialized knowledge not available in-house.

➤ Business is uncertain and it doesn't make sense to add fixed costs by adding more employees.

➤ You need someone to add credibility to an idea you want to present.

➤ The situation demands speed and flexibility.

But remember that consultants are not a panacea. They can help, but they aren't the end-all. In fact, they can cause problems and they aren't always in tune with your objectives. But if used properly, consultants can add quite a bit.

New Challenges Posed by the High-Tech World

Organizing people is not easy. It never has been, but now the challenge is even more interesting (yes, *interesting*, that's the word) with the advent of the global economy and the availability of high-tech tools. The people you organize in these times may not all be in the same building. You could be managing folks from around the world. And even if you're not, you are probably dealing with suppliers and customers from a broad area.

Thus, there is technology.

Technology helps you manage your employees so that everyone can communicate as easily, clearly, and quickly as possible. The only problem with technology is the fear that you could end up on overload. Keep it manageable. Use it as a tool, not an anchor.

Press Release

In 1991, for the first time, more money was invested in computers and services than in industrial equipment. The change signified a shift in the basic nature of management. We moved from a society based on goods and services to a society based on information. The information age offers incredible opportunities and wealth, just ask Bill Gates or Scott McNealy.

Allocating Resources to People

You'll never be able to satisfy everyone. It's impossible. Go to Las Vegas and bet the farm. It's not going to happen.

People who work for you are going to want more resources than you can provide. The more you can provide, the more they will want. It's a guarantee—just like death and taxes.

The result is that you'll have to decide on investments—and who specifically benefits from these investments. This is a dilemma if you have stock in an antacid company. After all, plenty of managers have worried themselves sick because the answers all have consequences. If you don't have stock in an antacid company, this is merely part of being a manager.

Answers = Resources.

Not only will some employees not like your decisions (because they didn't get what they want), but you can also count on some of your decisions directly affecting productivity. Make the right decision, and productivity goes way up. But make the wrong decision…

Coordination is very important. People need to know why you are making decisions. It will help ease things for everyone.

Techniques for Measuring Investments

You want to be consistent. It's a good trait.

The easiest way to be consistent in being a manager is to have a system. You, of course, need to first figure out what your objective is before you make decisions on where to invest your resources—human and financial. There are two well-tested techniques for measuring investments:

1. *Payback Analysis*. This method is used to calculate the time it takes to recover the cost of investments. The items with the fastest payback are rated highest.

2. *Return On Investment*. The life return on various possible investments are compared in this technique.

Sticking with the Plan or Going Beyond

Management is the art of dealing with change. Life is consistent in that everything changes. And now the truth—even your plan *could be* subject to change. There is a tendency to think of a plan—something you have *committed to*—as being something that can't change. It feels like changing religions.

But this is business. You *must* approach it with raw intellect (that includes but is not ruled by your emotions).

Simply Stated

A *sunset provision* is a methodology for automatically terminating a project. It gives every project a finite life, even when the project is considered good forever. When the time limit is up, the project must be reviewed and decided upon.

A plan is a tool, not a rigid commandment. Therefore, a strategy of versatility puts a sunset provision in every plan so that you can coordinate everything and you aren't stuck in something that doesn't work.

Of course, that doesn't answer the more serious dilemma—should you ever revise your plan in the middle of a year?

The answer is *maybe*.

Probably not.

But if the situation is serious enough or the opportunity great enough, then make the change. Who decides? Why, the manager.

The Least You Need to Know

➤ Organizational charts are a help and a hindrance. They clarify roles, but they can also lead to inflexibility and missed hand-offs.

➤ Consultants should be employed to do things that internal employees cannot do. Otherwise, you will encounter skepticism from employees regarding the cost and necessity of consultants.

➤ Given the exponential growth of society and the exponential need for change, managing will require more technological tools.

➤ Allocating resources is best done using a system. Inconsistent decision making gives fuel to those who disagree with the decisions you make.

Part 4
Dealing with Finances

Whoever said, "What you don't know won't hurt you" never ran a business. What you don't know can hurt you. Business is about a variety of things: philosophy, products, service, marketing, advertising, and more. But, at its core, it is really about numbers: What period of time? How do the numbers add up? How do they compare to your expectations? To last year's numbers?

If you only operate on intuition and inspiration, you are taking a very risky path. You have to know where you are and where you are going. You have to put this in terms of numbers, or you are going to be negatively surprised, to put it mildly.

This part of the book focuses on the building blocks of your business—numbers. It provides a description of what numbers you need, how to format them, and how to use them.

With these tools, you will learn how to control the business instead of having it control you. After all, isn't that what it's all about?

Chapter 16

Developing a Common Language— Numbers

In This Chapter

➤ Why numbers are critically important

➤ How to train people to understand numbers

➤ The difference between precision and speed

➤ Ways to evaluate competitive opportunities

Numbers are the common language of business. They spell out how much your company is making, how your stocks are doing, and how well your management is. All of the cool karma and motivational electricity you can create aren't going to matter a whole lot if you can't back it all up with cold, hard numbers. Like it or not, you will be judged on numbers.

Numbers give you reason—something to grasp. They are the opposite of ambiguity—they give form to your performance. They convert the abstract to the concrete and they enable you to be objective in your role as manager.

In this chapter, you will learn about numbers and why they are so important. I will discuss what numbers to look for, and how to use them to increase your effectiveness. You won't become a financial guru from reading this chapter, but you should be able to become a better manager. In this chapter, you'll learn to count all over again.

Why You Need Numbers

You *are* your numbers. You "own" them.

Numbers are clear, even if they are not. At least they can provide some common ground of understanding and offer a basis for making meaningful comparisons. As more businesses become global in a world with many languages, the benefits of clear numbers are even more obvious. But that's just the *next* step. Ignore them if you want, but no one else will. No one.

If you think numbers are just to impress your bank or your superiors, think again. Numbers are the life blood of your organization.

Press Release

The Small Business Administration reports that the primary cause of failure of businesses (more than 60 percent) is a lack of good paperwork and a lack of understanding of the numbers of business.

It is true that bad numbers will have bankers jumping out of windows, and great numbers are the cause of rejoicing in mahogany halls. It is true that a lot rides on numbers. But it is also true that numbers can be manipulated. They always mean something unless they mean *something else.*

Thus, you need numbers you can understand. You are going to be judged on a set of numbers. You will quickly learn that, in management, some numbers lead to other numbers. It can be quite circular, until you take control.

Which numbers?

That is the question.

The answer is that it will differ by company and by industry and you must follow the unique numbers that are critical to your organization. Here are some that are common to virtually every organization:

➤ Profit & Loss (P&L)
➤ Balance Sheet
➤ Cash Flow
➤ Budgets
➤ Sales
➤ Orders
➤ Costs and Prices

Great managers are constantly correcting their course. But they can only do this if they have two things—a course, and a regular measurement against it. Both must be grounded in a quantitative measurement.

Training Your People to Understand Numbers

Assume your people don't really understand numbers. If you assume that they understand numbers and it turns out they don't, you could have a disaster.

Train your people. In fact, while you're at it, get some training yourself, because your numbers are the currency of business. (Well, so is currency. But then, everyone knows that numbers and currency are related.)

First, be sure that there is money in your budget to train yourself and your people. Some managers like to get their employees to share training costs because they believe that it shows true commitment. I disagree. Your job as manager is to help employees do their best. If they look good, you look good. What they don't know could ruin you. On the other hand, excellence will reflect well on you.

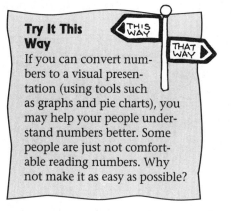

Try It This Way

If you can convert numbers to a visual presentation (using tools such as graphs and pie charts), you may help your people understand numbers better. Some people are just not comfortable reading numbers. Why not make it as easy as possible?

But excellence only comes from knowledge. If your people don't have access to the numbers they need, they can't do their jobs. Some managers and companies are so paranoid that they won't share anything. But paranoia is not a recommended strategy. If you encounter this, approach anyone trying to block the flow of information and speak logically. Try and get them to understand the need and the goal. Whatever you do, don't ever be the one to stifle information. It will come back to haunt you.

Some people, even if you give them numbers, will resist attempting to understand them because they are simply uncomfortable. Some people will do everything possible to avoid financial training. But don't let them. Training is essential if you think success is essential. And if you don't, why are you a manager?

There are numerous ways to do training. Some are easier than others, and some are more immediate. Pick the ones that are best for you and your team and then fit them into your budget. Push your people. Get it done.

Remember, the need for training is not a one-time thing. It's an ongoing matter that must be constantly addressed. Here are some ideas for financial training:

➤ *Outside classes.* Search these out. Don't wait for your people to bring them to you.

➤ *Bring in speakers.* Set up goals and objectives of topics to be covered.

➤ *Use budgeting as a training process.* Have your people go through the areas they control line by line. Then go through it all with them to show them what they may have missed or ignored. Pay attention to detail.

➤ *Do monthly financial reviews.* Check performance line by line. Don't just accept what has been presented. Ask why. Ask how it could have changed. Ask what could have been done differently. Ask what will happen in the future. Ask, ask, ask.

➤ *Analyze all reports.* Work with your people to analyze what is good and what is bad. Eliminate what is unnecessary and add what is needed.

Stressbusters

Get a number and a date. For example: How much profit by which date. Employees are happy to give one or the other, but not both. Get both. Hitting the profit number one year late doesn't get you what you need.

Simply Stated

Inventory turns are the number of times a year you sell (or turn over) your inventory. Divide the annual cost of goods sold by the inventory on hand.

Simply Stated

Receivables days is a measure of how fast you are collecting on the sales you have made. You calculate it by dividing the annual sales by the outstanding accounts receivable figure.

Quantifying Your Objectives— Replacing the Subjective with the Objective

If you haven't already learned it, you will soon. Employees are slippery as eels. Pinning them down on exactly what they are going to do is a Herculean task. And the more experienced employees are, the more experienced they are at avoiding commitment. So you need to tie them down. But how? Numbers. Use numbers to get a commitment.

Wherever possible, convert abstract goals into concrete ones. When you do, you add the three Ms—motivation, measurement, and methods—to your management. Here are some examples of the things that can and should be made into concrete goals:

➤ *Improve results.* You can quantify a number of things, such as *inventory turns* or *receivables days*.

➤ *Improve quality.* Quantify returns, warranty costs, and defects.

➤ *Improve efficiency.* Quantify sales per order, sales per square foot, turnaround time from orders to shipping, and speed of conversations on the phones.

➤ *Improve service.* Quantify delivery times, how many times a phone rings before it is answered, and the percentage fulfillment of an order.

It is easy to avoid non-quantitative objectives. It is also easy to think that working hard brings you closer to your objectives. But if you have a number as an objective, it can give you a dose of needed reality.

So Many Numbers, So Little Time

There are two different types of financial reports your company should generate:

1. *Financial accounting reports.* These periodically summarize your results for evaluation. The further you can break these down by internal departments and individual responsibilities of your people, the more beneficial they are. These are generally produced monthly and then summarized annually.

   Financial accounting reports enable you to evaluate your personnel and help you understand your company. They are formal reports produced with Generally Accepted Accounting Standards. Annual financial reports are often prepared by the company in conjunction with an outside auditing firm. The outside firm will summarize and present its numbers along with its "fairness opinion." This gives people additional confidence in the accuracy of the numbers.

2. *Operational reports.* These are more frequent and can be less precise than financial accounting reports. Operational reports are done internally; sometimes, but not always, by the accounting department. They are intended to keep you constantly alerted to the pulse of the company. They have as their primary quality the factor of time. These reports should be done promptly. Someone usually makes decisions or changes based on them, so speed is critical.

You will want some reports to be done daily. For example, sales versus forecast, accounts receivable, collection versus forecast, or cash bank balance are all reports you should consider doing on a daily basis.

Weekly reports could be payroll versus forecast, or purchase orders outstanding.

In operational reports, you don't need accuracy to the penny and dime; it's more important that they are timely so you can take any necessary corrective action.

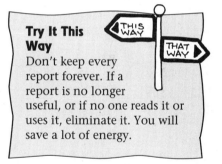

Try It This Way
Don't keep every report forever. If a report is no longer useful, or if no one reads it or uses it, eliminate it. You will save a lot of energy.

These reports and the constant evaluation of the reports are the responsibility of the manager. Your job is to evaluate, plan, and react.

But your first job is to decide what is measured. You know the critical variables. You have to ensure that reports are generated consistently and on time. You want the information disseminated to the people who make the decisions, and you want those people to actually read the information and act on it.

When all is said and done, though, the manager makes the final decisions. You are in charge. Act like it.

Financial Reporting = Precision

The purpose of financial reports is to give a periodic examination of the health of the business, taking into consideration such areas as Profit & Loss, Balance Sheet, and Sources and Uses of Funds statements.

Often, financial reports are given to outsiders such as banks, landlords, investors, and key suppliers. Typically, there will be a comparison to the prior to aid in the analysis of the progress or regression of the business. The outsiders will rely heavily on these results, so they must be done with precision.

Stressbusters
An integral part of all audited financial statements produced by independent accountants is the "Opinion Letter" at the beginning of each statement. There is a standard form letter that is used when everything is normal. If things aren't standard, the deviation needs special attention. letters with deviation are called a "Qualified Opinion."

Try It This Way
Set up a written schedule for the detailed accounting steps to be done to close the books. This is usually called a "closing schedule," and should ensure a timely arrival of financials. This is a day-by-day plan by which the books are closed. If you don't have this schedule, you may have completion dates that change from month to month and are not helpful to you as a manager.

These reports are normally prepared in-house on a monthly basis and then reviewed and approved on an annual basis by an independent outside accountant. This reviewed and approved annual report is called an "audited financial statement."

Business, like life, is funny. For instance, the greater the status of an outside accounting firm, the more reliability outsiders place on the report. Thus, many companies rely on the limited number of internationally known accounting firms. However, sometimes smaller firms can give better assistance.

What kind of firm you choose depends on what you need. Of course, as a new manager, you may not have a say in what firm is used. Large firms usually have specialists in things such as international business and taxes. Smaller firms may be able to give you more individual attention. As manager, you may just be stuck with whatever came before. That may not be bad—or it may be. You won't know until you assess your needs.

Financial reports are geared for one thing—precision. This precession takes time. Rushing the numbers increases your risk—the risk of inaccuracies and the risk of embarrassment if corrections must be made. You still have to make sure that reports are generated regularly. You need them. Life is better if you have some control of the financial department. But if the accounting department falls outside of your control, you still have to meet your goals.

Typically, monthly reports are generated within 15 days after the end of the month and the audited report is generated within 90 days after the end of the year. If inventories are large, taking a periodic physical inventory may delay the process a bit. But normally, 15 days is sufficient to get everything done. Smart managers ask to have a draft of the internal numbers presented to them and their people for review before the report is published. They want to make comments and ask questions before these numbers are shown to anyone else.

Flash Reporting = Speed

You could become frustrated with the sluggishness of financial reporting. I've been there. Done that. And frankly, the bean counters may love a slow, steady financial report, but, as a manager, it doesn't do a whole lot for me. And it won't for you either. It falls short of what you need.

You need fast information.

You need flash reports—stuff that comes to you *fast*. Flash reports are reports that come without the usual overcoat of bureaucracy, precision, and sluggishness.

Of course, with speed, you will experience a modest loss of precision. In many cases, managers don't need it anyway. They may be interested in the big picture, and timely decisions for them are more important than precision. You don't need to know the pennies when it's the dollars that are important to managers.

Hopefully, the reports you need can be spun off of the regular accounting and computer system. If you can just reformat and generate some new, quick reports, you can save duplicated effort and also make sure that all the numbers in the flash reports are tied to the more precise financials turned out later.

Unfortunately, much of what you want may not come from your existing system. You and your team will then have to generate the reports. If you need the reports and they are not there, the best way to get them is for your team to do the work. Besides, if you generate the reports yourself for a while, it will help you get a grounding in what your organization is doing. You may find, after time, that reports you thought you needed are unnecessary and something else is necessary. Figure out what you *really* need and then go to the *MIS* or accounting department. Give them the final format. Instead of asking them to do work that turns out unnecessary, figure it all out first. This will make you many friends and save political capital in the accounting and MIS departments.

Stressbusters
If your regularly scheduled financial reports don't show up on time, it's time to investigate. Usually, the absence of a timely report indicates a bigger problem. And, almost always, when the numbers finally show up, they are below par.

Simply Stated
MIS stands for Management Information Systems, the updated description of the computer systems found in a company.

Here are some examples of reports that are not normally generated but which could be helpful:

DAILY:

➤ Sales compared to forecast

➤ Cash-received compared to forecast, using a bank balance

MONTHLY:

➤ Orders this year versus last year, and versus forecast

➤ Sales per square foot (if you have retail)

➤ Sales per employee (best if you use a rolling, 12-month forecast)

➤ Accounts receivable (aging and average number of days)

➤ Inventory (listing of obsolete inventory and annual inventory turns

Reporting on Opportunities

There will be opportunities. They will come up, and not just once a year when you are doing your budgets.

Some opportunities need to be pursued—perhaps to increase results, perhaps to make up for some unexpected shortfall, or perhaps because you have found the opportunity of a lifetime. But some opportunities are best ignored, or at least deferred to a later date.

So. What do you do? You want to take advantage of opportunities while not hurting your basic plan. You want to balance the unknown against the known, the pessimists against the optimists. And then, once you've done the balancing, you need to explain your logic to your people or you will face questions about why you chose *this* and ignored *that*.

The best tool that I know and use is called the *Blueprint for Profitability*. It compares alternatives, assigns responsibility, and puts a date on expected results. These are all necessary components to successful projects. By looking at expected results, a number of projects can be dropped without even being included on the chart.

Some can be dropped because they show too few results. Others can be dropped because the results are so far away that they won't help in the necessary short term, and some will be dropped because an individual will be loaded down with other responsibilities and the opportunity just plain won't work.

People may notice that even though something may have a very high "Possible" result, if the "Probability" is low, the project may not look as attractive as one that has a lower "Possible" result combined with a higher "Probability."

This kind of decision making is logical, not emotional. That is good.

This chart should be discussed at every meeting. It should:

➤ Compare actual results to the month at hand.

➤ Update the "Possible Results" based on improved information.

➤ Update the "Probability" based on improved information.

➤ Recalculate the "Expected Results" based on latest expectations.

➤ Decide if some projects should be dropped.

➤ Decide if some projects should be added.

The Least You Need to Know

➤ For ease of management and evaluation, convert whatever you can into numbers.

➤ Financial reports such as Profit & Loss and Balance Sheet produced by the accounting staff are better for outside evaluation than they are for management.

➤ Flash reports give the pulse of an organization. If they cannot be generated by the accounting department, they must be generated by the manager

➤ Opportunities must be measured, or you won't know what to go for and what to stay away from.

Chapter 17

Know Your Numbers or Find Someone Who Does

In This Chapter

➤ What to measure and when

➤ Daily reports for timely decision making

➤ Using forecasting tools to improve your results

➤ Where, when, and why you may need to audit

There are many great managers who are not obsessed with numbers. But if they aren't, they hire someone who *is* obsessed with numbers. No matter what, it all has to add up. Great managers make the numbers work for them. So if this isn't your strong point, augment your staff with someone who can both understand and explain them to you.

There is a mountain of data in business. It grows and grows. You need to harness that data and get it moving, not accumulating. When you can do this, you will have mastered the art of making numbers work for you, and you'll be on your way to being a great manager.

Goal setting, of course, is one step, but it is not sufficient alone. You need to measure your progress against milestones along the way. And that means you have to measure a number of things a number of times within your work process.

In business, you don't want any surprises, not even positive ones—they will buffet your organization around too much.

Instead, you want numbers.

This is a chapter about the nitty-gritty world of numbers and how they will make you or break you. You will learn what to measure, when to measure, and how to use your measurements to improve your results. You will learn about audits and whether you need one and when. Read this chapter and discover how it all adds up.

What to Measure: Focusing on those that Make a Difference

You get numbers by measuring and monitoring. Then you respond to what the numbers tell you. That is management. Forecast and react. You need to do both. You need to get your people into a position so they can give you optimal results.

You do this by keeping track of numbers. You do it with accounting systems and by using the techniques mentioned in Chapter 16.

You want to at least report Profit & Loss (P&L) and Balance Sheet items on a regular basis. You need these numbers once a month within 15 days of the end of the preceding month.

You need these numbers for yourself. You also need to show these numbers to other people.

If you want a loan, banks will, at a minimum, want a summary of your P&L and Balance Sheet information—probably once a month. Investors will also require it, but not as often. Your key vendors may require your annual figures.

You will want the same information, but you will want it significantly expanded for your own use.

Every month, there are four vital reports that I rely on and that I've found most successful to other businesspeople too.

1. Compare financials to the budget.
2. Compare financials to last year.
3. Compare year-to-date financials to the budget.
4. Compare year-to-date financials to last year.

These reports presuppose that you have a monthly budget. I would not just presuppose this. I would insist on it. A monthly budget is an essential tool.

What to do with These Comparative Budgets

If your banks or an investor asks not only for the summaries but also for some of these comparisons, I recommend doing a second, more conservative budget and have comparisons to this to show them the best possible picture.

In-house budgets are very often aggressive and are set up that way to motivate employees. Good idea. Often, it works. But sometimes it doesn't, and the budget that you give to funding sources should be more conservative than your in-house budget to make certain you will reach goals. If you don't reach goals, bankers and investors will not be happy. So you probably need two sets of budgets.

And you need someone to do the budgets. Large companies usually have an internal accounting team. Smaller companies might also often have an internal accounting team. But often smaller companies use outside accountants.

Whichever way you choose to get your numbers, you need to see reports. You want information and you want it as quickly as possible.

The very first rule of financials is that the numbers must always tell the truth. Those are the numbers you need to know even if you don't like what they say. In other words, don't shoot the messenger.

> **Stressbusters**
> If you don't have a regular accounting system with monthly printouts, you need one NOW! Hire someone or set it up yourself. But do it, or you won't even see potential for trouble or growth. You really don't have a choice.

From there, you can find different ways of interpreting the numbers to present to others. This is called (only slightly tongue-in-cheek) creative accounting.

But first, you need to understand reality, or as I tell my clients, get the facts straight first.

Friendly Financials

In management, you need optimists in sales and pessimists in accounting—and both of these sides in your own personality. You need to understand the numbers to know which side to bring out.

You don't need or want complicated reports. You want your reports coming to you in a timely and readable fashion.

Timely reports have already been discussed in Chapter 16. As for making your financials readable, there are a few simple devices you can use to make them not only easy to grasp, but also friendly.

Percentages are always a key ingredient in making the reports reader friendly. They put things in perspective. They are numbers that mean something.

Press Release

A recent University of Pittsburgh study found that 90 percent of very successful companies kept proper financial records. The same study found that 90 percent of companies that failed did not keep proper financial records, and 40 percent of the companies with bad records ended up in trouble with the IRS. Something I wouldn't wish on my worst enemy.

Here are some ways to get friendly financials:

➤ *List expenses from the top down on your budget and your financials.* This way your eye can follow the largest expense down to the smallest. This helps you prioritize and lets you do a speed analysis because anything that is big and out of line jumps out at you. Don't get caught up in the smallest details. Normally, 20 percent of your categories will cover 80 percent of actual expenses.

➤ *Divide expenses into fixed and variable expenses.* This gives you a more precise look at the flux you may face.

➤ *Remember that some expenses are tied to sales.* If sales are up, it's logical to assume that some expenses, such as sales commissions, should also be up and variable. But some expenses like salaries or rent should stay fixed.

➤ *Don't rely on a comparison of bottom-line profits alone.* You need comparisons of the subcategories to give you a complete picture.

➤ *Set a budget and stick to it.* If you change it during the year, you are fooling yourself and giving employees wiggle room around their goals and objectives. It is confusing, and it goes against simplifying and focus.

One of my consulting clients was having a difficult time reaching his budget. He called me, depressed that he couldn't meet his budget. A short while later, he called again. "I figured it out," he said. He was ecstatic. He had redone his budget and lowered everything. "I met my budget," he said proudly. But he foolishly never looked at the underlying causes of his problems, so things just got worse.

This does not mean that you should not regularly re-forecast when you are going to be at the end of the year. Of course, you adjust as a situation presents itself. And of course, you should consider chasing new, great opportunities if you can afford them and if they don't undermine the attainment of your budget. But if you do, you must set up an entirely new budget for this project and manage it separately.

Measure Regularly and Consistently

Time is a great teacher, but unfortunately it kills all its pupils. Likewise, waiting for time to bring results will possibly kill your organization.

Late numbers, as I've said, can spell trouble. You just don't know what their lateness means.

Besides the fact that late numbers can spell trouble, late numbers are trouble by merely being late.

You need information in order to make timely decisions. And you need information to symbolically and precisely tell people what you think is right and wrong. It must be important if it is measured regularly and it certainly has an air of urgency.

As a manager, I've heard many excuses over the years as to why reports are late: from "My dog ate it," to "My husband is going to jail today." No excuse is satisfactory.

> **Stressbusters**
> If you don't receive information 15 days after the end of the month, something is probably wrong. Either the numbers you're going to get are not good, or they are not going to be accurate. If information is late, there's usually a reason.

I need numbers to run a business. I need people who will get them to me. And so do you. If you don't have those people, get new people. It's not a choice—it's essential.

Information is a powerful tool if it is used for a call to action. Some managers are actually afraid of sharing information and try to keep what they know close to the vest. In fact, they sometimes even try to shape the information. That's wrong.

For one thing, employees will make decisions whether they have information or not. That's their job. Your job is to make it easier for them to make correct decisions. Give them information.

Your people also need objective ways to measure their performance to give them job satisfaction. They need to be allowed to have access to information. Get the information you need and then share it with the appropriate people. You'll learn something about your company and your staff every time you do it.

Using Forecasting to Enhance Results

The primary tool that ties corporate goals to day-to-day efforts is a forecasted budget. The best *forecasting* is based on past information and is tied to specific individual areas of responsibility.

Someone once said, "Those who fail to study the past are doomed to repeat it." A business corollary might be, "Those who don't know the past will never do any better."

Simply Stated
Forecasting is a projection of expected numbers going forward. The most common forecast is the annual budget which includes profit and loss, balance sheet and sources, and uses of each.

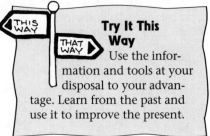

Try It This Way
Use the information and tools at your disposal to your advantage. Learn from the past and use it to improve the present.

Stressbusters
When building a budget, use actual figures, not budgets from prior years. Using budgets that deviate from reality will only compound errors from year to year.

Consider the story of how the British military handled the notoriously inept General William Winden during the War of 1812. During that war, a British force captured an American swell of troops that was under the "leadership" of Winden. It was an easy victory for the British. Winden was also captured.

After a brief interview and an assessment of the situation, the British realized they had in their hands a great weapon of war. And they knew that to use General Winden effectively, there was only one thing to do: Give him back to the Americans.

The U.S., after getting back the "heroic" General Winden, rewarded him by putting him in charge of Washington D.C. Shortly afterward, the British burned Washington D.C. to the ground. They knew a good weapon when they had one.

You want to use past information as a basis for future decisions. For instance, if your fiscal year starts January 1, you probably will do your budgeting in November. It's a good idea to put together a base year of financials for the prior 10 months (January–October) actual plus two months of estimated results. This gives you a fairly solid estimated fiscal year as a base for forecasting.

Use the information of the previous 10 months as a jumping-off point to start your budget. From there, try and identify the anomalies that happened last year and those that will happen next year and adjust your figures accordingly.

At this point, start your forecasting process. The more detail you have, the better, and the more people you involve, the better.

Remember, if an employee is involved in planning the budget, that employee is much more likely to meet the budget.

Using Waterfall Charts to Update Information

An easy way to collect and update information is to develop a number of rolling forecasts that I call waterfall charts. These work by keeping a 12-month forecast of key variables such as sales expenses or margins.

To use a waterfall chart, you chart those variables that you know are critical to your business. Every month you update your forecast, dropping off the month just completed and adding the same month in the future year.

There are many benefits to this chart. First, you are always updating it so that when it is time to do your annual budget, that procedure is much easier.

Second, you can look at trends and determine whether you were naturally too optimistic or pessimistic and begin to adjust your thinking and forecasting accordingly.

Third, by forecasting the same month of the year after just completing the month, you will better understand the idiosyncrasies that impacted your business than you probably will at the end of the year, when you are further away from the occurrences and are trying to deal with 11 additional months of data.

Flash Reports Versus Financial Reports

Flash reports, as you learned in the last chapter, are quick, timely reports that are used to help make operational management decisions. They are, by nature, different than financial reports.

Flash reports are internal reports designed to give you quick information. They don't need to be precise. They need to be reasonably accurate and very quick.

Flash reports can cover a number of critical variables, including:

➤ Daily sales

➤ Cash position in the bank versus your books

➤ Production progress

➤ Inventory levels

If you need information quickly, no matter what the subject, you should arrange to have regular flash reports.

But you don't want to be swamped with information on a daily basis. Your job is not to drown in paper. You want vital information and that is it. For instance, I only look at daily sales. I have decided that, for me, daily sales is a vital piece of information.

Some tips for using a flash report chart that you might find helpful:

➤ I normally cross out the weekend days so I can read the chart faster and do more meaningful comparisons to prior years, which will have weekends on different dates.

➤ I underline the week for quick, easier comparisons.

➤ Sometimes I put in a space for a comparison column of budget to actual month-to-date (MTD) for speedy analysis.

➤ Sometimes I put a section in for weekly percentage comparisons by the week for a quick overview.

Flash reports are not the same as financial reports, which are formal documents that often require audits (discussed next).

Audits: The Good, the Bad, and the Ugly

Audits are generally the most formal of all the operational financial reports and they are usually annual. They can be done internally, but more often they are done by outside accounting firms in conjunction with your people.

Simply Stated

An *audit* is a formal review of your books by an independent outside third party. Usually, but not always, this is part of your annual report of earnings. Other times it's just to validate the numbers you release.

Banks and creditors will often request an outside audit because an outside audit is more credible. Outside auditors double-check the integrity of your internal systems and reporting. It gives you and outsiders increased comfort. Outside auditors also bring an expertise in such arcane areas as taxes and new accounting rules that you may not want to pay for year-round.

Outside accountants could be public accountants (PAs) or certified public accountants (CPAs). A CPA is certified and has passed rigorous accounting exams. They have specialized skills and can be immensely helpful to a manager. Because of this, a CPA is often more acceptable to outsiders.

However, I have also seen many PAs who are just as good as, if not better than, many CPAs. The choice really depends on what you need, or what the people who you report to need.

If those making the decision are seeking outside capital from lending institutions, from investors, or from suppliers, you will almost certainly need a certified audit. The cost will be justified and you will get some benefits. If you are a public company, it is mandatory that you get an audit.

Press Release

The bigger your company and the more money you are seeking, the more you need a big, respected accounting firm. Outsiders know that big accounting firms are sticklers for detail and will not risk lawsuits for any of their clients.

However, don't just use the auditors for the credibility. Use them for their expertise. They see hundreds of companies and have developed a lot of knowledge. Ask them for it.

Periodically ask for a management report reviewing your operations. It costs more, but will give you the insight of experts.

The Least You Need to Know

➤ Financial accounting is usually done monthly and annually, long after the facts and events that created the numbers and well beyond the time needed to correct things.

➤ Daily and weekly operational reports will alert you to situations in time to correct them.

➤ You need regular consistent financial measurements to know where you are, how you are doing, and where you are going.

➤ If you plan to borrow money, take on an outside investor, or get significant credit from your suppliers, you need a formally audited financial statement.

How to Measure Performance Objectively

Decisions have to be made with cool calculation if you want to thrive. Management is not a place for the sentimental or the subjective. Step back and look at things objectively; that's the hallmark of the manager who is "going places."

In other words, you need *facts*. The world is full of reasons and excuses and mitigating circumstances that will not even buy you a newspaper without an additional 50 cents. That's right. Your life as a decision maker begins and ends with the facts and your ability to measure them objectively.

This is a chapter about how to make objective analysis possible. You will learn why you need to break everything up into units that you can analyze. I'll discuss the difference between fixed and variable costs, the role of the past in your analysis of the future, to whom you should compare your organization, and how to check your progress along the way.

Breaking Up Budgets, Projections, and Other Numbers, into Distinct, Assignable Units

Everybody loves a winner. But what is a winner? The purpose of measuring performance is to find the winners. Separate them out. Encourage them. Give them more opportunities.

On the other hand, losers need to be helped or be sent away. Certainly, their impact on the organization needs to be lessened until they can get their results up to expectation.

You need to discover early on who is winning and who is losing, the reasons for each, what you can do to encourage the winners, and whether the losers are worth helping.

But you want to avoid being bamboozled. You want facts, not glitz. You want objectivity. But that can be tough to come by because things are not always what they seem. For instance, great salespeople may not really be great—they may, in fact, be better at selling themselves to you than they are at selling your product to your customers. Be careful. As Joe Friday used to say, "Just the facts."

Press Release

Even the obvious is not always what it seems. For example, the Pacific end of the Panama Canal is east of the Atlantic end. If you didn't rely on the numbers of longitude and latitude, you could easily mistake this fact.

You may be subjective when you don't even know it. People you like may get a less rigorous analysis than someone you don't like. And quiet people may be overshadowed by gregarious types. It's easy to be subjective. After all, everyone has an opinion.

Objectivity, though, takes great discipline. Here are some ways to improve the objectivity of any analysis of your area of responsibility:

➤ Break up everything into small units, making them as small as is practical.

➤ Eliminate the *apples-and-oranges combination of disassociated numbers* that means nothing.

➤ Increase the ease of analysis by allowing the systems in your organization to do some analysis for you.

➤ Identify if units are profit centers, cost centers, or some other responsibility's centers.

➤ Assign an individual to head each unit, and give that person both responsibility and accountability.

➤ Delineate between team and individual assignments.

➤ If responsibility is given to a team of people, still put one individual in charge of a team, to ensure accountability and responsibility. Someone must have the ultimate responsibility.

Differentiating Between Fixed and Variable Costs

Not all costs are the same. Although they all show up on a Profit & Loss Statement, some vary with volume while some are constant. The difference is important.

Your analysis must take this into account. For instance, you cannot automatically think that expenses for sales and commissions are "bad." After all, commissions are given for sales. And sales are "good." Right?

The true measure of sales commissions is whether the variability is consistent with the increase in sales.

Thus, it is best to break up your expenses on the Profit & Loss Statement into four sections:

➤ *Fixed costs.* Costs that remain constant no matter what the fluctuations in business; for example, rent or management salaries.

➤ *Variable costs.* Costs that change in concert with some change in business. The most common and easiest things to measure for variations are costs related to sales volume; for example, sales commissions or shipping costs.

➤ *Semi-variable costs.* Costs that have some elements of fixed costs and some of variable costs. For example, some costs, such as phone and utilities, have a base cost that is fixed, and a variable element that is based on usage.

➤ *Allocated costs.* Costs that come from another department and are allocated on some basis by the accounting department. There could be Internet costs, marketing costs, or other overhead like accounting.

Breaking down expenses according to whether they are fixed, variable, semi-variable, or allocated is not the way most accountants like to turn out statements. They usually prefer an alphabetical listing or some other listing. You should, however, work to get them to break out the statements into these four categories. It will make your job a lot easier.

Once you do the breakout, you need to do a comparison of absolute numbers and of percentages. This separation allows an easy evaluation of the different components of performance. Fixed costs, which are more than the fixed dollar limit, then stand out. Here are some suggestions for keeping fixed costs down:

➤ Give bonuses instead of fixed raises.

➤ Pay people based on their performance, not just on the position they hold.

➤ Outsource activities that aren't essential so that you can eliminate them easily if times are difficult.

➤ Keep the head count down. Every person brings with him a lot of extra expenses—fringe benefits, phone, travel, supplies, space needs, computer, and so on.

When you break things out, variable costs that exceed the standard variable percentage will also stand out.

Semi-variable costs are a bit harder to analyze. But if you break them out, you at least avoid cluttering the other analysis.

Allocated costs are shown on a budget to allow a manager to understand that he or she is using resources that must be paid for by the company. Otherwise, a manager frequently forgets about these. The problem with allocated resources is that no one (and I really mean *no one*) will ever agree on the proper amount of allocated resources. Any deviation in the actual allocated amount from the budgeted amount will make the budget manager look bad. Nevertheless, these must be taken into consideration.

To Know Where You're Going, You've Got to Know Where You've Been

Ah, history. You should have been there. It's a great precursor of what is coming. It's also a reference of how you are doing.

That's right. You can't answer how you're doing unless you can compare how you're doing to something. It's like the old joke: "How's your spouse?" "Compared to what?"

The key is to come up with a valid measurement. The two best things to compare yourself to are:

➤ Last year's numbers

➤ This year's budget

Simply Stated

Zero-based budgeting is a technique in which every line item in the budget is put at zero. The figures are then built up from there. This is different than the normal technique of starting with last year's numbers and adjusting for expected changes. The idea is to be able to kill anything not justified. Everything starts at zero.

All actual results should be measured against these two. All dollars, percentages, and variations should be printed out by your computer system. Computers can save work. Although these two touchstones are important, my experience has shown that they are both usually derived from the same set of numbers—last year's figures. The only time this is not so is when *zero-based budgeting* is used.

In most cases, budgets are firmly rooted in what happened last year. I have no argument with that. It works, as long as it is thought out line by line and nothing major has changed within your company, your industry, or the economy.

You have to have some touchstones.

How are your results? Compared to what?

Once you know the history, you need to figure the future and be careful not to be so optimistic as to be unrealistic.

I have a friend who once submitted his forecast to a company and they said, "Not good, we need more." He upped his forecast by 20 percent. They said, "Not good, we need more."

Finally, my friend said, "Just put in what you want. You aren't interested in reality anyway." The next day, my friend started looking for a new job. He wasn't willing to trade one day of comfortable agreement for 12 months of questions as to why he didn't meet his forecast.

Remember, your forecast establishes your expectations and you need to manage those expectations.

Also consider that unrealistic sales expectations will usually lead to an increase in expenses and overhead. When these increase too much, they multiply the effects of a mediocre year.

> **Stressbusters**
> A forecast of future results is a great tool that can drive you. Or it can be an unrealistic dream that you will never meet—and thus look terrible when you miss your goal. A forecast must be accurate. If you forecast an unrealistic number and don't meet it, you've done a bad job. Period.

Rolling Forecasts

Numbers can swing wildly from month to month. That volatility can make comparisons in the short term seem somewhat meaningless. Retail stores are an example of this.

But there is a way to bring some clarity to your forecasts—a 12-month rolling analysis. In this, the average for the preceding 12 months is plotted on a graph. Each month, the latest month's average is added, and the corresponding month of the previous year is dropped.

This graph accomplishes a lot. It plots progress over time, giving you a feeling of the direction and cadence of the organization. It smoothes out distortions caused by things like strikes, bad weather, and seasonality. And it is visual.

Compare Your Organization to the Best

The idea is to win. The only way to chase greatness is to find greatness and put it in your sights. Sometimes it's a specific set of results. Sometimes, though, it's a specific organization—the one beating you. The one beating everybody.

Greatness resides in many places, and if you become too self-absorbed to understand that there is a world around you, you could miss it. It's easy to become complacent. If you think you are successful, you may miss the big picture.

In fact, your position relative to your competition, and specifically to the best organizations in your market, will be a key determinant of how well your business does.

Press Release

There once was a company in the outdoor clothing business that ignored its competition. Management was happy with a tiny profit. Sales were growing at about 3 percent a year. Everybody was happy and comfortable. Then, one day, they woke up to find that their competitors dominated the field. The only way they could compete was to lower their prices, so they did. And, overnight, profits evaporated. The moral to this story is that ignorance is not bliss—it's blind.

Comparing your organization to the best gives everyone a target. It can be tremendously motivating. It can, in fact, be electrifying. It brings focus.

On the other hand, if you compare yourself to mediocre competition, you will undermine your chances of success. "We're average!" is not exactly a battle cry.

Benchmarking—A Tool for Excellence

Who do you aim for if you are the best? For many organizations, the answer seems to be the companies in the middle. Too often, companies climb the mountain only to discover that the view from up there is often looking down. Then the fall begins.

The problem with success is the vision can get cloudy and the drive can diminish.

Try It This Way
Don't just aim to be the best in your industry. Aim to be simply *The Best*.

There is a way to fight this: *benchmarking*. This is a technique in which you look outside your market. Look at the best firms in business overall. That's right, compare yourself to the best of the best. Who does a particular thing—say marketing, or service, or distribution—the best in the world? How do you compare?

The things you can measure are probably as broad as your imagination. These are limited only by your ability to get information from the best in world. Here are some examples:

1. Compare your shipping.

   ➤ Measure the fulfillment rate to see how your shipping compares to the best in business. Order a range of products from these companies to establish your figures.

➤ Measure how long it takes to get an order delivered from some firm compared to your own.

2. Compare your customer service.

    ➤ Measure the number of unanswered calls.

    ➤ Measure the number of repeat customers.

3. Compare your quality.

    ➤ Compete for the Baldridge Award for best quality. Baldridge is a U.S. governmental quality control commendation awarded annually to the best companies in the U.S.

    ➤ Measure your defect and return rates.

Try It This Way
Call your own phone to see how your speed, your voice mail, your system, and your service compares to those who are the very best in the business.

4. Compare your financial results.

    ➤ Measure things such as inventory turns, receivables turns, return on sales, return on investment, and growth rate.

    ➤ Look at percentages for things like bad debt, warranty costs, and obsolesce to see if you really are as good as you tell everyone you are.

The list is limitless, but you should focus on a few vital things that make a difference for your organization. Don't confuse yourself with too many comparisons. And don't limit yourself to looking at domestic companies. Some of the best companies are foreign.

You can do a number of things with benchmarking and in many ways it will help you to stay motivated and to compete. But it only works if:

➤ There are regular comparisons.

➤ All data is accurate and updated.

➤ The information is shared with everyone in the company.

➤ You choose the best companies as your standards.

➤ You are willing to change to be more competitive.

Aim high. Benchmarking is a great way to improve your aim.

The Least You Need to Know

➤ Objective measurement starts with establishing a valid forecast, with clear measurement against both this forecast and last year's numbers.

➤ It's best to measure small units so you can pinpoint success and identify what needs work.

➤ Fixed costs remain constant without regard to business fluctuations, while variable costs surge and fall with some aspect of business.

➤ People need to be held accountable for things they can realistically control. Breaking out expenses, such as allocated expenses, clarifies the evaluation of employees' performance and eliminates a lot of bickering.

➤ Study the past to get a sense of whether you are making progress.

➤ Use benchmarking to compare yourself to the best in your industry and in the world. You will be driven and so will your people.

Chapter 19

Managing Financial Resources

In This Chapter

➤ The difference between cash flow and profit & loss

➤ Do's and don'ts for pricing

➤ Holding a monthly review session to guarantee good financial results

➤ How to maximize the use of your financial resources

➤ Sources of financing you may not be using

It's important to keep track of your resources. You have to know about them. You have to *know* them. Every nickel everywhere is known by you.

This is, of course, impossible.

In fact, different managers have different levels of control of their resources. But the more you know about your resources and the better you control them, the better off you are. Your results will be better; plus, you will have more options open to you. Efficiency and organization is good.

This is a chapter about thinking about opportunity and risk. I'll show you how to maximize opportunities so you can finally feel in control. You'll learn the basics, including the difference between cash flow and profit & loss and the different strategies for approaching each. You'll also discover how to maximize your existing resources, as well as find new resources if you need them.

The Importance of Cash Flow Versus Profit & Loss

Simply Stated
Cash flow is a term used to describe the flow of money into and out of a company, including loans and money invested.

Simply Stated
A *Profit & Loss Statement* is a document that records expenses and income during a set period. It does not rely on the timing of actual payments. Rather, it uses accruals and accounting conventions to spread costs over time.

Cash is king. It is true. Many in business assume that if they are generating increased sales and profits, everything is great. That may not be valid. Remember, cash is king.

Of course, everything depends on your situation. If you have the resources, you can chase the big profit. But if you need cash flow, you may not have the time to chase.

It's a simple fact that you need money to spend money. If you can't send money where it is supposed to go, some people are bound to be unhappy. Worse than that, without cash flow, opportunity is lost.

There is a difference between *cash flow* and *profit & loss (P&L)*. You need both, but sometimes you can't get P&L because you don't have cash flow.

Growing Yourself into Bankruptcy

It's easy in certain climates to lose focus on cash flow, which is the lifeblood of your organization. The problem with growth is that it often requires a commitment of capital before profits are put into the bank. Cash is usually needed for:

➤ Inventory
➤ Financing receivables
➤ Staffing
➤ Increase in fixed assets

You will not have access to unlimited capital. Not in the real world. No matter how large your company, you will face limits. You will still be competing with other divisions. It's always best to know what you have before you try to use it.

Internally Sustainable Rate of Growth

You generate funds. The question is, what rate of growth can you sustain on those funds? How fast can you grow without having to seek outside funds? It's a good question, and a critical one. If you don't take this into account, you may end up being stopped in your tracks just when everything is going great.

The key is the trade-off between your profitability and your cash flow. You have to take into account your terms of sale and your terms of purchase.

Keep this in mind as you consider everything: If you have to pay cash for all of your goods, and yet you extend terms to your customers to ensure sales, you are really acting as a bank. But you're not a bank—you're the manager of an organization that is trying to both survive and thrive. It can be tricky.

Thus, the Internally Sustainable Rate of Growth is a key number. Once you have this rate calculated, you will know if you can finance your growth internally or if you must seek funding from other sources.

The Internally Sustainable Rate of Growth is simply how much you can grow your company without having to go to outside sources for funds.

The easiest way to calculate this is if you take the historic relationship between the capitol you have in the business (equity plus retained earnings at the beginning of the year) and divide this into sales. This will tell you how many times you turn your capitol. Then if you take this number and multiply it by your projected cash flow, it will tell you how much growth you can handle based on the cash you expect to generate, thereby giving you the rate of growth that you can sustain from internal operations.

Price for Profit, Not Just for Survival

The key ingredient for financing your growth will inevitably be your profits, and profits usually start with pricing policies. Profit margins are the most important variable you will encounter.

Most companies are fearful of going out of business. Most companies are afraid to price aggressively. That's why most companies are like most *other* companies.

Your primary source for growth is the profits you make. Here are some Do's and Don'ts for pricing:

Do:

➤ Know all of your costs, including your indirect overhead.

➤ Know all of your competitor's prices and product offering.

➤ Realize that prices outside the U.S. will differ from those inside the country.

➤ Include terms and discounts when calculating your prices.

➤ Factor in the cost of "closing out" any excess merchandise that you may have at the end of a season.

➤ Price based on the value of your product or service to your customer.

Don't:

➤ Assume your competitors know their costs.

➤ Price to get 100 percent of the market.

➤ Price below your total costs.

➤ Price just to survive.

➤ Use only a standard constant percentage above costs.

➤ Assume everyone buys at the lowest price.

Press Release

For the first few years of its existence, Power Bar, the energy food company, didn't borrow any money. Instead, the company took all of its costs and doubled them to arrive at prices. It then reinvested half of the gain to make more energy bars and held the rest for payment for expanded overhead. Thus, the company grew within the bounds of its resources.

Holding a Monthly Financial Review

Managing financial resources requires constant attention. Just coming up with a budget is not enough. A budget is merely the beginning and merely a forecast. It is *not* reality.

Once you have a budget in place, you need to regularly measure your results against the budget and then take any corrective action that is necessary. There will almost always be some correction that needs to be made, because things inevitably deviate from projections. This is not Utopia, nor is it Heaven. This is Earth, the place of random occurrences. So, as an earthling and as a manager, you should keep track of random occurrences as well as regular occurrences.

I advocate a monthly review that is normally consistent with a company's financial reporting and with a company's monthly budgeting. Hold this meeting as early in the month as possible. The earlier that you hold the meeting during the ensuing month, the easier it will be to remember what happened in the previous month. Thus, the sooner you will be able to make corrections.

The key to all of this is to create a sense of urgency—you need results and you need them now. The meeting helps create this.

Who to involve:

➤ Yourself

➤ Someone from accounting who generated the numbers, or someone who can immediately find where the numbers originated

➤ Your employee who is in charge of the area of responsibility

➤ Someone to keep the minutes of the meeting and a record of the commitments that are made by the people involved

What to cover:

➤ Income statement (Profit & Loss Statement) items compared to budget

➤ Cash flow compared to budget

➤ Balance sheet items (inventories, accounts receivable, and major capital expenditures) compared to budget

➤ Blueprint for profitability (if you use it)

➤ Compare results to updated expectations stated at prior monthly meeting

What to do with deviations:

➤ Analyze for cause and impact

➤ Whenever possible, write a specific plan to get numbers back in line

➤ Monitor the plan

What to do when errors are found:

➤ Don't panic—understand that a lot of data will inevitably bring errors

➤ Don't let errors pollute your analysis

➤ Request that the accounting department adjust the historical figures (not just put them in next month)

➤ After the errors are corrected, look at the month again

> **Stressbusters**
> Keep your finger on the pulse of your organization and avoid surprises. Surprises are never good, even if you think you have come across a good surprise. For instance, if sales are higher than expected, you may run out of inventory.

> **Stressbusters**
> Don't expect things to always be corrected overnight. I have found that things inevitably take twice as long and cost three times as much as expected.

Maximizing Your Financial Resources

There are only so many resources to go around, and as a new manager you may find that not many of them are going to get around to you. In fact, one sure way to lose upper management support fast is to come in and immediately start asking for more resources. The honeymoon will end quickly.

Instead, you need to figure out a way to make do with the resources you have been given. Of course, you may find that you don't have all the resources you need. The truth is, that's typical.

First, Analyze Whether You Are Maximizing What You Have

Review your assets. Do you need them all? Can you sell the van? Can you get by with less?

Review your expenses. Almost every company can cut expenses 5 percent.

Review your terms to customers. Can you shorten the terms to get your cash sooner? Can you decrease the discounts to get yourself more profit?

Review your terms with suppliers. Are you paying too soon? Can you get extended terms with no interest charges? If so, this may be the cheapest cash you will ever find.

Review your pricing. Is there an opportunity to raise your profits and increase prices?

Don't always assume a price increase will hurt you. Take the time to do the math and project the impact of raising prices. Sometimes raising prices, while inhibiting sales, can actually give you more profit and requires you to tie up less cash in inventory. Do the math.

Second, Examine Your Present Financing for Existing Sources

If, in your management job, you control the financial department, you will have an easier time examining your present financing.

Simply Stated

Factors are organizations that loan money against accounts receivable. They are normally more aggressive than the bank and will often loan a higher percentage. Factors do their own credit checks and will not necessarily approve every account. When they loan against the receivable, they take ownership of the receivable as security.

Financing. That's right—loans. Loans are the standard source of funds that are used beyond those internally generated. But, of course, money costs money and is therefore precious.

The first step is to find out what the terms of your loans are and compare them to what is standard. Hopefully, you will find an opportunity to get better terms somewhere—whether a bank, a finance company, a *factor*, or whatever.

If you don't control the financial department, you will have to deal with them. If you are in charge of a department and the financial department deals with many departments, your concerns may not be theirs. They may do things that don't maximize your financial resources. Or maybe they just haven't looked in detail at your needs or opportunities.

Whatever their reason, if you have to ask for more money to run your organization, it's always best to go to the financial department with more than a request. Go with a solution.

Finding Other Financial Resources

Sometimes, you may need to go outside the box of tradition. If your company can't provide you the resources that you legitimately need, you do have other options. I'll list some. But remember, forcing people to think outside the box of tradition is difficult. Figure out how much political capital you have, then consider how much of it you need to spend to get what you need.

First, Consider This

Use common sense when looking for the money you need to accomplish your goals. Weigh the pluses and minuses. Frame your pitch in the best possible light and always be positive. That being said, remember:

➤ There are personal risks. If anything goes wrong with the solutions that you offer, you will be blamed.

➤ There are corporate risks. Your creative idea can be risky for everyone.

➤ If you bring your boss a suggested financing solution, you increase your chances of getting financing. Instead of saying, "I need…" it's better to say, "Let's try…"

➤ It is best to seek money *before* you need it.

Five Additional Sources of Financing

If you have guts, you can be creative. How creative depends on you. If you have a plan in which the risks justify the rewards, and you feel confident in your projections, it may be just the thing to catapult you up the corporate ladder and set your company apart from all those companies that stay "in the box" and don't take risks.

The following sources of financing aren't for everyone, but you may find they're just the thing for your company:

1. *Customer financing.* Sometimes, you can get financing from a customer beyond what is normal. This is called "channel financing." Customers can pay in advance, taking an "anticipatory discount," given to them for paying in advance. This works best in a hot market where the customer is concerned about availability of goods, exclusivity, or better prices.

   Customers can also pay with *Letters of Credit (L/C),* which you can then take to your bank to support your financing. L/Cs are more prevalent in international transactions, but are also used domestically.

Simply Stated

Letters of Credit (L/C) are formal commitments by a bank to pay an obligation on behalf of a company some time in the future. The L/C designates specifically what goods are to be purchased and when. Normally, these cannot extend beyond 180 days. The recipient collects directly from the bank. The bank, in turn, collects from the company that issued the L/C.

2. *Supplier financing.* This is another form of channel financing. Suppliers are another of your channels. In this, the supplier gives you extended terms on payment to help you increase your cash flow and presumably improve your business. The supplier is usually more liberal than a bank, because he gets a profit on what he sells you, and he receives interest on the balance that is outstanding. Thus, the supplier's risk/reward ratio is better than a traditional lender. Japanese trading companies frequently offer this kind of financing.

3. *Paying with something other than cash.* Suppliers will sometimes let you pay with a secured note or an L/C that has a deferred date. If you offer to pay some interest above and beyond their cost of money for the time delay, it may be even more attractive to them. Even without interest, though, many suppliers will find that it is to their advantage to help you out.

Internationally, L/Cs with dating are common and suppliers use this to back up their own financing. If your bank asks you to put up 100 percent collateral to back the L/C, it defeats the financing purpose. But frequently, banks will not ask for 100 percent collateralization.

4. *Production financing.* In the ramp-up (production) phase prior to shipping peaks, many fast-growing manufacturers may not have enough inventory or receivables to support their borrowing needs. They can be faced with a cash squeeze during the ramp-up phase. The irony, of course, is that cash flow, profit, and collateral are great once you ship. The question is how to get enough cash to produce so you *can* ship.

Simply Stated

Certificates of deposit (CDs) are bond notes that you buy from a bank that pay better interest than traditional savings accounts. These normally require that you stay invested for a fixed period of time, and are backed by the bank's credit worthiness.

Some financial companies understand this and provide L/Cs for the borrower to purchase from an outside contracted source. As security, they take title to the goods in production. They also ask for firm purchase orders that are, at a minimum, 120 percent of the amount of the advance. Then, when the goods are shipped to the customers, the manufacturer gets an accounts receivable advance and, in turn, repays the finance company.

5. *CDs or t-bills backing your loan.* Sometimes, you will find people or firms that support you but are unwilling to invest directly in your organization. There are ways to get help from them.

Ask them to put a *certificate of deposit (CD)* or *treasury bill (T-bill)* into your bank as collateral for your loan that your bank will make to you.

Your supporter then continues to earn interest on the CD/T-bill he has pledged to the bank. You pay him some additional interest (say 2 percent) on the money. When you pay back the loan, your supporter is free to take the collateral and do with it what he pleases. He gets the advantage of an increased return on his investment, and he can use the bank to do any necessary collections.

> **Simply Stated**
> *Treasury bills (T-bills)* are similar to CDs except that they are issued and backed by the federal government. Because of the federal guarantee, most people feel these offer more security than CDs. They are usually issued for a longer term than CDs.

The Least You Need to Know

> ➤ Don't just assume that growing sales and profits mean you are doing okay. Study cash flow to be sure you don't grow yourself into bankruptcy.

> ➤ A regular monthly review comparing actual results to projections is necessary to properly manage your financial resources.

> ➤ Before you go to your boss asking for money, look at your existing resources to see if you can cut any expenses.

> ➤ In a booming market, the channel of customer or supplier will often finance you. Trading companies will frequently be more liberal in financing their customers, who are also making a profit on these goods that are bought from them.

Part 5
Managing Sales and Marketing

Hey, look here. I've got things here. Stuff too. I've got things and stuff for sale. But what I offer is not mere vapor. I offer the real deal—hard, cold information at a reasonable cost. You've already bought the book. Now all you have to do is invest some time. My marketing worked. Now it's time to close the sale.

This part of the book is about what it takes to actually get to the point of a sale. You'll learn why you need stuff to sell stuff, and you'll discover the tools you need to get the sale. Finally, I'll teach you how to choose your customers. That's right, you get to choose your customers. In fact, I chose you. Do you see how that works? You will.

So come on inside. I can show you things.

Chapter 20

You Can't Sell Something You Don't Have

> ### In This Chapter
>
> ➤ How selling is tied to your finances
>
> ➤ What resources need to be factored into the marketing and sales decisions
>
> ➤ Why shipping normally happens at the end of the month and how to avoid it
>
> ➤ Managing the cost of sales in an era of uncertainty

A sale is not a sale until the products are delivered. And the products have to be paid for, too, or you really don't have a sale. Sales mean money. Until money changes hands, you don't have a sale and the only way to ensure that you actually get a sale is with corporate teamwork. There is a reliance on a lot of resources throughout the company to make a successful sale.

In many companies, there is mutual lack of respect between various departments. For instance, most sales and marketing teams want to stay as far away from the financial department as they can—there is simply a different mentality. And sales can suffer.

This is a chapter about the interrelationship of sales, marketing, and finance. You'll learn that all of the departments of a company are interwoven and must strive for the same goal. You'll discover why the sales department, particularly, has to use all of the company's resources in order to maximize its results. And I'll talk about why companies always ship at the end of the month and how to keep down the costs of sales in an uncertain market.

Know Your Resources

It's not uncommon to hear salespeople say, "Why don't they just leave me alone and let me sell?"

The answer: That's not reality. In the real world, everything is interwoven. As independent as salespeople want to be, they are still dependent on the rest of the company to give them the information and support necessary to execute sales.

If a salesperson launches off on the selling before taking the resources into account, the salesperson will inevitably overpromise and leave their customers disappointed. Mostly, salespeople need to take into account what is provided by finances and operations.

Stressbusters
Always write up a sales program in advance and get everyone to sign off on it before the salespeople go off on the road. Without firm guidelines, a lot of commitments can be made that the company may not be able to meet. Even if the company can meet the commitments, they could prove costly. Your people have to know what they are selling.

Finances provide:

➤ The capital to produce and warehouse the inventory

➤ The capital to finance receivables

➤ The information on costs to facilitate the pricing

➤ The credit analysis to see if the customer is creditworthy

➤ The collections on accounts receivable

Operations provide:

➤ The scheduling to know when products or services may be available

➤ The execution of getting the product or service to the plant or warehouse on time at the targeted costs

➤ The infrastructure to ensure accurate and timely shipping

➤ Quality control and quality support functions

If salespeople overpromise because they are unaware what the company can *really* deliver, the cost will be high. First, there will be costs—as in money. Second, there will be ill will. And third, sales levels will not be what they seem. Quite simply, sales require great coordination.

Resource Considerations for Sales and Marketing

There are, of course, traditional issues. What do we have to sell? Who do we want as customers? When will the products or services be available? But there are other issues too.

Cash and financial resources:

➤ Do you have a lot or a little compared to the competition?

➤ Can you use your terms (sale anticipation, discounts, offering extended dating on bills due to you, offering liberal credit limits, etc.) as a strength or are your competitors better focused and able to offer more so it is a weakness?

Research and development (R&D) effectiveness:

➤ Do you stand out for originality or is your firm one that quickly copies and responds to markets?

➤ Can you quickly change designs or are you slower and more orderly?

Production plan:

➤ Do you produce to order or to stock?

➤ Can you produce quickly or is there a long lead time between order and delivery?

Timeline:

➤ Are you faster or slower than your competitors?

➤ Are you earlier or later than your competitors?

Quality:

➤ Are you higher or lower than your competitors?

➤ Should you provide a guarantee?

The list could go on and on, but these are the most critical issues. If you don't know them and don't factor them in, you will most likely over- or under-commit.

Time May Be Your Most Precious Resource

Selling has to take into account an adequate lead time that is needed to execute a program. There are ways to overcome time delays, but they all have their costs. Sometimes, with all the scrambling, you still miss your deadlines and then you end up with cost increases and no sales to show for it. So be careful. Nevertheless, you can try these things:

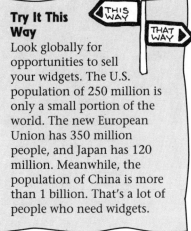

Try It This Way
Look globally for opportunities to sell your widgets. The U.S. population of 250 million is only a small portion of the world. The new European Union has 350 million people, and Japan has 120 million. Meanwhile, the population of China is more than 1 billion. That's a lot of people who need widgets.

➤ You can air-freight materials in (but that costs money).

➤ You can air-freight products to customers (but that costs money).

➤ You can piecemeal-deliver to customers (but that undermines your image).

➤ You can divert shipments to your best customers (but then you develop a reputation of being unreliable for the general market).

➤ You can have people work overtime (but that costs money).

It is true that time equals money and thus is a resource to be taken seriously.

Think Global

The world is getting smaller in many ways. Communication systems have become remarkably efficient. The relative cost of travel is decreasing while the speed of travel continually increases. And the popular culture of America is becoming, at least partially, the popular culture of the world.

This smaller world is there for you, if you know what to do. Companies can now shift labor and production to the most efficient markets on the globe. Even small companies now face global competition. You have resources around the world. It's up to you to find them and use them correctly.

Why Companies Always Ship at the End of the Month

The end of the month is shipping time. Sometimes, companies even hold open the books for one or two days after the end of the month just so they can get enough to ship out and record from that month.

Try It This Way
Many companies base their financing on month-end numbers (frequently inventories and receivables), which compounds the need to push all the shipping to the end of the month. Arranging with the lender to update numbers daily or periodically during the month can take some of the pressure off of month-end shipping.

There are a number of reasons why companies ship at the end of the month. The first is psychological. Reporting to outsiders (banks, owners, and so on) is normally done monthly. Everyone is driven to make these numbers meet or exceed budget, so in some ways, it's like the student cramming for final exams or doing the homework at the last minute. It has to be done.

Companies also ship at the end of the month because the proliferation of product lines makes full shipment harder, and because goals are usually set up monthly.

The peaks and valleys that result from end-of-the-month shipping can impact the finances and accounting of the organization. It's not pretty. It's not beneficial. And it's not appreciated by customers, either. There are steps you as a manager can take to change this habit and make everyone happier with your efficiency, and I recommend strongly that you consider them:

➤ Set up goals based on periods shorter than monthly. Weekly is best, but biweekly or every 15 days can also work.

➤ Write orders to be delivered in intervals shorter than one month. Traditionally, orders are written to be delivered in monthly increments. Cut that down and watch efficiency go up.

➤ No matter what you choose, it's critical that you measure results against projection for that time period.

➤ Don't just focus on one-month goals. A "ship to the walls" philosophy is short-sighted and will usually result in corresponding voids in the warehouse that take weeks to fill.

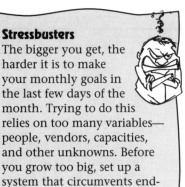

Stressbusters
The bigger you get, the harder it is to make your monthly goals in the last few days of the month. Trying to do this relies on too many variables—people, vendors, capacities, and other unknowns. Before you grow too big, set up a system that circumvents end-of-the-month shipping. If you do this, your success rate will increase.

The Time Value of Money

Money is money, right?

Wrong.

A dollar received today is worth more than a dollar you will get tomorrow. Here's why:

➤ If it is in your hand, it is certain. If it is coming, it is less certain.

➤ If you have it, you can invest it and get a return on your investment.

➤ If you have it, you have options of what you can do with it.

Therefore, you have to take into account the time value of money when you make decisions. If you extend dating to your customers as part of your terms of sale, this cost needs to be taken into account. If you plan to hold a lot of inventory to back up sales, you need to factor in the cost of capital.

Many companies break down their budgets functionally, and so the cost of financing ends up under the finance department. Thus, it is never related to the costs of the sales department.

On the surface, this may make sense, because the finance department is the one that usually negotiates the terms of the borrowing. But the amount of borrowing is usually determined by the terms of sale that are quoted. In some cases, if the terms are too liberal, you may run out of credit altogether. Then you will not have enough money to operate your business.

Try It This Way
The cost of terms, discounts, and financing must be reflected in the budgets. If these costs are not figured in, the people putting together the pricing and sales terms may overlook them and inadvertently make a wrong decision.

You can usually live by the rule that *cash is king,* and price and sell on those terms. However, sometimes it is commercially impractical to do so. In fact, if you have enough cash, you may find that you can make more money by selling on terms with a higher price.

So, how do you know what is best? Well, if you don't have any money to extend terms, your cost of money is infinite. You can't extend terms. Period. But if you do have the cash to extend terms, it doesn't mean you should automatically do so. Instead, do a comparison of the alternatives.

The comparison technique used most frequently is the Discounted Present Value, in which you convert all future streams of income to constant present-day dollars. Then choose the best alternative.

First, figure out your cost of capital (usually, this is your borrowing rate). Then, discount any future stream of income by that amount. Here's an example: You have two choices. You can choose a $100 cash sale or a sale for $108 that is paid in one year. Which do you choose?

Let's assume your borrowing rate is 10 percent. Then follow this calculation:

Gross Income	Less Discount	= Present Value
Cash sale	$100 – 0	= $100.00
1-year term	$108 – (10% × 1 yr. × $108) =	$ 97.20

Now the decision is obvious—choose the cash sale, even though the price sounds lower.

How to Manage Sales and Costs in an Era of Uncertainty

The world is uncertain. There are booming economies and there are recessions, and anyone who has been in business long enough knows that nothing lasts forever. Therefore, be very careful when setting yourself up with fixed expenses. Some may seem like a good idea in a booming economy, but just wait.

Press Release

There once was a snowboard company growing at 50 percent a year. Management assumed it would continue and increased all of their expenditures by 50 percent. When orders came in at the same level as the previous year, they were overspent by a huge amount. As I said, there once was a snowboard company...but there is no more. Be careful of spending money you haven't made yet.

Often, one of the largest expenses any company faces is the cost of its sales staff. I suggest making these expenses flexible and variable.

Companies starting out frequently have difficulty predicting sales and often choose to use independent commissioned sales representatives. Then, as business becomes larger and more predictable, they often move to in-house salespeople on fixed salaries. It is predictable. But sales still are not. Sometimes, the in-house people are on part salary and part commission.

The following tables list some advantages and disadvantages of both independent commissioned sales representatives and fixed-salaried, in-house representatives.

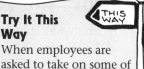

Try It This Way

When employees are asked to take on some of the risks of uncertainty, such as commissions based on results, or bonuses at the end of the year, they are taking on higher risk than strictly salaried people. As such, if the results are good, they should be rewarded more than salaried people. It's only fair.

Independent Commissioned Sales Representatives

Advantages	Disadvantages
Costs vary based on results.	You don't get all their time and maybe not your fair share.
More entrepreneurial and only rewarded if successful. It naturally weeds out weak ones.	May carry other products that conflict with yours.
Can use other products as leverage to get you into new customers.	Can use your products as leverage to get other products into new customers.
Usually finance their own expenses and improve your cash flow.	If they leave and owe you for samples or "draws" against future commissions, you may not be repaid.
	Normally, the cost is higher.

Fixed-Salaried, In-House Sales Representatives

Advantages	Disadvantages
You have 100 percent of their time and they only succeed if the company succeeds.	They have a cushion of a fixed job and may be less driven to succeed or to exceed expectations.
In large companies, the cost is lower.	If expense reductions are necessary due to sales shortfalls, it is difficult to reduce the cost.

The Least You Need to Know

➤ Promising something you can't provide is bad selling. Overcoming this requires knowledge of functional areas.

➤ Shipping everything at the end of the month is a bad habit that can be corrected by setting up weekly objectives for sales targets, for order writing, and for scheduling of internal activities.

➤ Cash is usually king. If your terms of sale include deferred payment, you need to factor this into your pricing and your cash-flow analysis to see if it makes sense.

➤ Using commissions as a method of paying salespeople makes your expenses fluctuate better with sales and reduces your fixed costs. But it is usually more expensive than fixed salaries.

Top-Line Focus—Sales and Marketing

In This Chapter

➤ Marketing strategies for optimum results

➤ The relationship and difference between sales and marketing

➤ The difference between features and benefits

➤ Pricing techniques to improve top- and bottom-line results

Selling is important. It is, in fact, of ultimate importance, because you have to sell to make money. And money is why you are in business. Right?

No company exists for very long without producing a good bottom line. And you don't get to the bottom line without starting at the top line. The top line is selling.

You require sales and marketing and it better be great in order to stand out, because the world is becoming saturated with products, promotions, and advertising. Some great marketing and sales may be simply alchemy. Some of it may be luck. But most of it is about step-by-step planning and execution.

This is a chapter about the differences between sales and marketing and how to make both of them phenomenal—independently and together. It gives a methodology and logic for approaching the process of sales and marketing, and highlights some topical ideas that are setting companies apart from one another in today's business world.

Marketing Creates Interest

Marketing creates the positive umbrella over your product or service that makes people want to buy. Marketing is the attempt to set yourself apart in the world and to give the customer a compelling reason to buy. It is image and it is a lot of details.

Press Release

The average American high-school graduate has watched 15,000 hours of television and has seen 350,000 commercials. The result is a generation of viewers oversaturated with brands and messages and who are very blasé toward ads, let alone convinced by one.

Understanding Who Buys and When They Buy

Not everyone thinks the same way. And not everyone buys the same way. Not all people respond quickly or in the same fashion to innovation. A small portion of people are risk takers, while others wait to see how these risk takers like something.

In fact, the process and sequence in which people try products is a predictable sociological pattern based on the customer's make-up. I illustrate this below in a bell-shaped graph called "the diffusion process."

The more revolutionary the product, the longer the cycle takes. Mass advertising as a tool may speed the process, but it is still a process. This is why overnight successes usually take years, and this explains why it's often best to defer huge marketing expenditures until they bring success.

Use One Strategy or Another, Not Both

If you are selling through retailers to the ultimate consumers, you will probably have to have two strategies—one for the retailers and one for the consumers. But the strategies have to mesh to be effective.

Although you should approach retailers and consumers differently, you need to decide first which one to focus on. There are two common strategies, the *push strategy* and the *pull strategy*.

The push strategy is one in which all marketing emphasis is on trying to get your products on retailer's shelves. This is normally used to introduce a product or when a company is not as well known as its competitors.

The pull strategy is one in which all marketing emphasis is placed on the end consumer. This is normally used when your product is established, the market is large, and you are seeking much greater representation by the retailer. Often, it is used to expand product differentiation.

I advocate a push strategy until about the third season, when enough product is on the shelf to satisfy customers. Here is the normal purchasing pattern:

➤ **First season:** Quite small orders. The retailer is testing to see if the company delivers on time and delivers the same products shown as samples. Retailers are skeptics, but they figure they can always sell a few of the items to someone.

➤ **Second season:** If the first test is met, then a second, larger order is placed. This is now to see how much customers like the products, and which products are liked best. The retailer is now looking for discernible patterns and a feeling of the real market demand.

➤ **Third season:** Assuming the second season also went well, and the retailer has good information, the retailer will now place major orders. Finally, they are "on board."

Increase Your Market Share

Research shows that from zero percent market share to 30 percent share, there is a direct correlation between increased market share and the increased return on investment, which should be one of your major profit goals. Thus, all of your marketing strategies should be geared toward increasing your market share. You want to move up—to get better and bigger. The four cornerstones of doing this are:

1. Market segmentation. This helps clarify the customer and target advertising and promotions.

2. Product innovation. This give a competitive advantage and a reason to buy your product over others, and usually at a higher price.

3. Distribution innovation. this offers a method to either be more efficient, more timely, or lower cost, all of which are competitive advantages.

4. Promotional innovation. This allows you to stand out in a world of too many ads, too much information, and too much similarity.

Focus on Benefits, Not Just Features

Customers use your products, and so they are interested in how this product helps them. They want to know the benefits, not features. Don't tell them things they aren't interested in, tell them instead how the product helps them, saves them money, and is wonderful for them.

Think of it this way. Features are the things designers and engineers talk about—weight, speed, size, durability, color, and so on. Benefits are what those features actually mean to the customer—long life, low price, image, status, ease of use, and so on.

Remember the diffusion process that I mentioned earlier? The innovators lead the charge. The innovators are actually interested in features because they are knowledgeable and they are risk takers. They have the ability to translate features into benefits. The best example of this is the computer industry. Innovators want to know all the technical specifications. But the further you go into the customer base, the less the customer knows and the less the customer cares. He just wants to know: What does this mean to me? What does this do for me?

Another example is the success of the initial advertising campaigns for Lexus and Infiniti cars. They avoided talking about 4-wheel brakes, air bags, V-8 engines, and other features. Instead, the ads concentrated on the feeling the person would get from driving the car.

Market Concepts, Not Just Products or Services

Do you sell your products for about a million dollars each? If not, you probably don't want to sell your products one at a time either. Instead, you want to sell *concepts*.

Selling concepts clarifies who you are and positions you in the mind of the consumers. You want clarity.

For instance, there are bookstores that only sell New York Times best sellers. The Sunglass Hut focuses on sunglasses.

If customers can relate your product to a concept, you have a better chance of standing out.

Bundle Products or Services Together

Do more with less. The idea of marketing is to get the most bang for your buck, so get it all to fit together for yourself and, more importantly, in the mind of the consumer.

Press Release

In the outdoor business, companies make a broad range of clothes. Businesses have put pieces together and sold them to retailers as a concept. After all, retailers don't have time to see everything, so companies have promoted the concept of dressing in layers and bundled clothes together—underwear, mid-layer (sweaters), and outerwear. Instead of selling one product, many are sold.

You as a manager know that, in business, time is money and money is your goal. So how do you save time? Simple, elegantly simple. Don't sell one of a kind. Sell a bunch.

Engage in Partnership Marketing

If you can find a partner with similar customers, you can share resources. Think of the Energizer Bunny—the ultimate partner. Partnership marketing is often advertising, but sometimes it is more.

Partnering with customers or suppliers is even better. The economics of partnership marketing improves because there is a coordination of effort and a reduction in the duplication of tasks. Everyone wins.

Press Release

A number of textile mills combined with pants manufacturers and retailers in a strategic alliance. The results were astounding:

➤ Wal-Mart/Seminole Pants/Milliken Mills combined—Seminole sales went up 31 percent. Inventory turns increased 30 percent.

➤ J.C. Penney/Lanier Pants/Burlington Mills combined—Lanier sales went up 59 percent. Inventory turns went up 90 percent.

Create a Brand Identity

When you sell only a product, you have created one sale at a time. When you create a brand name, you have created an annuity. Putting your brand on every product will make your product your salesman—your cheapest salesman.

Logos, images, and brand names that are registered are a great asset. Most products can be copied or at least mimicked, and product life cycles keep shrinking. But brand names can go on forever.

Constantly Innovate

Innovate or die. Quite simply, you need to change, to get better, to think of new ideas. People get bored. You'd better not.

The list of companies that haven't succeeded is very, very long. These are companies that didn't evolve as the markets changed, and didn't innovate through research and development to perpetuate their survival. Five and Dime retailers kept their format until they died. Head skis dominated the market with a huge market share until they refused to shift from metal to fiberglass. This just about put the company out of business.

Bring Customers Back

Customers appreciate quality. A happy customer is a customer who comes back, and, as you'll learn in Chapter 23, your best customer is the one you already have. Concentrate on those folks. Besides being good customers, they will help sell your product. Remember, a happy customer tells five other people. An unhappy customer tells 25.

Selling = Money

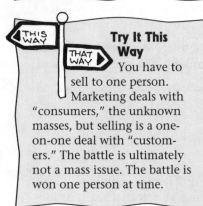

Stressbusters
Don't wait for customers to find you, because they will probably find someone else instead. A few years ago, the Dayton Hudson department stores concluded that there are enough stores in the U.S. to serve 450 million people. But there are only 250 million people living here. Someone is selling to 200 million non-existent people. Be careful that someone isn't you!

Try It This Way
You have to sell to one person. Marketing deals with "consumers," the unknown masses, but selling is a one-on-one deal with "customers." The battle is ultimately not a mass issue. The battle is won one person at time.

Selling is closing. Selling is cash. Selling is what ultimately determines your success in business. Sometimes, managers forget this because they are wrapped up in other things. But the truth is, without sales, your organization won't exist.

There is an even more basic truth: You have to ask for sales. If you don't ask, the customer won't buy.

The simplest demonstration I ever saw of this was on the floor of a ski shop I was visiting. There was a customer who was there for hours. He was interested in a ski package, but clearly he was hesitant.

The customer kept eyeing an expensive set of skis, boots, poles, and bindings. Everything was perfect, but the customer was reticent. He wanted the set. Then again, he wasn't sure. Perhaps it was the price. Perhaps it was something else. Finally, the salesman just asked, "Well, do you want them?"

The customer responded, "Yes, but..."

"But what?" asked the salesman. "Quit talking and just buy it."

Guess what happened next? That's right. The customer pulled out his checkbook and headed to the register.

You Need a Strategy to Sell

There are two major strategies that work in reaching customers. One is a *top-down strategy*, the other is a *bottoms-up strategy*. Both take into account the way sales work in any industry.

The top-down strategy works by first attempting to influence the "trendsetters" (at the top of the pyramid) and then having them influence everyone else. This strategy is often used in businesses such as the computer and sporting goods industries. It uses the influence of experts. Yes, it is elitist, but it works.

Press Release

Regis McKenna, the Silicon Valley public relations and advertising guru, has helped many companies become successful by using the top-down strategy. He estimates that no more than 100 people influence the entire computer industry.

The bottoms-up strategy is often used by Asian companies. These companies come into the market with lower prices and try to garner maximum market share and drive the competition out based on pricing. When the field has narrowed, these companies gradually and deliberately move up the pyramid in both products and pricing.

Sometimes, the baggage and stigma associated with a lower-priced product is too difficult to overcome in the effort to climb. In that case, the manufacturer must create new brands. Lexus and Infiniti automobiles are examples of how Toyota and Honda did it.

To Sell, You Need to Stand Out

You need people to notice you. If they don't notice, it's going to be very hard to get them to buy anything. It's so simple that it is often ignored. But don't automatically expect people to notice you—you need to *make* them notice.

The easiest way to sell is to differentiate yourself from the competition—in product, segmentation, pricing, distribution, and communication.

To Sell, Keep Asking Questions

Do you want to know what the customer wants? Sure you do. So, ask. Ask questions of your customers. Ask questions of yourself.

➤ What is it that you are selling?

➤ What do your customers want from you?

➤ Who is the competition?

➤ What are the customers getting from the competition?

➤ What is the financial health of existing customers?

➤ Who are the new customers in the market?

➤ How can you reach customers most efficiently?

To Sell, Avoid Sales Killers

Sometimes, doing the right thing is just not doing the *wrong* thing. A lot of sales is personalized and you have to avoid obvious things that could kill a sale, such as:

➤ *Lack of product knowledge.* If the customer knows more than you, they won't buy from you.

➤ *Pricing based on cost, not value.* Customer need is what should determine prices.

➤ *Promising things you can't deliver.* If you know your capabilities and your lead time, it will improve your sales now and in the future.

➤ *Trying to be smarter than your customer.* You may know more, but no customer likes you to prove it.

➤ *Not looking and dressing appropriately.* Every industry has its style and norm. If you violate the norm, you risk not being taken seriously.

➤ *Not being precise.* Approximations and guesswork will give you unhappy customers.

➤ *Not giving post-sale reinforcement.* Your best long-term customer is a satisfied customer.

Pricing: A Major Component of Sales

You have to sell at a profit. You don't want to give your product away, yet you don't want to price it so high that no one is interested. You want to optimize your profits, which doesn't always mean maximizing your profits. Instead, you must price consistently with your objectives.

Press Release

Beefeater Gin entered the Australian market and decided it could price low and succeed. Unfortunately, there were a lot of low-end competitors, and Beefeater was not considered low end. Their efforts failed. So, upon entering America, Beefeater reversed course. They approached the U.S. market with a high-end profile and had a runaway success.

It's a balancing act that takes careful management. After all, you want to make money, not just sell product. Some managers think that selling low will bring more sales. That happens sometimes, but certainly not always.

Press Release

Absolut Vodka had an advantage coming into the U.S. market. The duty on Absolut, which comes from Sweden, was much lower than all vodka from Russia. Absolut could have priced low, but they wanted a high-end image and priced accordingly. They used the extra margin to launch an expensive advertising campaign to make Absolut be perceived as the best. Absolut now dominates the vodka market.

Avoid Profit Eroders

There are a number of factors that can reduce your profit margin and you need to avoid them in order to find success. If you're not selling at a profit, you will have to raise your prices. If you find the market won't pay the higher prices, you will have to change your prices. Or you may have to change your products. Or your costs. Or your promotions. If you're not making a profit, something sure has to change, or you will soon be changing jobs.

Here are some profit eroders:

➤ *Wrong pricing.* Check and then double-check the prices you quote and the prices on your invoices or sales tags. More times than you would expect, there are human errors.

➤ *Shrinkage.* If you sell goods, you will have damaged goods and stolen goods. It is irksome but inevitable, so the cost of this must be taken into account.

➤ *Pricing based on old or incorrect costs.* Update and verify your costs regularly. "Close enough" is never close enough in pricing.

➤ *Too large a product line.* This will result in excess inventory and products that you will have to close out and mark down. Don't be afraid to say no to product proliferation.

➤ *Not factoring in the cost of bad debts.* A sale is not a sale until it is paid. Most companies end up with bad debts, and this needs to be taken into account in your pricing.

➤ *Not factoring in the cost of returned goods.* If you get something back and then have to sell it at a discount, your margins suffer.

➤ *Failure to mark down and swiftly move obsolete product.* Your first loss is your least loss. As soon as you realize something is obsolete, mark it down and sell it. Like old fish, it never gets better or more valuable and it becomes increasingly difficult to sell.

➤ *Failure to consider the risk of fashion or far away sourcing.* This cost is real, so put something in the cost to cover it.

Pricing Techniques to Improve Results

You can get better results. This should be your mantra: *I can get better results.* Of course, like everything else in management, you have to have a method. A strategy. There are techniques.

Try It This Way
There is no more profitable situation than to have a specialty product in a commodity market. For example, the Air Jordan Nike shoe has done quite well.

Before you make any final decisions on what to do, you want to have both your total costs and your competitors' prices in hand. And, of course, you want to constantly measure to compare your results to your expectations.

Here are some well-proven pricing techniques that can ensure great results:

➤ *Loss leaders.* A few products are priced low to get customers to buy, with the assumption that the customer will continue buying once the customer is in the store.

➤ *Economies of scale pricing.* The price is based on the volume that is expected to be sold. The prices are based on the cost efficiencies that will occur once you actually reach the expected high volume, not what the costs are today.

➤ *Incremental cost pricing.* Different prices are charged in different markets that require different support. For example, a product that has already been developed and sold domestically could be sold internationally for a lower price because the price would not have to support its research and development or domestic advertising.

The Least You Need to Know

➤ Customers are most concerned about how your product or service enhances their lives, not what makes up the product.

➤ Combining your marketing efforts and dollars with other companies (customers, suppliers, or other companies going for the same customer) will make your marketing efforts go further.

➤ Try to establish sales and marketing momentum and then aggressively capitalize upon it.

➤ Sales and marketing are greatly enhanced by differentiating yourself from your competitors. Similarity breeds confusion and confusion paralyzes buyers.

➤ Pricing should be established by three things: your total costs, your customer's expectations, and your objectives.

Public Relations and Advertising— Imperfect but Necessary Tools

In This Chapter

➤ The benefits of having clear objectives

➤ Advertising that works

➤ How to get yourself known and save money

➤ Why and how to measure results

Suppose you work for a circus. (Hey, it could happen.)

Suppose there are rumors going around. The elephant trainer wants your job in the front office. Some members of the board are trying to move you out, so the word is out.

You are the advance person, a manager charged with selling tickets for the traveling circus. Sell lots and you win. Sell little, and you're looking for a new job. You could use advertising, public relations (PR), promotion, and publicity to attract customers. These are your tools. Luckily you knew to be prepared for such a situation, because weird things happen in business all the time. People want your job because they think they can do better. You know that you have to use all of the tools you have to your maximum advantage.

Now suppose that in your job you have a trained tiger to help you sell tickets. What would you do with the tiger? See, the circus business is interesting, so you better know how to operate, how to manage if you want to remain here in the circus. You better do this tiger thing right. That's the word, because everyone knows the elephant trainer could do it right.

So how do you use the tools available to you to your best advantage?

If you wanted to *advertise*, you could put up posters in the next town that you are to visit.

If you wanted to use a *sales promotion,* you could parade your trained tiger through the next town.

If you wanted to use *publicity,* you could lead your tiger through the town's city council meeting.

And if you wanted *public relations,* you could get the tiger to perform tiger tricks in the city council meeting and get everyone to smile at the tiger's talent.

These tools are all different, yet they are all interrelated. This is a chapter about how to use the tools available to you to promote your business. You'll learn about the tools of PR and advertising and their advantages and limitations.

I wrote this chapter once and it was already great. But then I rewrote it. That's what you do with tools like PR and advertising. You constantly reinvent to make things better. That's this chapter. Now, this chapter is *new and improved.* So, come on in—let's go to the circus!

Start, as Always, with a Plan and Objectives

Focus. That's the word. It's always the word.

It's a big world, and there are lots of options for getting the word out—the work about who you are, where you are, and what you sell. You can do it any number of ways, but you must first gauge your objectives and then develop a plan that fits. If you want long-term results, you want a long-term plan that won't wear thin. If you want to give people perspective, you have to offer a point of view.

Press Release

Sometimes the best results come from the simplest advertising. Eric the Red encouraged his Norse followers to emigrate to the cold, barren land west of Iceland by naming it Greenland. Sometimes adding a tagline to your company helps clarify in a similar way what you are doing.

The plan must be in synch with the corporate objectives and, to be effective, it must:

➤ Be in writing

➤ Have measurable objectives

➤ Be constantly measured against objectives

➤ Have a sense of urgency

I have found that the best point of view is to be one that stands out. And I have learned that you can never stand out by being the same.

In fact, if you ever find yourself describing your company by saying, "Well, we're just like [name a company] except…" look out! You're in trouble. Your job is in jeopardy, because you are doing nothing to stand out.

At first glance, the odds of standing out are not great. A consumer sees an average of 560 advertisements a day. You have a finite budget and can only do so much. Right? Well, actually, you can do more. You can be creative. Stand out. Take risks. Go for it all. You have to get yourself noticed, because the meek will inherit nothing. And do you know what? That's all right with the meek. I'm here to tell you, don't be meek.

Press Release

Mike Dunne's construction company in Los Angeles competes in the business of renovations to fire-damaged buildings. He works for insurance companies. He had a plan to stand out in the business: *Give us the job and we'll move in immediately and meet or beat your deadline. If we beat your deadline, you give us a bonus.*

Because insurance companies often pay for their customer to occupy alternate sites, and because construction companies are notorious for missing deadlines, Dunne easily stood out, and, not surprisingly, he quickly received lots of business. His company, in fact, became the darling of the Los Angeles insurance world.

The Facets of Advertising

The media world is a big world. Thus, the world of advertising has many manifestations—from television to billboards to direct mail flyers to *P.O.P.* (Point of Purchase). You name it, and there is a media outlet out there ready to attract attention—or to be ignored.

207

Simply Stated

P.O.P. is short for *point of purchase*, and refers to materials used at the point of sale in a store. These materials are used to stimulate a customer's interest in a product and to convert that interest into a sale. They can be attention-getting or information-packed, or both. For example, the display rack for L'Eggs hosiery which clearly makes it stand out in retail stores.

In all of that, you want to find someone to pay attention. That's advertising. You want to influence either the ultimate customer or the retailer, or both. But no matter what, you need objectives in this diverse world. All good advertising has the same basic premises:

➤ *It doesn't try to accomplish too much.* Keep it simple.

➤ *The message is clear.* Cute isn't cute if it is confusing.

➤ *It is consistent.* The idea is to build up an image through consistency and repetition.

➤ *It is targeted.* The consumer is known and only the customers with the highest-probability of purchasing your product or services are targeted.

➤ *It is cost-effective.* Options need to be weighed on the potential number of people who will see the ad and the number of times they will see it.

Looking for Results

The important thing is how you spend what you spend. Once you know what you can spend, then you can put together the plan that can only be geared toward one thing—improving results.

Stressbusters

Great-looking ads can be a thing of vanity. Great ads are often like a personal reflection. But great ads can make you look pretty silly if you don't get results.

So revisit your long-range plan and your specific marketing plan. Figure out the most direct path for getting where you want to go. And then launch.

Work back from the customer to you. Who are the customers? Where are they located? What do they want? What do you provide that is unique? Now clearly, concisely, and in a novel way, develop a comprehensive program to execute this. Doing so with a well-coordinated plan and a well coordinated objective will maximize results at a minimum cost.

Focusing on Good Advertising: Making Every Penny Count

A famous retailer once said, "I know that half of my advertising dollars are wasted, but I don't know which half." The retailer was right.

If you don't know which half of your advertising is wasted and which half connects, what do you do? You might spend both halves for fear of getting zero, but then you'll run out of money. Or you might spend zero and do nothing, but then no one will find out about you. Neither solution is effective.

So, what do you do? Ah, yes, there's that word again: Focus.

The rules for effective campaigns can be boiled down to the following easy to follow list:

➤ Start with clear objectives.

➤ Lead, don't follow, the competition.

➤ Find your audience, and don't try to be all things to all people.

➤ Connect your marketing objectives to company objectives.

➤ Stick with your program and give it a chance to succeed.

➤ Think your way though *everything*.

The best way to maximize the effectiveness of your advertising and PR campaign is to understand your market position and then behave accordingly.

Save Money by Using Guerrilla Tactics

You *can* beat the system—the system of mass marketing that is trying to turn America into a generic five-brand country. Yes, there is such a thing as mass marketing, and for those few companies with more resources than a five-star general, it works.

But for the rest of us, it's more fun to be urban guerrillas, hitting quick and with passion and using creativity as a substitute for muscle. Generic, we are not.

Reebok didn't try to compete with number one when it first came out. It aimed at becoming number three. Reebok representatives went to the famous retailer Nordstrom and said, "We know that your salesmen always show three different shoes to a customer. We don't expect to be number one or number two, but make us number three. We are different. We make a softer, more comfortable shoe."

Nordstrom listened, and Reebok went on from its modest introduction to become *Reebok*, the remarkably successful maker of athletic shoes and apparel world round.

Try It This Way
Do it the Leonardo da Vinci way—all at once. An ambidextrous workaholic, he sketched with his right hand while he simultaneously wrote with his left. It should be easy for you to run two programs at once if you are organized. Follow rigid timelines and maintain logical check points along the way. All of us can walk and chew gum at the same time if we try.

Save Money on Advertising

Do you really need to advertise? If so, why?

If you also consider PR, promotions, packaging, and giveaways, you will be surprised at how often you will find that you really don't need to advertise. But if you still think you should advertise, there are many ways to make your dollars go farther. For example:

Simply Stated

Gang printing is the process of printing many different projects at one time. It saves time and money by cutting down on the setup time, improving the length of the press run, and getting economies of scale in the purchase of paper (the more you buy, the less it costs.)

Try It This Way

Ask a magazine for copies of the page of your advertisement. All magazines run extra pages. Then send the actual tear sheet out to retailers to let them know about your ad campaign. You'll find twice as many retailers will now know of your campaign. I know. I've tested it.

➤ *Create an in-house ad agency.* Magazines and others dealing with advertising normally give a 15 percent discount to agencies. Thus, doing it yourself can save that 15 percent.

➤ *Undertake in-house desktop publishing.* There are tremendous computer graphics programs that can make in-house advertising faster and cheaper.

➤ *Allow proper lead times.* Poor planning results in a lot of unnecessary rush charges. If you plan far enough in advance, you can really save money by *gang printing* many items at the same time.

➤ *Barter for ads.* Some magazines will trade you ad space for your product or service. And some companies specialize in barter trade, where they take your excess goods in trade for ad space that they have secured.

➤ *Be flexible.* At the last minute, television, radio, and magazines may have open slots which they offer at a much lower rate.

➤ *Make people aware of your advertising.* Retailers always ask a manufacturer to advertise to bring people into their stores. Tell them where and when you will run ads.

➤ *Use partners.* You can co-op with your suppliers or customers to multiply your dollars. Sometimes, because they have more frequency than you, their rates can be much lower than yours.

Save Money on Public Relations

Public relations is the act of calling attention to the company with the anticipation that the media will pick up the story at no cost to you. Sometimes it's as simple as calling attention to one of your products. It can sometimes be difficult to control, but within boundaries, almost any publicity is good publicity.

While there is no cost for the space you finally get, there is a cost to getting the appropriate information to the appropriate people. If you don't do the PR professionally, the chances of anything getting published quickly diminishes. Here are some guidelines to getting publicity cheaply:

➤ *Send out stories a second time*. A lot of times, a first mailing doesn't get printed. Maybe it wasn't noticed. Maybe no one thought it worthy. But as soon as someone publishes your PR, it gives it credibility. Send this out a second time, with the newly published article, and you will get a great response.

➤ *Figure out the media's schedule*. Most magazines and newspapers have a planned schedule for what they are going to write. Being there with the right information at the right time increases your probability of publication. The media is starved for stories, but they need the right story at the right time.

➤ *Always put your name and telephone number on the stories you send out*. If the media is intrigued by your story, they may need more information. Make their job easy.

Follow Your Money—Measure It

Marketing is an investment. It should have clear objectives and its success should be measured against these objectives.

You, of course, will want to start by measuring where your money is allocated. Ineffective companies like to spread their money around. Effective ones target a few expenditures and lump their money to get over the threshold of recognition—way over the threshold of recognition.

You will inevitably make some poor guesses and investments with advertising. That's no big deal. Everyone does it. The smart managers, however, learn from it. You can learn by setting up expectations and measuring against them. Key your ads with different response codes, and then measure the actual cost and effectiveness of each ad. Project the response to programs using *C.P.T.* (cost per thousand) as a measurement and then measure actual results against it. Repeat what is great, or even increase it. Drop what doesn't work. Don't ever be afraid to make decisions.

Simply Stated

C.P.T. (cost per thousand) is the methodology used to compare differing media for advertising. It takes the cost of the ad and divides that number by the legitimate number of observers (expressed in terms of thousands) of the ad (not always the total audience, because not all may be potential purchasers). The resulting number is then used to compare and rank diverse options.

The Least You Need to Know

➤ Don't be afraid to fail because half of the stuff you try usually won't work. Instead, try to figure out which half.

➤ You want to have an objective, a goal to focus on achieving. Measure against the objective and pursue those that were successful. Your best overall objective is to stand out.

➤ The best advertising is focused. Targeted ad and marketing expenditures are more effective than those that are spread out and never exceed the threshold of customer awareness.

➤ You can save money by being creative and efficient in your advertising and public relations.

➤ Analyze your results and make corrections from there. Replicating the dollars spent by your competition is no guarantee of success.

Who (and Where) Is the Customer?

The customer chooses you.

But, if you are a smart manager you understand that first, you choose the customer.

It's not as circular as it seems. You see, customers buy what they need, not necessarily what you are selling. And so they ultimately choose you. But you choose the ones to chase. And you'd better be right. If you aren't approaching the right customer, if you aren't concise, if you aren't clear, and if you aren't convincing, you are toast.

This is a chapter about the hunt for the right customer. You'll learn how to narrow down the list of potential customers into those who are your best customers, and then find out what they want. In essence, in this chapter you'll learn how to develop a customer-led business.

You Already Have Your Best Customers

You can look high and low for customers, but the best place to look is in your order book.

Remember, it is unusual to make a profit on your first sale to a customer, but you will make a profit if you keep the customer. There are a lot of costs associated with finding a customer—marketing, sales, advertising, product diversity, and so on. These are really more than you can expect to be repaid in an initial purchase.

If you lose a customer after a first sale, it costs a lot to replace them. But if you keep them, you are on your way to profits and success. The key to success is reaching, understanding, and staying in touch with your customer. You need to establish a relationship. You want them to feel like *your* customer. You want them to think, "This is *my* company."

Customers are predictably skeptical. No matter how great your product or service, they are not exactly racing out to buy from you. They have other priorities. After all, most have a life. They are not obsessed with you and your products. Instead, they are bombarded with companies pitching their products every day. You not only have to make customers aware of your products, you have to make them *want* your products.

Customers follow a slow yet predictable path to get to you. This path is what I call the Awareness Cycle.

The first two phases (Awareness and Interest) are normally the focus of your marketing programs.

The next three steps (Conviction, Trial, and Repeat Purchase) are where selling takes over and where your sales dollars should be targeted. Your sales and marketing programs must be in synch to capture the customer and for this to work smoothly. The hand-off must be seamless.

You need to allow all the necessary time for your customers (potential customers, that is) to mentally go through the process until they are ready to purchase. Your thinking, planning, and financial projections all have to take this into account. Clearly, you want repeat customers. Working with repeat customers gives you the following advantages:

➤ There is little additional cost to attract them back.

➤ They know where to find you.

➤ They have already made a commitment to you.

➤ You already know who they are and what you are selling.

➤ They have established some relationship or bond with you.

Think about this: People seldom change their dentist or doctor. Why? Because they have established a relationship based on trust. Successful managers do the same with their customers.

Cling-To Marketing

Once you get a customer in your grasp, don't let go. Focus on your best probability sale and then deliver what you promise. Always deliver.

Remember: It costs five times as much to attract a new customer as it does to keep an old one.

Stressbusters
Don't let your salespeople give up too early or become discouraged by failure. Salespeople who cold-call on new accounts know that it takes three calls or visits just to get in the door, and five calls or visits to make the first sale.

Stratifying Your Customers

Some of your customers are better than others. Remember, the Pareto Principle says that 80 percent of your business comes from 20 percent of your customers. Thus, you need to identify that 20 percent and then tailor your resources to them.

Frankly, unless you are a mortician and everybody is a potential customer, you really need to use your precious sales time and devote it to the people and the companies which will give you the best results. After all, business is about results.

The idea is to stratify your customers according to the potential volume or profits that they provide and then tailor your offer, your time, and your promotional dollars in line with the potential. I suggest dividing your customers into three categories:

➤ *A-Level Customers.* Those 20 percent who can provide 80 percent of your business.

➤ *B-Level Customers.* Those customers who have the potential to become A-Level Customers, or who have such a unique position that no one can replace them.

➤ *C-Level Customers.* The rest of the market. These may very well be the customers you truly enjoy working with, but who have very limited potential for growth.

Offer Post-Sale Reinforcement

Customers want to know that they've made a good decision. Sure, if they spend the cash, they clearly have a degree of confidence about their decision. But it never hurts to let them know how smart they are being by purchasing your products. Simply having a person at the cash register comment on what a great purchase the customer has made is an excellent reinforcer. Another good strategy is to make a follow-up phone call to see if the customer is happy.

Press Release

Paula the Balloon Lady was contacted by a customer from 1,000 miles away. The customer wanted balloons taken to his elderly father for his birthday. Paula understood how to keep customers. Instead of just delivering the balloons, Paula followed up with a handwritten note and a photograph of the father with the balloons. The customer never went to another balloon purveyor again.

Use Data-Based Marketing

When you have customers, keep in touch. Get their names—perhaps from a warranty card, sales order, or sign up, or just ask. Keep the names in your files and constantly go back to them. They have already voted with their checkbooks.

Direct mail companies are experts at this. They record the amount of purchase, the number of purchases, the frequency of purchases, and how recently the customer made a purchase. The customers that fall into the highest category are the best customers. Obviously.

Inside-Out Marketing

There is nothing like a friendly face, especially when you are trying to sell. The people who know you best will be the most supportive of your plans and the most accessible. They probably already consider themselves to be "insiders" and know of your reliability. They should not be a hard sell.

The best way to approach this is to rank the people you or your team know from those closest to you to those farthest away. Then, focus your efforts and your promotions on those closest to you—the best customers. I see it as a circle, radiating from you outward.

What Happens If You Don't Get Results?

In a word, persevere!

That's right. If at first you don't succeed, try to hide your astonishment. It is hard to succeed at first. The truth is (this is a dirty little secret of the world of success) that overnight success usually takes years. Even in the computer industry, where we have all heard stories of rapid success, it still usually takes a lot of time. Those who succeed are willing to fight through failure.

Of course, you will have some resistance. This is normal. You've got to live the cliché and give 110 percent. You have to care. You have to have passion. You have to care so much that if you lose a sale, you will actually cry. When you care that much, you won't lose many sales.

Of course, you still have to keep track of your results and compare them to your step-by-step plan. If you do, you are on your way to success.

There are times when it simply doesn't make sense to continue to chase a customer. Sometimes you have to cut your losses and move forward. It's a tough call, especially if you have the necessary confidence to succeed. But, with regular analysis and common sense, you will know when it's time to move on to other customers. Don't do it prematurely. But when it is time, do it. Don't hesitate any longer.

For example, if you have been making regular phone calls to a customer and now they have become impossible to reach or you always get put into voice mail, you can conclude that it's time to write-off this customer and move on.

The Era of Niche Marketing

The era of "Big" is gone. Uniformity has gone the way of the black Model T. Sure, Henry Ford got away with making one car in one color, but that was long ago. Even in the 1950s, there were a few magazines (*Life*, *Look*, the *Post*), mostly U.S. automobiles, and a lot of similarity in taste. Who could have different taste? There was nothing else to taste. Chocolate or vanilla? Those were your choices.

But times have changed. Now the world has exploded like a Technicolor dream.

> **Try It This Way**
> Set up goals along the way to the sale—baby steps, if you will—so that you and your team can measure your progress. Don't just focus on the distant goal of the sale. As manager, keep everyone informed on how the sale is progressing. It will help morale and the esprit de corps.

> **Press Release**
> The average U.S. consumer is deluged with more than 750,000 ad impressions a year and faced with 500,000 registered brand names. And you want to stand out? It is very hard to do with a limited budget, and few of us have the saturation budget of Coke, Nike, Budweiser, or Chevrolet. The only logical response to this is to find some area that is too small or too specialized to be attractive to the large advertisers. Find your niche in the markets where you can stand out with your smaller budget.

The impact of the 1960s and the technological revolution of recent years have fragmented society. There are now all sorts of new customers demanding all sorts of new products. There are now *niche markets*.

Simply Stated
Niche markets are those subsegments of markets that have enough similarities and unique differences to become markets themselves.

Stressbusters
Register your brand names in anticipation of expanding business. Many companies have found out the hard way why this is important—someone already owns their name and their rights and it may cost a small fortune to get them back. In fact, some companies actually do nothing but register other companies' names. You often have to register country by country, but it is worthwhile.

Try It This Way
It is too expensive to register in every category in every country. Figure out where you are likely to do business and register there.

Geographical Niches

In this increasingly smaller world, there is a lot more potential competition. But the glass is more than half full, because there are also a lot more markets. Technology and travel have certainly telescoped the world, but in that close-up view there are many opportunities that don't have geographical boundaries inside or outside the U.S. Smart managers know that a company focused merely on every Tom, Dick, and Harry may miss Gunther, Pierre, and Akio.

Product Niches

Most customers already have the things that they need. They are instead looking for the things they want and the things that make them different. Everyone wants to feel like they are special, part of a special market.

Here's an example. Years ago, there was the "camping" market, which included a whole lot more than just camping. But it was all lumped together. Now, there are niches like backpacking, trekking, ice climbing, rock climbing, mountaineering, rafting, kayaking, and fly fishing. There are, in fact, excellent companies out there that cater to all of these individual needs—each is a niche.

Demographic Niches

Which generation are you? Based on the surplus of products available, there are many generations out there with products to match. There are hearing aids and Ensure for older people. There are snowboards for younger people. The list is as long as life. In addition, the age groups are constantly shifting. After all, if you are old, you used to be young. By focusing, you can find opportunities that bigger companies pass right over.

Press Release
Of all the people who have lived to the age of 65 in the history of the world, more than half are now living. What this means is that there is a huge new market appearing for products needed by older people that never existed before. Food supplements, products to help people with arthritis, managed care facilities, and the list goes on and on.

The Role of Market Research—Helping You Focus

It's wise to study your customers. Learning, remember, is good. Sure, you need to use intuition, but it never hurts to feed your intuition with information. One of the best ways to do that is with *market research.*

There are many types of market research. Some are more specific than others, yet all are geared toward helping the company find customers. It can include a consumer survey, library research, or actual research right out in the market.

Many companies don't have the in-house talent necessary to run these studies. There are companies that can be hired on a short-term basis to help. Here are a few common types of market research:

Simply Stated
Market research is the formal collection of data on the markets and the customers that an organization is pursuing. It helps companies make decisions. Usually, the data is quantitative and statistical and measures the hypothesis of managers.

➤ *Focus groups.* Small groups are given general questions and then observed while they discuss the issues. The results are generally non-quantitative, but they give direction.

➤ *Data-based research.* Data that is available in libraries and records is analyzed for market opportunities. The advent of computers has greatly helped this type of research.

➤ *Customer-based research.* Actual customers are asked questions about their needs and desires. This is then summarized into theoretical results.

Try It This Way
One of the easiest and best ways to get customers involved in the product-design phase is to solicit their advice and recommendations. Customers are usually eager to help out and to show off their knowledge. Quite simply, ask what they want and then provide it.

➤ *Test-market research.* Products are actually put into a market to test their acceptability. Sometimes different prices are tested to see the impact of this variable.

No matter what, find a way to do your market research in a cost-effective way. You have to find customers, but you certainly don't need the time, expense, or aggravation of a fishing expedition. You need to be smart. You need an objective to your research. Here are four steps I suggest to make sure your research is focused:

1. Get personally involved in the market. Be there, do some of it. Don't leave it to someone else.

2. Do some research of your own. Informally poll your people, your suppliers, and your trusted customers. Listen. Check out any written materials you can find.

3. Do some barstool research. Sit down for a beer or a cup of coffee and start up a conversation with the person next to you. It's amazing what you can learn for the cost of a libation.

4. Define your objectives. Define the potential benefits and keep boundaries on costs.

Customer-Led Businesses

Ask customers what they want and then give it to them. Sure, it doesn't sound like the stuff of an MBA—but there it is.

A lot of businesses just don't "get it." Some think that customers actually get in the way. It's a weird philosophy, but common. A lot of managers have zero respect for customers. Most of those managers don't stay managers for long.

Think about it. Remember the last time you tried to get your telephone hooked up in a timely fashion? How about the last time you stood in line at a checkout counter waiting for people to wade through all the technology? You were made to feel "in the way." It's common.

Have you ever called a business and spent five minutes or more going through various voice-mail prompts only to find that no one answers their phone anyway? Of course you have. We all have. Have you tried calling your own phone system? Please do. It may be a real eye-opener on how you are perceived.

Customers who are treated badly soon look elsewhere. It is human nature. No one likes to be treated like they are worthless. Yet, that is the message many businesses send to customers: *We don't need you.*

But don't kid yourself. Customers are king. They are always right—even when they are wrong. Your role is not to drive them away or make them feel unwanted. You are not there to belittle people who would buy something from your organization. Gosh, no. And don't condescend. It doesn't work. Never has, never will.

Press Release

Your customer base will change. You cannot automatically assume things will stay the same. For example, by the year 2000, nearly one-third of the U.S. population will be non-white or Hispanic. And, by the same year, nearly one-third of the population will be older than 50.

Your role is more than just to satisfy customers. Your role is to delight them, make them love you, and love your product or service. You want them to talk about your product. You need to remember that word of mouth is a powerful thing. And not only that, but you need repeat customers if you are going to survive.

Remember, customers can be fickle. They can change their minds and yes, even be annoying. But customers pay your bills and keep you in business.

The Least You Need to Know

➤ Your best customer is the one you already have. The easiest people to sell to are those who already know you.

➤ "Overnight" sales success is generally the result of years of work.

➤ Market research can be used to focus your efforts and escape the costs of trial-and-error searches for sales.

➤ All major markets are fragmenting into niche markets. This opens up tremendous new sales opportunities.

➤ The customer is king. Treat them like one and you can become wealthy royalty too.

Part 6
What to Do When Problems Arise

This is all so interesting—this attempt to systematize human nature. Management is full of interesting facts. Some would say that management is simply full of it.

You will find that you are not always the hero. And you will find that the cloud doesn't always have a silver lining, and yet, you will also find that only when you experience things (the real life occurrences associated with the ups and downs of business) do you come out with answers. In this part of the book, you'll learn how to be ready for the inevitable problems in results and in personnel, and how to push on to get past them. You will learn what it takes to accomplish. To dream. And to revel.

Protecting Against Adversity

A crisis is coming.

No matter what you want to think about, you are going to face a crisis of some sort or another if you are a manager. That's why you plan. That's why you prepare for problems, because when they come you are going to be expected to take action. Your job as manager is to make the necessary adjustments, and so you need to start with options.

It's not as if life is a choice between *risk* and *no risk*. Life is actually a series of competing risks and you need to weigh them carefully, prepare yourself, and then take action.

It just happens faster in a crisis.

This is a chapter about adversity and its role in management. You'll learn about layoffs and how to deal with them. I'll tell you about the best approach to a crisis and how to act calmly and decisively in an 11th-hour crisis. The crisis is coming, but don't panic. Keep reading.

Things Don't Always Go as Planned

Here it comes. You don't know where or when or even what, but you *know*. It's going to be different. You can only count on change. There will be problems. The smart manager won't allow a disaster to turn into a *disaster*.

There may be a fire, a flood, a roof collapse, or a big customer will walk away. Financing can dry up. Interest rates have hit 21 percent. Customers die. It happens. It all happens.

And so you've just plain got to figure a way to gauge the impact of a crisis on your company, and the impact on yourself.

The Impact on Your Company

Is it a big crisis? Or is it simply a problem? How can you tell the difference?

The Difference Between a Crisis and a Problem

Crisis	Problem
Losing your biggest customer	Losing a couple of customers
The bank calling your loan	Cash flow slowing down
An earthquake	A short-term UPS strike
Loss of your key designer	Turnover of personnel
Losing your patent coverage	Having your product copied
Having your product fail	Getting bad press in an industry publication
Inaccurate computer information	Crashing computer system or slow computer output

The difference, and you have to measure, decides the difference in your strategy and reactions. Small blips on the radar screen need to be taken in stride and handled in an orderly manner.

But a big crisis that threatens the entire corporation requires an extraordinary response. Throw the routine away. You have to act.

Press Release

Eskimos make great kayaks, made of seal skin and designed for the frigid waters of the Arctic. But if there is a hole under the water line, it is a true crisis. They don't have time for committee meetings. They know how to act. They never go out without a rescue plan. They act.

The best solution is to have a back-up plan in advance, and protective measures such as insurance, limited fixed costs, and back-up sourcing already lined up. There is no time for hindsight. It's too late.

You have to take action, perhaps a radical reaction. Your team wants you to have confidence. It will give them confidence. Here are some steps to show you believe in your ability to change things:

➤ Develop an easily understood plan to solve the matter and ensure that it doesn't happen again.

➤ Change your managing routine.

➤ Don't allow others to fall back into their routine in a crisis.

➤ Get people involved in solving things—doing helps overcome their feelings of helplessness.

➤ Allocate specific responsibilities and spread the workload.

➤ Create urgency with short-term deadlines.

➤ Keep people busy thinking of successes you have already had, big or small. Confidence is self fueling.

> **Stressbusters**
> Don't cry wolf all the time. There is a general rule that applies about problems: Don't tell people about them. It is another one of those 80/20 rules—80 percent don't care and 20 percent are glad you have your problems.

The Impact on You

You are on stage. This is your moment, the reason you were hired, so if you don't revel in the crisis, then you just don't get your role. You are the person, so suck it up and take risks, smart risks. But, just as the company has to have a back-up plan, so do you, because not all risks will work out well. I suggest a plan that's based on keeping yourself visible in the market place:

➤ Put together a well-polished, updated resume.

➤ Keep an ongoing dialog with industry head-hunters (perhaps under the guise of finding employees or in helping find employees for someone else).

➤ Write articles for industry publications.

➤ Attend industry functions.

➤ Speak at industry functions.

➤ Set up and maintain additional personal credit lines in case you need to go some time without a full income.

> **Stressbusters**
> Security in today's job market is diminishing, but one axiom does apply. The best performers have the highest chance of keeping their job and the best opportunity to find alternate great opportunities.

Crisis and Its Impact on People

There is no time to reflect in a crisis. People either panic, or they jump to help out. And at the end of it you learn that experience is what you get if you don't get what you want. You learn. You always learn. And so should the people who work for you.

The reactions of people to a crisis are often due to the effectiveness of the leader. In a crisis, a leader needs to be in the front of the pack. People will not only listen to what you say, they will look for clues as to what you feel, and they will certainly find clues. Your face and your manner will give things away. If you have conviction, they will know it.

Panic begets panic. Calm begets calm. Which do you want to beget? Here are some suggestions for maintaining a sense of calm in a crisis:

➤ Go to an autocratic style of management. Under crisis, democracy doesn't work. If you want to reach for a large, seemingly unattainable goal, you have to clearly take charge.

➤ Be honest with people. Don't sugar-coat the issues, because as soon as the negatives show up, your credibility will be shot.

➤ Make some quick, solid decisions. Make small, easy decisions first. It creates a feeling of progress and reestablishes confidence in you.

➤ Be decisive. People will want to be told what to do.

➤ Focus on your best people. They are normally the ones who can leave your company most easily, and the ones you ultimately need to keep around. By getting them heavily involved, you use up their time and allow them a chance to show their worth. If they are not part of the solution, they may become part of the problem.

Cutting the Costs of Labor

Jobs. That's what bad management costs. That's the target of a bad economy. In a crisis, jobs are lost. In a crisis, the first need is often to cut costs, and that usually means, yes, jobs. Call it downsizing, rightsizing, decruiting, reducing overhead, cutting fat, tightening the ship, creating a lean machine, layoffs, or seasonal cutbacks. Call it whatever you like. The impact is the same.

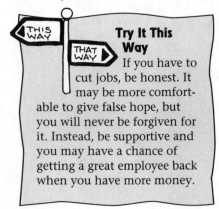

Try It This Way
If you have to cut jobs, be honest. It may be more comfortable to give false hope, but you will never be forgiven for it. Instead, be supportive and you may have a chance of getting a great employee back when you have more money.

It can happen. It probably will happen. You may have to deal with it. If and when you do, you will be making a vital impact on the health of your company. Cultures are built on stories, and the stories of your layoffs will become known. It speaks to how you feel about your people. Moreover, layoffs are regulated. If they are handled poorly, you run the risk of expensive litigation. Everyone, including and especially those who stay on, will be watching.

If you want to move people around inside your company, you need to take into account the views and rights of a lot of constituencies such as the government, unions, labor boards, and insurance companies. Labor law is complex. You really need a labor lawyer. But here is a quick summary.

Federal Government

Large companies are required to give 60 days written notice prior to a mass layoff or a major reduction in hours. The government uses the Worker Adjustment and Retraining Notification (WARN) Act to regulate the treatment of mass layoffs or reduction in hours in companies with 100 or more employees.

Unions

Most union contracts specify the exact procedure for dealing with employees in cutback situations, and in rehiring. Seniority is common. Often, seniority in a certain type of job counts the most. Unfortunately, this may cost you a number of your best employees while you are forced to keep some mediocre people. You may want to keep the best of the best, but the union contract will ultimately prevail.

Insurance Companies

When employees are laid off, they are still entitled to health insurance—at least for a time. The government passed the Consolidated Omnibus Budget Reconciliation Act (COBRA), which requires companies with 20 or more employees to offer to continue insurance plans for 18 months. The employee has to assume the obligation to pay the premium, but it is at the company rate—usually much less than what an individual could get on their own.

Government Labor Boards

There is societal concern with discrimination and it shows in government labor laws. Labor boards, set up to enforce laws, are particularly concerned with discrimination in any cutbacks. Recent efforts to hire minorities have paid off in the hiring. But going by the seniority system clearly puts minorities at a disadvantage, so there are laws.

The problem is that the laws have confusing parts and exceptions. The best advice I can give you is to consult your labor lawyer. It may be cheap compared to pretending to know.

Handling Temporary Layoffs

Temporary layoffs can be seasonal, or they can be random, based on business conditions. The layoffs are not always negative, although they certainly may be. But sometimes, employees may actually want the time off to do other things—ranging from painting the house to visiting relatives to going fishing.

Press Release

L.L. Bean, the successful outdoor products mail order firm, hires more than 300 seasonal workers every Christmas season. They are hired to handle the seasonal upswing in business. Instead of being laid off, people are hired for a short period of time and then they leave after the season. Most employees come back year after year.

Here are some suggestions for handling temporary layoffs correctly:

➤ Give employees two weeks' written notice.

➤ If there is a union contract, make sure you abide by it faithfully.

➤ Explain any known, ongoing relationships (Cobra benefits, rehiring timing and procedure, separation pay) to employees.

➤ Thank employees for their work with the company.

➤ Be brief. Don't give employees any reason to think they can change your mind. A layoff is a layoff.

Rehiring Right

Strict seniority as a basis for employment has its drawbacks. If you lay off this way, it can ruin affirmative action programs. It can result in creating departments of people who have no experience. It can break up teams of employees. And it can certainly result in you laying off some of your best people.

Thus, I suggest writing up a seniority policy long before you need it.

Finally, when you have employees who are on layoff, keep in touch with them. Let them know you have not forgotten them. Help them understand your struggle. Let them know they are in your plans for the future. And then, when you can finally afford to bring them back, they will most likely be part of your team.

Handling Permanent Layoffs

Permanent layoffs are, well, permanent, so you need to give employees plenty of notice. Although it isn't written in stone, common courtesy would suggest that a permanent layoff demands a longer period for a notice than two weeks—perhaps a month. When you give notice to employees, tell them about the employment benefits that are theirs in this situation. In addition, keep these points in mind:

➤ Firmly adhere to your written seniority system. If there is a union contract, use that as a basis.

➤ Offer to give employees a letter of recommendation. You might also offer to help them find another job, or maybe even pay for a job recruiter.

➤ Get any company property back. Any tools, IDs, computers, keys, and passwords should be returned.

➤ Hold an exit interview. You can learn from them.

➤ Answer employees' questions.

➤ Give them their final check, or arrange for it to be sent to them, for salaries and expenses.

Press Release

If you don't pay the employee what is owed on the day they leave, you are obligated to pay them ongoing salary and benefits until the day they are paid. The burden is on the employer to prove when it was paid and that the amount is correct. If you can get the employee to sign a statement to this effect, it goes a long way to proving your case.

➤ Thank the employees and wish them luck.

Finally, whether it's a temporary layoff or a permanent one, it always helps to have two people present from the company when you give the employee the news. It keeps the record straight and helps keep a difficult meeting on a professional level.

It Could Happen to You

Five times in seven months, Mark Sevelovitz prepared paychecks for the pinkslipped of International Designer Accessories Inc. That was part of his job. He got the list of the pinkslipped and prepared their final payment.

So, the story goes, one week Sevelovitz went to the payroll department for the list of soon-to-be pinkslipped. But that week, when he asked, he was told the list of doomed employees was not available yet. He went again the next day, and still the list was not ready.

The next morning, he asked again.

"We'll let you know when the HR rep gets here," he was told.

And, in that moment, he knew one of the names on the list: his own.

Alternatives to Layoffs

There are alternatives to layoffs. None are great, but layoffs aren't great, either. Sometimes you have to make tough choices. In these times, you can find out what your team is made of. Don't kid yourself. People aren't going to be ecstatic. All you can ask is that people hear you out and try to be as open-minded as possible.

Here are some alternatives to layoffs:

➤ *Implement a company-wide reduction of fixed compensation.* Cut salaries across the board, but then include a carrot via a specific program for people to get a bonus at the end of the year to earn some, or all of the cut back if the company is put back on track.

➤ *Implement across-the-board pay cuts.* Equal percentages work best.

➤ *Offer early retirement to employees.* It can only be an offer, you cannot force people.

➤ *Implement work sharing.* This keeps teams together and has the additional psychological advantage of one employee helping another. The fact that all employees keep their benefits keeps costs higher, but it also brings about a lot of employee appreciation.

➤ *Close down the entire facility for a few weeks.* This keeps teams together and treats people similarly. Also, if the reason for the problem is a sales slowdown, this will help get inventories back in line.

Use common sense. The salary cutbacks really only work if you include everyone—especially management. You will have a disaster on your hands if you only ask the rank-and-file to take the hit.

Dealing with 11th-Hour Crises—A Usual Occurrence in Business

Try It This Way
Preparation mitigates panic. When things go wrong, the best antidote is to have an immediate alternate plan ready. No waiting. No pregnant pauses. No hand wringing. Just action.

You can expect a crisis at the 11th hour because, well, just because that's when they seem to happen most often. Things go wrong just before they are supposed go right. That's some kind of law, I believe.

Knowing they will happen is the key to dealing with them. Don't be surprised by the surprising. You can now learn to anticipate the unexpected. If you have clarity and an inner calm when the crisis hits, your team will quickly be drawn to your confidence. So, don't act surprised.

Insurance, Protection Against Adversity

The most obvious and best program for unknown disasters is insurance. Insurance, like a lot of parts of business, is tricky. Unless you are lucky enough to have an insurance expert on the staff of your company, you need to find one. Usually, that means finding a good agent.

There are low-cost programs from companies with shaky futures. Avoid these. Likewise, you could jump from agent to agent. But that is counterproductive.

I recommend instead finding an agent you can trust. I know from my experience with a devastating fire one year, when my loyal agent fought for me and my company. I had been loyal to him for years. He proved that I was right to be loyal.

A bit of loyalty is always worth more than a cheap, quick deal. Always do your homework before you pledge loyalty. Meet with the agent. Find out what your coverage is and develop a rapport with your agent. You may need that person. If anything goes wrong, you will be held accountable for picking the agent, so take the time to develop trust.

Try It This Way

Insure against those occurrences which, if they happened, would send the company into a tailspin. Consider self-insuring for anything else. Examples of catastrophes to protect against are: fire, floods, hurricanes, earthquakes, roof collapses, huge accounts going out of business, and people getting injured using your products.

Of course, if someone else in the company makes the insurance decision, your task is harder. But certainly, your starting point is making sure you have enough of the right type of insurance.

"Plan B"

A fallback plan is something you cannot ignore. Write it up and then put it away until you need it. Then you will be ready to act immediately. Your immediate need in a crisis is to focus critical goal-getting energy on problem solving, not on the problem. You want to have some first steps in place.

Press Release

It took an optimist to build an airplane, but it took a pessimist to build a parachute. You need both to succeed, but make sure the optimists—the possibility thinkers—are predominant.

Of course, you cannot anticipate everything, nor do you want to focus on problems and create a self-fulfilling prophecy. You simply want a plan that is flexible, realistic, simple, and bare bones. Something to get you started.

Once the fallback plan is finished, put it away. Concentrate on the tasks at hand. In other words, get to work.

The Least You Need to Know

➤ You can count on adversity, so you should plan for it.

➤ Laying off people for the short term or long term has all sorts of legal implications. Get a good labor lawyer involved to advise you before you finalize your program.

➤ Look for alternatives to laying off that may help bring your team together to solve the problem.

➤ Anticipate the 11th-hour crisis—it is common.

➤ Have a fallback plan ready to be implemented when things go wrong to focus energy on something other than the problem. Focus on solutions and start taking action.

Chapter 25

Eliminating Fiefdoms and Hidden Agendas

In This Chapter

➤ Why people may be torpedoing you and what to do about it

➤ Techniques for dealing with power grabbers

➤ The problem with naysayers and what to do about them

➤ Why firing is sometimes the only solution

Why?

You may ask. Why are the employees making it so much harder for me when I'm trying to make it easier for them?

Why? Because.

This is human nature. Because not everyone may be happy that you got the manager's job. Because...that's the way it is in business. There will be problems, folks won't agree with you. That's life. That's why you get the big bucks.

It's a culture thing, actually. Even the greatest organizations are simply not *great enough* for most Americans. The organizations all have a glitch—to work efficiently, they require that people sublimate their individuality to the greater good of the organization. But America is a country of individuals. Folks need to believe they are acting of free will.

Individual rights. They are part of our national psyche.

This is a chapter about individual rights and the greater good and why they can mesh. This chapter will explain that some people abuse individual rights and you will have to deal with them. And it will offer alternatives to get people on the same page.

Why? Because people are human.

Human Nature—Time Changes All Relationships

There will be personal bonds in your company, and they may not all be with you. You must understand that friendship is a good thing, but when there are cliques and hidden agendas, there is trouble. You walk a fine line.

Your perspective will depend a lot on how you moved into your position as manager. There are four basic avenues that managers take in getting their jobs, which we'll look at in the following sections. Each has a different dynamic, but all of them result in a relatively volatile crucible of human emotion. It all changes and evolves over your first year of managing.

Moving Up From a Lesser Position

The advantages for this manager are that she already knows the lay of the land. The employees are familiar. The cliques are known and the secrets are not so secret.

But the disadvantages are that an employee who is elevated over peers in a managerial position will often be the subject of jealousy. This manager, who was recently an equal, suddenly has to command respect and may have to distance herself from former close friends. It can be awkward. The uncomfortable shift can lead some to think the manager has become "big-headed."

A Lateral Move From a Similar Position Elsewhere in the Company

This manager may or may not know team members, and if this manager knows anyone, it may only be as a passing acquaintance. The depth of knowledge will play a large role in determining how quickly things begin to click.

If the relationship is new, lots of time will be spent at the water cooler trying to find out what kind of a person the new boss is, and what the employees should expect. Stories will be shared.

There will be a honeymoon period of change and adjustment.

Hired From the Outside—To Deal with Disaster

In a disaster, tension is high. There is a need for dramatic action, so the outsider will be expected to act dramatically. The outsider will make tough decisions. Jobs may be lost. The survivors will be hardened.

This manager's challenge is to convert the relationship that initially blends fear, anxiety, and hope into a new relationship of respect and teamwork. The manager's challenge is to get complete commitment. One note of caution: Arrogance is often the disease of successful companies. It often leads to a feeling that nothing needs to be changed. It makes the task of a new manager charged with the responsibility of changing things very challenging indeed. This may be the appropriate point to bring in an outside consultant with credibility to suggest changes. Of course, they too may encounter real resistance, but at least the focal point of their antagonism will be someone other than yourself.

Stressbusters

If you can shape people, those employees who create problems may turn out to be some of your best employees. Acting out is often a way of dealing with frustrations of things not being done well. Give people a chance to strive for excellence.

Hired From the Outside—To Continue Good Results

Happy honeymoon. This is a great situation—coming into an already winning situation. People here are already confident in what they are doing and will help things evolve. There is time to establish a positive manager-employee relationship.

Why you might ask, do you bring someone new in if things are going well? There are many reasons to do this: The star manager is promoted, they retire, they are hired away, or they ask to move to another job where there are new challenges.

Watch out however, sometimes a manager sees that the future is not nearly as good as the present and moves on to keep their career progress unblemished. On the surface, things look great, but... I say watch out because whoever is "on watch" when disaster hits is going to be held accountable—even is the causes were not his. President Herbert Hoover learned this lesson during the Depression.

Why Do These Relationships Change?

You have power. It's that simple. Relationships change as the power base changes. Authority differs from influence, clearly, but the overall goal must always be in your mind as you decide how to use your new power. And as you decide, folks are deciding how to react to you.

In your first few months, there will be jousting. It is human nature that people try and find a way to make the relationship work or justify why it doesn't work. You cannot just let things run their course. You have to be aware of causes and risk.

Some causes of friction with new personnel include:

➤ *Employees who have personal insecurity*. These people are afraid of the unknown and lack self-confidence.

Try It This Way Give employees credit and recognition for good work. If they don't get credit, they may resort to chasing negativity for recognition. It's true. One of the few ways someone can stand out in this complex, individuality-crushing society is by being negative.

➤ *Employees who are control freaks.* They can't stand being out of control and the change has taken control from their hands and introduced a new element of uncertainty.

➤ *Employees who seek power.* Usually they see the manager and the company thwarting their quest for power.

➤ *Employees who seek personal advancement.* Competitiveness is a big issue with these people.

➤ *Changes in style.* A new person has a new style and a new personality, and that is a change.

Direct Changes Toward Positive Ends

Personal relationships take hard work. You need to work to get people to perform at their optimum and bring about positive results. And the essential ingredient is clearly open communication—a dialogue which is both formal and informal. There should be one-on-one meetings, informal sessions such as company celebrations, and after-work activities such as a company softball team or a get-together for a few beers. The more levels of communication you have open, the better. Better for you, better for the employee, and better especially for the company's results.

Press Release

Many Silicon Valley companies such as Netscape and Oracle have Friday afternoon bands, beer, and soft drinks to give people a chance to recharge their batteries. It lets people relax and relate to one another. Some companies do it almost every Friday. Some do it during the summer months. Others do it around company anniversaries and to celebrate new products or sales successes. Try it, it works!

An informal network is very important, so don't ignore this aspect. If your informal network is really working well, it will inform you about problems well before they impact you. You also can learn of opportunities when they are just beginning to gel.

Redirecting the Thirst for Corporate Power to Improve Corporate Results

A thirst for power is a common phenomena. People who thirst for power will challenge you as a manager every day. These are disruptive people. They may, in fact, be out to get you or your job. And if you are one of the managers who has been elevated from the ranks, there will be some residual jealousy. You will have to deal with all of it, because ignoring it can be fatal.

Sometimes, you will see the actions of the power seekers. They will be blatant. But most of the time, they will be working behind the scenes and you have to be alert to their motivations. Or maybe your informal network will inform you. No matter how you find out, once you find out, you have to take action before action takes you. Don't wait for the coup to occur. Squash it like a bug.

Here are some tools you can use to quell the actions of power seekers:

Try It This Way
If you have meetings to discuss views and ideas, don't let them dwell on negatives too long or turn them into complaint sessions.

➤ *Hold meetings and ask everyone to voice their opinions.* Anyone who doesn't speak up but then complains behind the scenes will start losing credibility with their peers.

➤ *Create hit teams to solve problems.* Constantly rotate the leadership of these. This spreads power around and will help break up cliques.

➤ *Hold strategic planning meetings.* Get people's positions on a number of subjects and then work toward an agreement on the direction of the company. As much as possible, show people that their ideas are incorporated into the plan. If you don't have time for a complete plan, at least opt for a truncated one.

➤ *Define what is important and what is not so important.* Delegate the right to make the not-so-important decisions to your team. It will satisfy some of the quest for power. It will save you some work. It will not add measurably to your risks. It is win-win.

➤ *Take baby steps when making your initial decisions.* Look for a high probability of success. This minimizes the chance for someone to undermine you or to criticize your leadership. It starts building your credibility and respect within the team and with your boss.

➤ *Explain to your people why the company can't afford to wait for perfect information.* Let them know that you expect them to make decisions and you know that they may be forced to decide before they know all the facts. That's all right. You want urgency and drive, not perfection.

➤ *Eliminate cliques quickly, or you will never truly be in charge.* If you hesitate, you will not survive. Cliques develop a life of their own and seem to derive their appeal by being exclusive or negative. This creates destructive divisiveness on your team.

Press Release

Jack Simplot, the remarkably successful Idaho entrepreneur and the acknowledged potato king of the U.S., says, "Nothing will ever be accomplished if all possible objections must first be overcome."

Dealing with Naysayers

The easiest way to eliminate *naysayers* is not to hire them in the first place. If you are searching and have some doubts, don't hire the person. Keep looking. The extra time searching is more than justified by the time you'll save by not having to get rid of a bad employee.

Simply Stated
Naysayers are negative people who always complain, but never offer results.

But if you're stuck with naysayers on your team, know that they are not purposefully out to get you as power grabbers. But if left unchecked, they can be devastating to both the morale and results of the group. Naysayers can create a malaise in the organization. If you're not careful, they can set the tone.

You can't allow it if you want to be successful. Deal with these people. Don't let them take control. Here is how you work to get everyone on your side, and not on the side of the naysayers:

Stressbusters
Don't set yourself up for criticism by trying to solve things that you can't. You won't solve every problem, so don't give the naysayers ammunition.

➤ Reward the positive people with the better opportunities. The symbolism will not be lost on your people.

➤ Give more of your personal time to those who are good employees. Avoid the attention seeking of negative employees.

➤ Have one-on-one meetings with all employees. Praise in public, reprimand in private. Always listen.

➤ Have a "possibility thinking" period in all meetings. Don't let anyone voice objections or be negative during this period.

➤ Always split up naysayers when you develop teams. Keep the naysayers in the minority.

Surgery, Sometimes Even Radical Surgery, Saves the Patient

It doesn't always work—not for everyone. So, you have to remember that your role as manager is not to run a social experiment or to save anyone. Your job is to make things run. If things don't run well, you have to find the cause. The cause, unfortunately, is sometimes a person. Sometimes, you need to get rid of someone. Remember, Somerset Maughm said, "Mediocre people are always at their best."

But in today's world of unions, discrimination suits, and governmental intrusion into business, getting rid of someone even for legitimate reasons can be difficult. And the ones who are most likely to use these resources against you are also the ones who are most likely to be trouble. So be smart. Follow these tips:

➤ Consider transferring the person to another department. This only works if the problem is between you and that person. If you are sending a truly bad employee to another manager, count on that manager getting back at you some day.

➤ Discuss the matter with your boss before you do anything. Get your boss to back you or to lower his expectations for your results. If the boss doesn't back you after a couple of incidents, polish your résumé. It's time to move on.

➤ Consider offering an attractive separation package. Recognize, however, that whatever you do is setting a precedent.

➤ Keep careful records. As mentioned in Chapter 14, if you have to fire someone, do it the right way. Document legitimate issues and then confront the employee with facts.

The Least You Need to Know

➤ Your relationship with employees will change over time. It is up to you to positively manage this relationship.

➤ Not all of your people will want to help you out. Some are jealous, some want power, and some may dislike you or your style. Anticipate these issues and defuse them.

➤ Negativity is a self-fulfilling prophecy which you cannot allow to flourish.

➤ Firing employees is sometimes the only way to get your results. Don't shy away from it, but be sure to do it right.

Taking It to the Next Level—The Calm After the Storm

In This Chapter

➤ How to turn failure into a good experience

➤ What to do after you've survived the crisis

➤ Methods for getting your creativity back

➤ Ways to revitalize the organization for the next step

➤ Keeping the vision fresh

Learning how to become a great manager takes time. It's a journey. Frankly, a never ending journey. Each new employee, each new competitor, and each new challenge is a step along the way.

That's the bad news and the good news. Being a manager is a constant challenge, but that's the part of what keeps the job fresh and interesting.

You succeed or you fail, and if you fail you will just bounce back. And you will continue. On the path. Through the life. Learning lessons and earning cash, and discovering that the more you learn, the more you earn.

You know it won't be easy. That's not my promise. I promise the opposite. You will work hard. Very hard.

And you will fail from time to time as you proceed along the path. But if you are a real manager, if you've learned the philosophy and techniques needed, you will turn the hard work and the lessons into a great success. But even then you will not rest on your laurels. You will instead add your laurels to the hard work and lessons to create even more success. And *it's fun*. It's fun to win and feel like a winner. And it's fun to have money.

This final chapter is about the steps that get you beyond the crisis and back onto the path to success. You'll learn about rejuvenation and what important lessons failure can teach you. You will finally be shown why it's impossible to get the glory if you don't chase the glory, and why the glory is part of the journey, not an end-all. The job doesn't end when you get your first set of good results. The challenges just grow, and you can grow with them. The more you learn, the more you earn.

After the Crisis

Now what? That is the question. You made it (or maybe you didn't), but now what?

It doesn't end with the outcome. You actually have to move on, no matter what.

After any crisis is solved, there is the human tendency to kick back, breathe a sigh of relief, and coast for awhile. The adrenaline has worn off. The long, taxing hours endured during the crisis have made you tired and the euphoria of victory can make you complacent.

As I explained elsewhere, crises in business are like weeds. They spring up everywhere. The best managers are the diligent managers, the ones constantly on the alert and who nip most problems in the bud.

Failing Forward

That's right, failing forward. This is a concept I love and I advocate for every manager. What it implies is making mistakes, learning from them, and moving forward. The manager who makes no mistakes never tried anything, at least not anything new and adventurous.

As long as the cost of failure is tolerable to the organization, the benefits of trying something, learning, and moving forward greatly outweigh the costs of the failure.

Mickey Rooney once joked, "You always pass failure on your way to success." But it's no joke.

Failure happens. It happens every day and the lessons are usually great. It is brutal and sad and all too interesting and the winners always learn from it.

Winners fail. That's right. All winners have failed—that's one of the few traits that they all share. R.H. Macy failed seven times before his store in New York caught on. Babe Ruth struck out 1,330 times on his way to hitting 714 home runs.

Press Release

In the 1952 Olympics, Milt Campbell won the silver medal in the decathlon. Four years later, Campbell won the gold medal and Rafer Johnson won the silver. Four years later, Johnson won the gold and C.K Yang won the silver. And, four years later, Yang set a new world record while winning the gold. The principle of failing forward is perfectly exemplified in this progression: Think, plan, and persevere, and you will eventually succeed.

You are much better off if you have tried something and failed than if you have tried nothing and succeeded. Failure is closer to success than mediocrity is. Paralysis, of course, is not an option.

There will be some skeptics. There are always skeptics after a setback. And there will be employees who become like attack dogs, but you cannot let them get in the way. I explained about them in the previous chapter. Just believe and then make it happen. Focus on energizing the winners. The ones who "get it" will go with you to the next level.

Don't sweat the bad stuff. It can even help your career. Overcoming setbacks, and even failing, is considered a highly desirable management experience.

When You Escape the Crisis

You have probably been working night and day to overcome obstacles that threatened your business and now you have finally found your way to daylight. You are probably tired. You may even be sick and tired.

Call it burnout. Call it feeling let down. Call it anything you want, but you better call it something that you have to face. Because here it is: You probably need to revitalize.

You may even find that you are locked into one way of thinking. Trapped in a box, if you will. So, how do you break out? How do you move on? I suggest the following:

➤ Analyze the cost to maintain the status quo. Many people only look at the costs of new projects, but the status quo has costs that also need to be compared. Admittedly they are different, but often quite expensive.

➤ Analyze what to do to get out of the box. Changing a way of thinking or doing will cause perturbations. Change creates friction, and your goal is to figure out how to do it elegantly.

➤ Analyze what to do when you are out of the box. Don't just change for the sake of change, or because you are fed up with doing it the "same old way." Change with the goal of getting better and understand with that change comes a whole new set of challenges that you need to anticipate.

➤ Analyze the cost to get out of the box. As said, ad nauseum, earlier in this book, business is about numbers and a manger's role is to control them. The costs and benefits of changing should be estimated before moving on—to ensure the change is worth it, to ensure the resources are in place to properly execute the plan, and to keep from being surprised by unplanned costs. Surprise is the great manager's biggest enemy.

Put names, numbers, and dates to the exercise. It can be intellectually liberating—something that needs to be done, but without the urgency of a crisis.

Press Release

There once was a company that was undergoing major operating problems. So, it decided to build an even stronger box. It scheduled 365 meetings (one a day) for the following year. The company held the meetings, but they lost sight of the market. The company declared bankruptcy, and subsequent meetings were canceled.

Give yourself messages. *Life is the sum total of your experiences, and now you are even better prepared.* Move forward with your growth. Grow the cash flow. Grow the profits. Grow yourself.

Revitalize Yourself Through Creativity

As a manager, you know that you need ideas. You need to know how to react with creativity. You know you need to think new thoughts. You may need to create a new vision. You will at least need to revitalize an existing one.

It's up to you. You are the manager.

And so, you cannot ignore your need for personal growth. Especially after an especially tense time, you will need some time for quiet thought and reflection. You will find that escaping to goof off may be the most productive thing you can do for your company and yourself. Or, you may find that intellectual fantasizing with team members may be the key. You may just need to recharge. But, as in everything, you should go with a plan, even if it is merely to absorb.

Building up the organization, you will find, starts with revitalizing yourself. It's not going to come from anywhere else. You are the leader.

If you hit the wall, you need to recharge. Take some time and think. Try laughing. Sit down with key team members and try brainstorming, possibility thinking. Look at things from new perspectives. Throw out old assumptions. Start again by thinking of positive risk taking. It is time, once again, to go for it.

Here are some suggested ways to get the creative juices flowing:

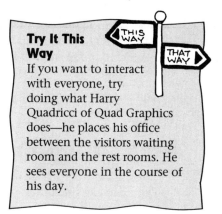

Try It This Way

If you want to interact with everyone, try doing what Harry Quadricci of Quad Graphics does—he places his office between the visitors waiting room and the rest rooms. He sees everyone in the course of his day.

➤ *Take a trip.* A changed environment gives a changed perspective.

➤ *Look for the wrong answers.* Sometimes wrong answers become right answers.

➤ *Change the scale of things…tiny versus giant.* The unusual always suggests new ideas.

➤ *Contemplate opposites.* Extremes have power.

➤ *Act like a child.* Observe, wonder, doubt, and disbelieve. You'd be amazed at the illogical things you just accept.

➤ *Play word games.* You will hear ideas in answers.

➤ *Look for humor everywhere.* Genuine laughter is good for the body, mind, and soul. Laugh. It's all pretty funny.

➤ *Do something creative.* Write, paint, sing, or make up a story. Invent. Get beyond your mind and into your heart.

➤ *Use free association in a group discussion.* Good ideas can be shaken loose.

➤ *Look for incongruities.* They offer unique approaches to common situations.

➤ *Experiment.* Think it up and then try it.

Press Release

At Cornell University, there was a test of lateral thinking and decision making by individuals. There were two groups taking the same test. One group did nothing special. The other group watched Mickey Mouse movies and read *MAD* magazine. The Mickey Mouse group, of course, scored much better. Fun works. Fun stimulates creative thinking and it brings a joy and spontaneity to work that helps people come alive.

Creativity does not just happen. It is work. But it is *fun* work, and fun is a tool for rejuvenating everyone. Do you have a smile? Are you laughing? Do you know a good joke? Do you have a good idea for everyone to do together? You are on your way to rejuvenating yourself and your company.

You only need to learn to accomplish things. The only rule of creativity is that there are no rules.

Getting It Together Again

There is nothing wrong or unusual about setbacks or failures in business. All companies experience them, and so do all employees—especially all successful employees.

But perhaps your people don't understand. Perhaps your recent setback is their first. Perhaps they are just licking their wounds or are afraid to move forward. Your job as manager is to move people forward. Don't let them get into a paralyzing self-analysis. There is still work to be done, and you can't let pride get in the way of commerce.

Instead, opt to reawaken self-confidence. People want to feel like winners, and managers have the power to help them realize that they are winners. Setbacks, of course, don't make people winners. But successfully dealing with setbacks does. People never learn anything if they never do anything wrong.

A good first step is to explain to your people that a crisis is actually rather common. Help them lose their worry. Help them understand that the key to a crisis is in solving it. Professor Larry E. Griener, a Harvard Business School professor at that, came up with a graph that explains this rather well.

While this graph covers crises of managing, and is far from being comprehensive or covering all the crises a company may encounter, it is instructional. In general, the graph says:

➤ Due to the evolution of business, every company is guaranteed to have some crises.

➤ Even if you've just finished a crisis, another one will crop up. So be prepared.

➤ It is okay to have a crisis, as long as you deal with it and are not paralyzed, as explained in Chapter 25.

Using the Same Tools, but Making Them Fresh

So, you got through it. You made it past the crisis and now you want to move forward and use the same tools you started with, but you want to make them fresh. You want to go for excellence, because if you are not reaching for the top, you may as well stop.

It is time for a new goal—an audacious, awe-inspiring goal. You want a goal so compelling that it erases concerns about history and gets everyone focused instead on the future. Excellence usually comes from radical actions.

It is time to start again at the beginning, like at the start of this book, but this time using your newfound experience and wisdom. Don't make the same old mistakes. New mistakes are much better.

Try It This Way
When you want to move everyone to the next level, you want to create big, wild, adrenaline-inducing goals. Go to the moon.

Don't just trot out your old business plan and say *"Go for it."* People are looking for you to change things, to always make things better, to give them a reason to strive. Use the old tools, but use them in new ways. Tweak. Give a feeling that you are entering a new and prosperous era, because you are. Let your mind race. Here are some of my ideas for your next meeting (add some of your own):

➤ Hold the meeting off-site, in a place you've never been before.

➤ Consider physical activities such as rope courses, river running, and mountain biking.

➤ Bring in speakers and leaders. Learn about Zen, meditation, and other cultures. Imagine how applying different outlooks and practices might revamp your business.

➤ Set up awards and new motivations. Consider changing titles and the basis of compensation.

➤ Consider a new line of business.

➤ Consider getting rid of established lines of business.

➤ Put a huge pile of cash on a table in front of the room and tell everyone that this is their bonus if they hit their goal.

➤ Conjure up the biggest, baddest, greatest, most awe-inspiring goal you can, and then go for it.

Renew the Vision

The point is, management has to have a vision, a compelling reason, and it should be transferred to those who are managed. Sweep people up. Go for the big hit. Live the life. Enjoy. It's like climbing in the Himalayas—when you reach one peak, look for the next one and just keep climbing.

Of course, weave in your new experiences and wisdom, but don't ever lose the dream. Fantasize. Visualize. Imagine. Then, in your gut, feel the excitement and the rush of pure adrenaline.

This is a new corporate life you have built. It is built on your sweat and your pure devotion to greatness. So enjoy it. Grow with it. Then, go for it all again. Put the finishing touch on it and start all over with the four concepts of great management:

1. *Simplification.* Keep things simple and understandable.

2. *Urgency.* Go for it now.

3. *Common sense.* Think. Just think.

4. *Passion.* You've just got to want it, whatever "it" is, and then you have to go for it with everything you've got.

Press Release

Henry Kaiser established the first Health Maintenance Organization (HMO) in the country. He explained, "It's pretty simple. If my workers aren't healthy, they can't work and then I don't make money." As Kaiser understood, business is people—at its heart and core. Pretty simple stuff. Very valuable stuff.

Passion, common sense, urgency, and simplification are the four cornerstones of great management. These are all things that reside in every one of us. They are not founded by education, race, gender, language, or wealth. They have to do with caring and honesty.

They all have to do with what is inside a manager. They great ones have these driving feelings inside and are not afraid to whip them out in front of everyone. They are not afraid because they know that the quest to be the best provides the results and feelings that can change the world for the better. And after all, isn't that what "it" is all about?

The Least You Need to Know

➤ It's natural to have some letdown after a crisis. It is the manager's job to rejuvenate the organization and let people know that the sun always rises.

➤ The first thing you as a manager must do to motivate people to new goals is to revitalize yourself. This is most easily done with a judicious use of creativity and possibility thinking.

➤ The process of goal setting and motivating is the same as when starting out, but to be effective it must be done in fresh ways.

➤ Setting a huge, inspiring, audacious new goal is the key to getting everyone to go to the next level.

Glossary

Age Discrimination Act   A law that clearly protects people over the age of 40 from discrimination.

Allocated costs   Those costs that come from another department and that are distributed on some basis by the accounting department to a variety of departments. For example, a graphics department may do work for a variety of divisions. The accountants would then come up with an equitable way to disperse these costs to the various divisions.

Americans With Disability Act (ADA)   This law says that medical tests can only be given after a decision to hire the person has been made. If you ask for a medical test before and then you don't hire the person, you could face a discrimination suit.

Big Culture Management   A style of management that is generally, but not always, used in a big company. It is characterized by lots of meetings, teams, and shared responsibilities. There are many layers of management, formal decisions are made with approvals from superiors, the span of authority is clearly defined, and even product introductions are done in an orderly way and approved by many people.

Cash flow   A term used to describe the flow of money into and out of a company, including loans and money invested. Often this is more important than profit because it can dictate survival.

Certificates of Deposit (CDs)   Bond notes that you buy from a bank that pay better interest than traditional savings accounts. These normally require that you stay invested for a fixed period of time, and are backed by the bank's credit worthiness.

Consolidated Omnibus Budget Reconciliation Act (COBRA)   A law that requires companies with 20 or more employees to offer to continue insurance plans for 18 months. The employee has to assume the obligation to pay the premium, but it is at the company rate—usually much less than what an individual could get on his or her own.

Core competency   The thing that you do best. The real core is inside of the people. It is the raw nerve, the answer to "Why are we here?"

Cost centers   Those areas of a company where management only has control of expenses, not revenues or profits. This includes departments such as finance, office management, or shipping.

Cost per thousand (C.P.T.)   The methodology used to compare differing media for advertising. It takes the cost of the ad and divides that number by the legitimate number of observers (expressed in terms of thousands) of the ad (not always the total audience, because not all may be potential purchasers). The resulting number is then used to compare and rank diverse options.

Economies of scale pricing   The technique for pricing where the price is based on the volume that is expected to be sold. The prices are based on the large volume efficiencies that will occur once you actually reach the expected high volume, not what the costs are today.

Employment at will   A legal term that says an employee can be hired or fired at the descretion of management. It clarifies that an employee has no employment contract—written or implied—greatly simplifying the firing process. This information should be included in all employee communications—the employee application form, the employee welcome letter, and all personnel manuals to avoid costly litigations in the event of a firing.

Entrepreneurial management   A management style that believes in maximizing opportunity. Entrepreneurism is about making fast decisions with limited information. It has a high tolerance for risk and a strong capacity to deal with ambiguity. Entrepreneurism is opportunistic. The mantra of an entrepreneurial manager is "Go for it!"

Employee Stock Option Program (ESOP)   A program that allows all employees to have ownership in their own company. The concept is that the company buys back its shares from existing owners and then resells the shares to employees. The resell to employees can be immediate or over time, but the stock is all held together in one lump sum and managed by an outside administrator. This employee stock purchase can come out of salary, bonuses, or the employee's own investment. There is a favorable tax treatment for ESOPs.

Factors   Organizations that loan money against accounts receivable. They are normally more aggressive than the bank and will often loan a higher percentage. Factors do their own credit checks and will not necessarily approve every account. When they loan against the receivable, they take ownership of the receivable as security.

Fixed costs   Those costs that remain constant no matter what the fluctuations in business. Examples are rent or management salaries.

401k   A retirement program in which employees regularly put funds into a retirement account. The money is put in pretax and it accumulates and compounds over the years without being taxed until the funds are distributed. The company has the option of matching a portion of the funds, also without taxation to the employees until distribution.

Gang printing   The process of printing many different projects at one time. It saves time and money by cutting down the setup time, improving the length of the press run, and getting economies of scale in the purchase of paper.

Incremental cost pricing   Different prices are charged in different markets that require different support. For instance, a product that has already been developed and sold domestically could be sold internationally for a lower price because the price would not have to support research and development or domestic advertising.

Interview   The place to ask probing questions to understand motivations as well as skill of a job applicant.

Inventory turns   The number of times a year that you sell (or turn over) your inventory. You calculate this by dividing the annual cost of goods sold by the inventory on hand. Generally, it's better to add the beginning and ending inventory and divide by two to arrive at the average inventory prior to your calculations. This avoids distortions in analyzing businesses that are growing or contracting.

Japanese way of decision making   A system in which everyone in the company is consulted before a decision is made. Also called the Ringi system, it is based on a concept of a ring in which everyone in the various facets of the company is consulted prior to a decision. Hence, things move slow in the decision phase, but execution is smooth.

Job description   A snapshot of how you see a particular job at a certain point in time. It is almost a contract: *This is what we expect, and this is what you get.*

Leadership   The ability to motivate and direct others to predesignated goals.

Letters of Credit (L/C)   Formal commitments by a bank to pay an obligation on behalf of a company some time in the future. They designate specifically what goods are to be purchased and when. Normally, these cannot extend beyond 180 days. The recipient collects directly from the bank. The bank, in turn, collects from the company that issued the L/C.

Loss leaders   This is a technique of pricing where a few products are priced low to get customers to buy. The assumption is the customer will continue buying once they start buying.

Management   A process of getting things done, mostly by making decisions to allocate people and money. Management also serves as an inspirational source to get the most productivity from employees.

Management by exception   A management style that works this way: You set up standards you want met. Then you set up an allowed variance (say 5 percent). Let anything that comes within the allowed variance be. Your job within this system is to look closely at only those things that vary widely.

Management by objective   This is similar to management by exception. The idea here is to set up objectives for subordinates. You want to avoid micromanaging and taking away authority or incentive. You care about results.

Market research   The formal collection of data on the markets and the customers that an organization is pursuing. It helps companies make decisions. Usually, the data is quantitative and statistical and measures the hypothesis of managers.

Management Information Systems (MIS)   The updated description of the computer systems found in a company. This was previously called data processing.

Non-Qualified Options   Stock options that require registration before being sold and, thus, are not as liquid as *qualified options*.

Options   The right to buy stock in a company at a certain price. This allows the holder to benefit if the company does well, and, at least in theory, helps align the interests of the employees with those of the owners because the employees are essentially owners.

Organizational chart   A graphic showing who reports to whom in an organization.

Outsourcing   The hiring of individuals or firms outside of a company to do work for the company that is normally done by internal employees. Any number of things—such as warehousing and shipping, accounting, or marketing—can be outsourced. The idea is to save money, reduce fixed costs, and to have a small internal team focused only on the core.

Overhead   Any cost of goods or services that is not directly related to its production. Utility bills, salaries, and mortgages are some examples of overhead.

The Pareto Principle   A principle that states that 80 percent of business comes from 20 percent of the customers.

Payback analysis   A method used to calculate the time it takes to recover the cost of investments. Usually investments with the fastest payback are rated highest.

Phantom options   Options that are not registered with securities officials. They are simply a commitment by the company to give rights that act like shares (and, thus, move up or down with the value of shares). They can later be redeemed with the company without actually having to buy or sell shares.

Point of Purchase (P.O.P.)   Materials used at the point of sale in a store. They are used to stimulate interest in a product and to convert the customer's interest into a sale. They may be attention-getting or information-packed, or both.

Possibility thinking   When you encourage employees to come up with what might seem like outlandish ideas: "What if…?" "What if" is a great tool. It can overcome so-called experts who always find reasons something won't work. Ask yourself, what if the experts are wrong?

Prioritizing   The practice of listing your tasks and organizing them from the most important (in terms of organization results) to the least important. Focus on those tasks at the top of the list at the expense of those at the bottom. If you can, hand off the lower-ranked tasks to others. Some things will simply be left undone.

Profit & Loss Statement   A document that records expenses and income during a set period. It does not rely on the timing of actual payments. Rather, it uses accruals and accounting conventions to spread costs over time.

Profit centers   Those areas of responsibility where an individual is responsible for revenues as well as costs. Thus, they can be held accountable for making a profit or loss for a certain subset of the company. Two examples are a geographic subset of your division, or a division such as sales and marketing. This form can be used for regular measurement and guidance for your employees.

Pull strategy   A strategy that places all marketing emphasis on the end consumer. This is normally used when your product is established, the market is large, and you are seeking much greater representation by the retailer. Often, it is used to expand product differentiation.

Push strategy   A strategy that places all marketing emphasis on trying to get your products on retailer's shelves. This is normally used to introduce a product or when a company is not as well known as its competitors.

Qualified options   In the most simplified form, the right to buy registered stock, salable upon exercise. These options have a purchase price that employees pay upon exercising them. Once they are exercised, the employee has shares of stock just like all other shareholders.

Receivables days   A measure of how fast you are collecting on the sales you have made. You calculate this by dividing the annual sales by the outstanding accounts receivable figure. This tells you the number of times you turn over the receivables in a year. It will show you exactly how long it is taking people to pay you.

Reticular activating system   The part of the human brain that filters information from the awareness. It is where information is disseminated and where decisions are made. It includes "the gut" and "the will" parts of your thought processes. It allows you to focus.

Return on investment   A technique that compares the life return on various possible investments.

Semi-variable costs   Those costs that have some elements of *fixed costs* and some of *variable costs*. For instance, some costs, such as phone and utilities, have a base cost that is fixed but a variable element based on usage.

Spontaneous dismissal   An immediate dismissal for cause. Cause includes such things as fraud, theft, and dishonesty. Very few things meet the test for a spontaneous dismissal. Check with your labor lawyer before you are "spontaneous."

255

Strategic alliances   These occur when an organization teams up with another organization. One organization uses the other one's services in some area, such as accounting, that was formally done in-house.

Treasury bills (t-bills)   These are similar to *CDs*, except that they are issued and backed by the federal government. Because of the federal guarantee, most people feel these offer more security than CDs. They are usually issued for a longer term than CDs.

Variable costs   Those costs that change in concert with some change in business. The most common and easiest thing to measure for variations are things related to sales volume—for example, sales commissions or shipping costs.

Western way of decision making   A system in which an individual, consulting a few people, makes a decision. People hear of it, challenge it, and it gets tweaked in a stall-and-proceed mode. The result is herky-jerky execution as it proceeds through levels of specifics in the organization.

Zero-based budgeting   A technique in which every line item in the budget is put at zero. The figures are then built up from there. This is different than the normal technique of starting with last year's numbers and adjusting for expected changes. The idea is to be able to kill anything that is not justified. Everything starts at zero.

Index

F

T

U - V

W - Z